GREEK LIFE AND THOUGHT

COLUMBIA UNIVERSITY PRESS
Columbia University
New York

———

FOREIGN AGENT
OXFORD UNIVERSITY PRESS
Humphrey Milford
Amen House, London, E. C.

FIG. 1. VIEW OF THE ACROPOLIS FROM THE WEST

Feb 44

GREEK LIFE AND THOUGHT

A PORTRAYAL OF GREEK CIVILIZATION

BY

LA RUE VAN HOOK, Ph.D. 1877-

PROFESSOR OF GREEK AND LATIN IN BARNARD COLLEGE
COLUMBIA UNIVERSITY

Revised Edition

DOMINICAN COLLEGE
LIBRARY
SAN RAFAEL, CALIF.

New York
COLUMBIA UNIVERSITY PRESS
1930

913.38
V316g

23-15286

COPYRIGHT, 1923, 1930
COLUMBIA UNIVERSITY PRESS

———

1st Printing September, 1923
2d Printing November, 1924
Revised Edition October, 1930

21327

"*The greatest single gift in Education is to infect the average man with the spirit of the Humanities.*" — SIR WILLIAM OSLER.

"*We should have scant capital to trade on were we to throw away the wisdom we have inherited and seek our fortunes with the slender stock we ourselves have accumulated.*" — WOODROW WILSON.

"*Nothing makes a man more interesting to himself or to others than that wide knowledge of men and life, that wide knowledge of the globe and of man's past and present on the globe, which is given by a liberal or cultural education in which the study of classical literature is an essential element.*" — THEODORE ROOSEVELT.

"*A fine grasp upon the meaning of Greek and Roman thought and institutional life gives new significance to one's knowledge of natural science, a deeper meaning to one's participation in political organization and activity and a sure standard for the determination and appreciation of excellence in letters and in art.*" — NICHOLAS MURRAY BUTLER.

PREFACE

MODERN conditions have caused a great decrease in the number of those who study Greek at first-hand. It is, however, coming to be more and more realized that an education which aims at being truly liberal and yet ignores or neglects the source of that which is culturally best in modern civilization is inadequate. In consequence, many colleges are prescribing, or strongly recommending to *all* students courses of study in Classical Civilization. Ever increasing interest, too, in ancient Greece, which has bequeathed to the modern world a priceless heritage, is being shown by intelligent readers in general, and in the last ten or fifteen years many books devoted to one or another aspect of Hellenic civilization have appeared and have received a warm welcome. All the modern western nations have affection and veneration for ancient Greece. Amid all their strife and rivalries, the peoples of Europe and America have this common interest, devotion, and bond — all admire and cherish the Greek elements in modern culture.

Numerous indeed are the books that deal with some aspect or other of ancient Greek life and thought and seek to interpret the Greek genius and achievements. Is there need, then, of another? I think there is. None of the existing books suits the needs of the reader I have in mind. The available treatises in English are either too comprehensive in treatment or too limited in scope and purpose. Some are too brief and superficial, others are too technical. There are excellent volumes devoted to Greek History (e. g., Botsford, Bury), to Greek Art and Archaeology (Fowler and Wheeler), to the Theater and Drama (Norwood), to Private and Public Life (Gulick), to Education (K. G. Freeman), to Religious Thought (C. H. Moore), to Economics (Zimmern), and to the Greek Genius and the Legacy of Greece (Livingstone). But these books are largely of restricted subject. On the other hand, the lexicons, the handbooks, and the Manuals of Classical Antiquities (e.g., the admirable *Companion to Greek Studies,* edited by Whibley) cover too wide a field and are too detailed and encyclopaedic; they are works for consultation rather than perusal and frequently assume some knowledge of the Greek language and civilization.

It is obvious that no one book, and especially one of brief compass, can adequately present or interpret ancient Greek civilization in its entirety. No such presumptuous illusion is entertained by the writer of this volume. My aim is this: To present to the reader, who may or may not have some previous knowledge of the Greek language or civilization, certain aspects of ancient Greek life and thought. Since " life and thought " really comprise the entire civilization in all its manifold manifestations, only special topics have been, and obviously could be, chosen for consideration. In general, I have preferred to omit discussion of many details of Greek Private Life, such as Clothing, Food, Sickness, Burial and Marriage Ceremonies, etc. It is not what the Greeks ate or wore that is of compelling interest and importance to us today; it is what they thought and achieved. This surely is true — every subject discussed in this book is of importance for modern life.

While ancient Greece as a whole from earliest times to the Graeco-Roman Age necessarily is under our survey, limitations of time and place must generally be observed. Strong emphasis, therefore, will be laid upon Athens at the time of her greatest glory, the Age of Pericles, and the period immediately subsequent thereto.

The chapters are necessarily brief and should be regarded as largely introductory to the subjects discussed. The interested reader and the serious student should supplement these pages by consulting the more detailed and extensive treatment to be found in the appropriate works which are cited for each chapter in the Bibliographical Appendix at the end of this volume.

It is my hope that this book may prove of value not merely as a text-book, but may fulfil a wider purpose. These are its earnest aims no doubt imperfectly achieved: To assist those who wish a better understanding of ancient Greek civilization and culture; to help readers to obtain a more intelligent appreciation of the Greek genius; and to convey a clearer realization of the great indebtedness of the world today to our Hellenic antecedents.

I wish to express my thanks and obligations to my friends Professors Edward Capps and Donald Clive Stuart of Princeton University, and to my colleagues Professors Charles Knapp, Edward Delavan Perry, and Clarence H. Young. These scholars have read portions of the manuscript and made numerous helpful suggestions. For the illustrations I am greatly indebted to Professor Young, who generously put at my service his collection of Greek photographs.

NEW YORK, April, 1923

LA RUE VAN HOOK

PREFACE TO REVISED EDITION

It is gratifying that still another printing of this volume on Greek Life and Thought is needed. For it is but another indication that interest in the achievements of ancient Greece, even in our modern time, steadily continues and increases. This third printing has afforded an opportunity for the correction of certain minor errors in the original edition and has also permitted revision of the Bibliography and the addition, in a Supplement to the Bibliographical Appendix, of titles of some recent valuable studies.

NEW YORK, August, 1930

L. V. H

CONTENTS

ILLUSTRATIONS

GREEK LIFE AND THOUGHT

A PORTRAYAL OF GREEK CIVILIZATION

CHAPTER I

THE SOURCES OF OUR INFORMATION

" To Greece we owe the love of Science, the love of Art, the
love of Freedom: not Science alone, Art alone, or Freedom alone,
but these vitally correlated with one another and brought into
organic union. And in this union we recognize the distinctive
features of the West. The Greek genius is the European genius
in its first and brightest bloom." — S. H. BUTCHER.

THE ancient literature and the monuments are
our chief sources of information in obtaining
a knowledge of Greek life and thought. Greek
literature, originally of great bulk, has suffered grievously in the course of the centuries for reasons subsequently to be related; yet in spite of the great losses
which it has sustained we fortunately possess a literary
heritage of very considerable extent and priceless value.
For the early period the epic poetry of Homer, the didactic verse of Hesiod, and the fragmentary poems of
the lyricists are the only literary sources of knowledge,
but for the fifth and succeeding centuries voluminous
prose writings throw a flood of light particularly upon
Athenian life. Historical events are narrated by Herodotus, Thucydides, and Xenophon; public and private
life and legal, political, and social conditions are revealed in the speeches of Demosthenes, Lysias, and the
other Attic orators; Plato's philosophical writings are
preserved in their entirety and the numerous works of
Aristotle are a mine of information of all kinds.
Thirty-three tragedies of Aeschylus, Sophocles, and
Euripides, rich in religious and ethical ideas, give evidence of the nature and importance of the theater and

drama; while eleven comedies of Aristophanes reflect, although in the mirror of caricature, contemporary political, social, and educational conditions and public and private life generally. The commentaries and literary collections of the Alexandrian scholars and writers and the Greek authors of the Roman Age explain much that would otherwise be obscure. Here and there, too, in Latin literature are to be found illuminating comments on Greek civilization.

Until about fifty years ago the modern world knew ancient Greece largely through the literature alone. Now, fortunately, the situation is vastly different, because of archaeological excavations and studies. In fact we of today are in a position to know far more of *early* Greece than Plato and Aristotle because of the illuminating revelations of the spade. Excavations in the island of Crete have unearthed the palace of King Minos at Cnossos and a remarkable civilization which flourished about 2800–1100 B.C. Homeric Troy has been uncovered in Asia Minor. Excavations have been and are being prosecuted throughout the Greek world yielding important treasures. Olympia, Delphi, Corinth, Athens, Eleusis, Epidaurus, Argos, Mycenae, Tiryns and Sparta in Greece itself; Troy, Sardes, Pergamum, Ephesus, and Colophon in Asia Minor; Delos, Melos, Thera, and Crete of the islands; Akragas (Agrigentum), Syracuse, Selinus, and Segesta in Sicily; these are some of the more important sites that have richly repaid the labors of the archaeologist and, after many centuries, their monuments and civilization again stand revealed to the light of day. These monuments, for the most part, we may classify as examples of architecture, sculpture, painting, ceramics, inscriptions, and coins.

Imposing and beautiful remains of ancient structures are to be found in all parts of the Greek world — in Sicily, in Magna Graecia, in Asia Minor, and in Greece proper, while in Athens itself and on its sacred Acropolis are still to be seen the marble ruins of the old-time temples and buildings. Temples and theaters are the chief examples of architecture preserved.

The museums of the world are stocked with Greek sculptures of marble and bronze. Works of art found in Greece may no longer be taken from that country, and consequently the museums of Athens and of lesser centers, e.g., Olympia, Delphi, Corinth, Sparta, Thebes, and Eleusis, possess, in numbers ever increasing, artistic treasures. The museums of Italy, in particular that of the Vatican in Rome, have many masterpieces. The British Museum in London contains the priceless Elgin Marbles from the Parthenon. The Louvre in Paris has the world's most famous statue, the Aphrodite of Melos (Venus of Milo), and the Victory from Samothrace. In Munich are the marbles from Aegina and in Berlin the sculptures from Pergamum. In the museums of Boston and New York are a number of excellent examples of Greek art. These statues, grave-reliefs, and terra-cottas are not only beautiful as works of art, but they contribute to our knowledge of Greek dress, costume, and physical characteristics.

Greek painting, being naturally of perishable nature, has not survived to the present day. It is true that painted grave monuments of considerable merit have been unearthed in Thessaly. Some Greek portraits of late date have been found in Egyptian excavations. The Pompeian mural paintings show Greek influence. But the great works of such renowned artists as Apelles and Polygnotus have perished. The artistic drawings on the indestructible terra-cotta vases abide, however, and countless specimens of this lovely art-form reveal in manifold ways the dress and appearance, the manners and customs of the ancient Hellenes.

Inscriptions tell us much of life in ancient Greece. All the important Athenian laws were inscribed on stone. Hundreds of these imperishable witnesses have been preserved, handing down the letter of the laws. We possess also numerous other inscriptions of greatest value informing us of important facts in matters his-

DOMINICAN COLLEGE
LIBRARY
SAN RAFAEL

torical, biographical, religious, medical, economic, theatrical, and commercial.

Coins, too, have their value in this connection. Each
city-state had its own coinage. These coins are not
only noteworthy as examples of art, but they are informative for trade and commerce.

Modern Greece to a limited extent contributes to our
knowledge of the life and customs of ancient Hellas.
Much in the life of the modern Greeks has its origin
in the ancient land. It must not be forgotten that the
Greeks and their language and literature have had a
continuous history from Homeric times to the present
day, thereby revealing a vitality of language and genius
almost without parallel. It cannot be expected that
the ancient Greek racial stock should have come down
in all its purity, when it is recalled how many grievous
political vicissitudes Hellas has suffered. Romans,
Slavs, Venetians, Germans, Albanians, and Turks over-
running and subjugating Greece inevitably have left
their mark on the people. Now and then, however, in
traveling in Greece one may see, especially in remote
valley or settlement, a youth or maiden of classic features and mien who might have served as a model for
an ancient statue or for a graceful figure depicted on
a vase.

The language has survived in a remarkable manner.
It is a mistake to speak of Greek as a *dead* language.
Although, as has been well said, no language can be
called dead which is the vehicle of an immortal literature, Latin, in a sense, is no longer a living language,
since it is not in every-day use by a modern people
as a spoken language. It has been superseded by its
daughters, the Romance tongues. But the Greek language and literature have had an uninterrupted history
throughout the ages. Certain changes of pronunciation, of idiom, and of syntax naturally have been
effected, since a language is a living organism that constantly changes, but modern Greek is essentially the
ancient language. Demosthenes would find little diffi-

culty in reading the better class periodicals published in Athens today.

These, then, are the chief sources of our information: the literature, continually being re-interpreted by each successive generation; the monuments, ever increasing through the labors of archaeologists.

CHAPTER II

GREEK STATES APART FROM ATTICA

A cypress dark against the blue
That deepens up to such a hue
As never painter dared or drew;

A marble shaft that stands alone
Above a wreck of sculptured stone
With grey-green aloes overgrown;

A hillside scored with hollow veins
Through age-long wash of autumn rains,
As purple as with vintage stains;

And rocks that while the hours run
Show all their jewels one by one
For pastime of the summer sun;

A crescent sail upon the sea,
So calm and fair and ripple-free,
You wonder storms can ever be;

A shore with deep indented bays,
And, o'er the gleaming waterways,
A glimpse of islands in the haze;

A face bronzed dark to red and gold,
With mountain eyes which seem to hold
The freshness of the world of old;

A shepherd's crook, a coat of fleece,
A grazing flock — the sense of peace —
The long sweet silence — this is Greece.
— RENNELL RODD.

ALTHOUGH our primary interest lies in Attica and Athens, it will be illuminating to survey briefly other parts of Greece in an effort to discover their nature, and that we may discern what rôles these states played in Hellenic affairs and what contributions they made to Greek life and thought, particularly in comparison with, or in contrast to, Attica.

A few words about the land and the people as a whole may fittingly preface this chapter.

The Hellenic race occupied the Balkan peninsula, a land of small area (about 25,000 square miles) extending southward into the Mediterranean Sea. The peculiar physical character of the land profoundly influenced the life and history of the people. The country is divided into a number of small plains or plateaux by numerous chains of mountains of limestone. These mountains are not of great height, yet they are sufficiently lofty and precipitous to form imposing barriers to people in ancient days when methods of travel and communication were primitive in nature. The highest

6

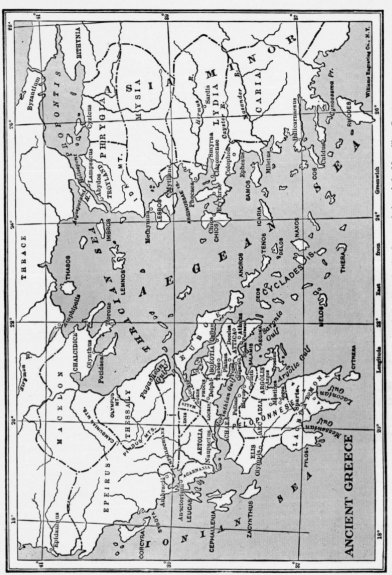

From "Hellenic History" by George W. Botsford. Reproduction by permission of the Macmillan Company.

ANCIENT GREECE

mountain is Mt. Olympus (Fig. 3), in northern Greece, nearly 10,000 feet in height, the fabled home of the gods. Between 7000 and 8000 feet high are Parnassus, north of Delphi, beloved of the Muses; Taÿgetus, which towers above the plain of Sparta; and Cyllene and Erymanthus, mountains of pastoral Arcadia, the former known to Hermes, the latter the haunt of the wild boar slain by Heracles.

Of even greater influence upon the people was the sea, which everywhere cuts into the land, forming innumerable inlets, bays, and gulfs. The gulf of Corinth, in fact, well-nigh cuts off the Peloponnese. The coastline of Greece is therefore of truly remarkable length and afforded numerous harbors, an encouragement to navigation. The Greeks in consequence were a maritime folk and commerce and colonization naturally flourished.

The climate of Greece is profoundly affected by the varying altitudes of the mountains and by the proximity of the sea. The temperature is mild, although bracing except in the dry, hot summer season. The winter, which is the wet season, is short and not severe. The winds are quite constant, a boon to sailors. The rivers for the most part are insignificant because of the shortness of their courses, and often dry up almost completely in the dry season. Only the Peneus and the Spercheus in northern Greece, the Achelous in Aetolia, and the Alpheus in Elis may be designated rivers in the real sense of the word, although even these streams are not navigable for modern vessels. The rocky soil of Hellas is thin and not very fertile except in a few districts, as, for example, Thessaly, although the grape and the olive flourished and smaller live-stock, such as goats, sheep, and swine, were abundant.

The scenery of Greece, although neither opulent in its nature nor majestic in character, is of appealing beauty and abiding charm. Particularly in the loveliness produced by color may the observer find pleasure. No sea is bluer than the Aegean, no sky, no atmosphere clearer than those of Hellas. The pink tones of rock and mountain, the greens of the scattered vegetation, the brilliance of the many wild-flowers, the play of light and shadow on mountain walls, the purples and violets of reflected glories as the sun sinks at evening — all these delight the eye and entrance the soul.

The origin of the Greek people is lost in obscurity. The Hellenes, a branch of the Indo-Europeans, and consisting of a number of tribes, began soon after 2000 B.C., perhaps, moving southward from the region of the Black Sea and the Danube, and in successive waves of invasion gradually occupied the whole peninsula to the south. They found the land already occupied, as at the citadels of Tiryns and Mycenae in the Peloponnesus, by a people which we call the Aegean or Mediterranean race, but the native inhabitants, who possessed a flourishing civilization, were conquered or dispossessed. The islands of the Aegean of which the most important was Crete, the seat of a remarkable civilization, and the coast of Asia Minor were next conquered and occupied, in the south by those Greeks called Dorians, in the middle portions by the Ionians, and in the north by the Aeolians.

Thus it came about that the Greek race of the historical period was the result of a fusion of the original Greek with the native Aegean stock. But it was the Greek language that triumphed and became universal (the old Aegean language of which we have an example in Crete has not yet been deciphered), and although the Greek elements were widely scattered over the whole eastern Mediterranean world and spoke different dialects, yet a common blood, language, religion, ideals, and characteristics made kindred the whole race called Hellenes. So it was that the Aegean Civilization of the Bronze Age (*ca.* 3000–1000 B.C.) was followed by the Greek Civilization which arose about 1000 B.C., the beginning of the Iron Age. The succeeding centuries saw the remarkable rise, development, culmination, and gradual decline of the Greek civilization.

The ages of the kings, nobles, and tyrants were succeeded by the rise and triumph in the fifth and fourth
centuries B.C. of the empire and cultured democracy
of Athens and the power of the military states, Sparta
and Thebes. The Macedonian phalanxes of Philip
trampled under foot the army of Athens at Chaeronea
in Boeotia in 338 B.C. Philip's son Alexander extended
his father's conquests. But along with the armies of
Alexander, as he subjugated Asia and Africa, went the
Greek language and civilization to usher in the Hellenistic Age with Alexandria, founded in 332 B.C., as its
center. Finally, with the capture of Corinth by the
Roman consul Mummius in 146 B.C., Greece became
politically a Roman province. But, as Horace well
says, " Greece when captured took captive her rough
captor " (*Graecia capta ferum victorem cepit. Ep.* II.
1. 156).

To the north of Greece proper lies Macedonia. While
the Macedonians were not regarded as genuine Greeks,
yet they spoke a Greek dialect. They have left no literature and were of no political importance until, in the
fourth century B.C., Philip established his monarchy
and built up that formidable military machine which
finally succeeded in crushing Athenian supremacy.
Demosthenes, the unremitting foe of Philip as revealed
in his *Philippic* and *Olynthiac* orations, in an eloquent
passage, thus contrasts Philip and his provincial Macedonian capital with the Athenians and their culture:
" Verily, no one indeed would dare assert this — that
it was fitting that he who was reared in Pella, a place
without repute at that time and insignificant, should
possess such ambition as to set his heart on ruling the
Greeks and should entertain this great ambition, while
you who are in truth Athenians, who daily in all you
see and hear contemplate memorials of your ancestors'
virtues, have in your natures such great baseness as
to yield up voluntarily to Philip your freedom! Surely
no man would dare affirm this! " Philip, however, as
a youth had resided as a hostage in Thebes, where he

received a Greek education and a military training, and this, coupled with great natural ability, enabled him to overcome all obstacles and eventually to become political master of Greece.

To the south of Macedon lies Thessaly, the northernmost province of Greece proper. The Thessalians, a people of many tribes of which some were not of pure Greek stock, occupied the largest and most fertile plain in Greece. This district, drained by the Peneus, was famous for its crops, its horses and oxen. The latter part of the course of the Peneus is through that rocky mountain gorge and pass, the Vale of Tempe, whose scenic beauty is extolled in ancient and modern verse, " the long divine Peneian pass " of Tennyson. Herodotus asserts that formerly all Thessaly was a vast lake, but that Poseidon, as men say, drained it by cleaving with a powerful blow of his trident the mountain wall between Mounts Olympus and Ossa. This statement of the Father of History is doubtless correct, although modern geologists would not use identical terminology.

At an early period, when Athens was an insignificant settlement, Thessaly was inhabited by powerful tribes and ruled by a proud nobility and princes. The hero of the *Iliad*, the warrior Achilles, was a Thessalian. But in later days the Thessalians were contemned as boors by the cultured Athenians, and were even called traitors, as they were accused of favoring the Persians and later the Macedonians. In behalf of the Thessalians it may be said that because of their geographical situation they were constantly exposed, as a border state, to incursions of enemies from the north. For southern Greece they constituted a buffer state. It is difficult for a people thus situated to progress in arts and literature. No literature and no important ruins are of Thessalian origin. Yet the Thessalians were not altogether cut off from intercourse with the more southern Greeks. Pindar and Simonides wrote odes in praise of Thessalian princes, and archaeologists have discovered in Thessaly painted grave-reliefs of some merit.

FIG. 3. MOUNT OLYMPUS AND PETRA PASS

FIG. 4. DELPHI: THEATER, TEMPLE OF APOLLO, AND VALLEY

FIG. 5. MYCENAE: THE LIONS' GATE

FIG. 6. CORINTH: TEMPLE OF APOLLO AND ACRO-CORINTH

Between Thessaly on the north and Attica on the south the most important state was Boeotia. The nimble-witted and highly cultivated Athenians had contempt for their somewhat stolid neighbors to the north and designated them as stupid and " swinish." The result is that even today the term *Boeotian* is applied to a boorish, slow-witted, or unesthetic person. It is true that Thebes never rivaled Athens except during the few years between the victory of Leuctra (371 B.C.) and the defeat at Mantinea (362 B.C.), when she held brief military and political hegemony. Thebes has bequeathed us no extensive literature and no important works of art. Architecturally the capital city was mean and insignificant. But it must not be forgotten that Pindar, the great lyric poet, was a Theban, and that Hesiod lived in Ascra, a Boeotian village. Furthermore, at a small village in southern Boeotia have been excavated fine examples of those charming and artistic little terra-cottas which bear the name *Tanagra figurines* from the place where first they were found. Of the ancient capital-city, Thebes, with its famous seven gates as described in the *Persians* of Aeschylus and its citadel, the *Cadmea* of Thebes, the seat of rule of Cadmus, of Laius, and of Oedipus, almost nothing remains. The level plains of Boeotia were the scenes of several fateful battles, Plataea (479 B.C.), where the invading Persians were decisively defeated, Leuctra (371 B.C.), where Epaminondas by his victory over Sparta won temporary supremacy for Thebes in Grecian affairs, and Chaeronea (338 B.C.), where Athens fell before Philip of Macedon. Near Boeotia's western boundary rises Mount Helicon, the storied abode of the Muses, while on the south, on the Attic frontier, stretches the lofty mountain wall of Cithaeron, on whose slopes the infant Oedipus, so ran the myth, was exposed. Thebes is only some fifty miles distant from Athens, but the two cities were a thousand miles apart so far as sympathies and intellectual and cultural intercourse were concerned.

To the west of Boeotia lay Phocis, a small state, but

of great importance, as the seat of Delphi. Here, amid splendid and awe-inspiring scenery on the side of Mount Parnassus, were the center of Apollo's worship, the home of his temple and oracle, and the sacred Castalian spring. The cult of the Pythian Apollo at Delphi was one of the most important manifestations of Greek religion. The greater states of Greece built permanent treasure houses at Delphi wherein to house their costly dedicatory offerings to the god of prophecy, of health, and of light. The Amphictyonic League met annually in the spring at Delphi. Here the Pythian Games were celebrated every four years. Deputations bearing gifts to the god from every part of the Greek world were constantly arriving to consult the Pythian oracle. No visitor today should fail to see Delphi (Fig. 4), where the French excavations have uncovered the whole sacred precinct with the ruins of the Pythian temple, the treasuries, theater, stadium, and winding sacred road.

To the west of Phocis were Aetolia and Acarnania, flourishing states, but comparatively negligible in Greek political and literary history of the classical period.

South of the Corinthian Gulf is the Peloponnesus, the southern part of Greece, containing a number of places of importance.

The city of Corinth, a great commercial center, stood at the western extremity of the Isthmus. At the foot of the lofty Acro-Corinth (Fig. 6) is the site of the ancient city, where for some years the American School of Classical Studies at Athens has conducted excavations. The fountains of Pirene and Glauce have been disclosed, a sacred way and ruins of a theater revealed, and the foundations of numerous buildings uncovered. The excavations have not yielded many important works of art, and this is not surprising when we recall that in 146 B.C. Mummius, the Roman consul, sacked Corinth and despoiled the city of its artistic treasures. It may be explained that the carrying off of Greek works of art by the Romans became a regular practice and shiploads of statues were sent to Italy to adorn Roman buildings and villas. Not many years ago sponge-divers engaged in their occupation off the island of Cythera, south of the Peloponnesus, were astonished to find strewn on the bottom of the sea some fifty statues, the cargo of some wrecked Roman galley. Unhappily the action of the sea-water through the centuries had seriously marred their beauty, but one statue, a splendid bronze figure of a youth, is now a prized possession of the National Museum in Athens.

In Argolis, south of Corinth, are several cities of great importance in pre-historic days, celebrated in Homer and of great interest to the student of today, namely, Mycenae, " rich-in-gold," the capital city of Agamemnon, leader of the Trojan expedition, and Tiryns, mighty castle-fortress. Argos, too, and the Argive Heraeum excavated by the Americans are near. The excavations of Dr. Schliemann at Mycenae made the world first acquainted with that flourishing and early era called *Mycenaean* (1500–1200 B.C.). At Mycenae within the well-known Lions' Gate (Fig. 5) and below the citadel Dr. Schliemann excavated five tombs which contained many treasures such as masks, cups, and daggers wrought largely of gold and beautifully and artistically fashioned.

The latest investigations (1921) at Mycenae by the British School " leave the question open whether the power and the wealth of the city was due to conquest and colonization from Crete or to peaceful penetration by trade and the like. Whatever the cause, the culture of the mainland suddenly became saturated with Minoan influence."

Also in Argolis was Epidaurus, the center of the worship of the god of healing, Asclepius (the Roman *Aesculapius*). Here many interesting inscriptions have been unearthed which were carved in honor of the god and testify to miraculous cures effected by the deity. The theater of Epidaurus is the best preserved of all the ancient Greek structures of its kind and seated perhaps thirty thousand spectators.

In northwestern Peloponnesus Elis was politically of little importance as a state, but it contained Olympia, on the river Alpheus, the scene of the celebration of the great Panhellenic festival-games in honor of Zeus, which were held every four years and attracted visitors from every part of the Greek world. Excavations here by the Germans have uncovered the whole *Altis* or sacred precinct, with the foundations of many buildings, chief of which are the temples of Zeus and Hera. A museum erected at Olympia contains the works of art discovered there, including the famous statue of Hermes by Praxiteles, the Victory of Paeonius, and the sculptured pediment groups from the temple of Zeus.

In central Peloponnesus was mountainous and pastoral Arcadia and, in the southern part, lay Messenia.

Chief of all the Peloponnesian states was, of course, Sparta, Athens' great and only rival in ancient Greece — a rival, not in literature, as Spartan writers were few and their literary remains are scanty; a rival, not in art or architecture, as Sparta had no Phidias, no Polygnotus. Nor were the Spartans comparable with the Athenians in refinement or polish. But the two states clashed over the political hegemony of Greece and long and bitterly did they contest in the Peloponnesian War from 431 B.C., until, in 403 B.C., the Spartans triumphed. In political ideals the two states were poles apart, as Sparta believed that the individual exists for the State; Athens, that the State exists for the individual. The aim of Spartan education was to produce the brave and hardy soldier; the Athenian ideal was to prepare the youth for citizenship and for life in the fullest sense. And yet it should be added that the Spartan constitution, government, and laws were admired for their efficiency, and were approved by Plato and Aristotle in their writings devoted to the ideal commonwealth. But these thinkers were not in entire sympathy with a democratic form of government.

It is natural to attribute to a country itself the characteristics of its inhabitants, and so, recalling the Spartan as we know him — severe, rugged, and martial — we might well picture him living in a stern, unattractive land. Yet hardly any city in Greece has a lovelier situation than Sparta, which lies at the foot of Mt. Taÿgetus, towering over " hollow Lacedaemon." Flowing through the town is the shallow, rippling Eurotas, which waters in its course the flourishing fruit orchards, today mainly orange and olive. It is a beautiful spot, although it was unloved by the Muses and Graces. The modern town of the same name is built on the ancient site and has the same broad streets, unusual in eastern lands, which characterized the city in Homer's poetry.

Recent excavations by the British at Sparta seem to show that the Spartans were not always so severe in their attitude towards life. In early times they were patrons of art and poetry, but after the end of the seventh century B.C., with the conscious adoption of a rigorous constitution and military ideals, their civilization suffered a drastic change.

When we think of Greek civilization we naturally think of Greece proper and especially of Athens. And yet it must not be forgotten that the Greeks were scattered over a wide area and each far-flung colony or center made its contribution. In Asia Minor, Ionia gave birth to thinkers and writers of History, Geography, Geology, Cosmogony, Science, Philosophy, and Sophistic. In Lesbos, Ceos, and other Aegean isles lived and sang such gifted poets as Sappho, Alcaeus, Simonides, and Archilochus. To the west in Sicily and southern Italy (called *Magna Graecia*), early colonized by Hellenes, were established numerous cities destined to become richer and more populous even than their mother-cities. The founders of formal Greek rhetoric, of literary comedy, and of pastoral poetry were of Sicily. Imposing ruins of ancient temples and buildings may be seen today at Paestum in Italy, and at Segesta, Selinus, Syracuse, and Girgenti (the Greek *Akragas*, the Roman *Agrigentum*) in Sicily, — monuments which still bear witness to the wealth and glory of those western tyrants and patrons of the arts such as Hieron and Theron. The importance of Sicily in the history of Greek civilization should not be underestimated.

CHAPTER III

ATTICA AND ATHENS

"Athens, the eye of Greece, mother of arts
And eloquence." — MILTON.

OF ALL the many places inhabited by the Greeks, Attica preëminently claims our attention. It is a tiny district judged by our generous standards of territorial area. Indeed, it is not as large as our smallest state, Rhode Island, yet because of the genius and accomplishments of its inhabitants, only a few hundred thousand in number, it will ever be venerated.

Attica is a rocky triangular district stretching southeastward from Boeotia to Cape Sunium. The northwestern boundary was the mountain wall formed by Parnes (some 4600 feet in height) and Cithaeron, the passes over which were guarded by frontier forts. The sea surrounds the small district on all sides except on the west, where the narrow Megarian province connects it with the Isthmus of Corinth, the bridge to the Peloponnesus. A series of small plains is formed by the mountain spurs projecting to the south, namely, the plain of Eleusis on the west, the plain of Athens with its two small streams, the Cephisus and the Ilissus, the *Mesogaea* or midland plain east of Hymettus, and finally a fertile stretch along the eastern and northeastern coast. The total area available for cultivation was small indeed, and the thin soil, while favorable to the olive, was quite inadequate to supply the inhabitants with food and produce. Although the available land was industriously cultivated, the population was compelled for support to turn to manufactures, to fishing, and commerce on the sea. Wheat and general produce were imported from foreign lands. The early inhabitants of Attica may therefore be differentiated thus in regard to place of habitation and occupation: the people of the mountains were shepherds, those of the plain were farmers, while the dwellers by the sea were seamen or fishers. Originally, we are told, there were twelve independent towns in Attica, e.g., Eleusis, Marathon, and others, but Theseus, mythical hero-king, joined all these scattered communities into one federation, which became the greatest city-state, Athens. In consequence, all inhabitants of Attica were citizens of Athens, and Athens and Attica were politically identical.

Two mountains rise near Athens, Pentelicus and Hymettus. Pentelicus (Fig. 7), some 3600 feet in height, lies to the northeast and was, and still is, the source of an admirable marble (Pentelic) extensively used for building purposes. All the temples of the city and structures on the Acropolis were built of this material. Pausanias, the ancient Greek traveler of the second century after Christ, who wrote the valuable extant guide-book or description of Greece, tells the story that the building of the Athenian stadium of Pentelic marble by Herodes Atticus in the second century A.D. well-nigh exhausted his quarries on the mountain. But in recent years with marble from this same source the stadium has been reclothed and many buildings erected and a mountain of marble still remains. The traveler by sea while still far from land can see the great white gashes and scars on the sides of Pentelicus where the quarrying has been done. It was truly a great boon for Athens to have at its doors this source of building material. There is considerable iron present in Pentelic marble and this becomes oxidized by exposure to the weather, so that Athenian ruins, e.g., the Parthenon, are not pure white but have assumed a golden brown color due to the *patina*. Immediately to the northeast of Pentelicus lies the little plain of Marathon, some twenty-four miles from Athens, the site of the

FIG. 7. MT. PENTELICUS FROM THE S. E.

FIG. 8. MARATHON: THE BURIAL-MOUND

FIG. 9. MT. HYMETTUS: VIEW FROM THE PARTHENON

FIG. 10. SUNIUM: THE TEMPLE OF POSEIDON

critical battle in 490 B.C., when the Persian host met complete defeat at the hands of the Athenian defending army under Miltiades. Over the Athenian dead was heaped a *tumulus* (*soros*) (Fig. 8) on the plain which the visitor may behold today. Recent exploration of this mound brought to light vases and relics of those heroes, the men of Marathon.

Separated from Pentelicus by an interval of some two miles is Hymettus (Fig. 9), 3300 feet in height, a mountain wall some twelve miles in length stretching like the back of a great whale from north to south. It is a prominent feature of the Attic landscape. Particularly at sunset is the mountain a spectacle of beauty as the entranced spectator watches upon its surface as upon a great screen the play of changing colors, the pinkish, violet, and purple glow, as Ovid says, *purpureos colles florentis Hymetti*. Hymettus was renowned for its bees and delicious honey, antiquity's substitute for sugar, and likewise for its building stone, a bluish and streaked marble: the reference of Horace will be recalled, *non trabes Hymettiae* (Odes 2.18.3). This stone was a special favorite in Hellenistic and Roman times.

Attica terminates in the promontory of Sunium, a narrow, rocky, and lofty height on which from afar still shine in sunshine and gleam in moonlight the milk-white columns of the temple of Poseidon, the "Sunium's marble steep" of Byron (Fig. 10).

Near Sunium were the silver mines of Laurium, an important source of revenue for ancient Athens and even today still worked for baser metals.

As Athens was an inland town, a few miles distant from the sea, a harbor was necessary. Originally the open bay and roadstead of Phalerum, three miles away, had sufficed, but in the fifth century a safer and better maritime haven was needed and this was found at Piraeus. Here, through the efforts of Themistocles and later of Pericles, a flourishing ship-station and town arose. In fact, after the destruction of Athens by the Persians in 480 B.C., Themistocles urged the Athenians

to move their city to Piraeus for greater convenience of
commerce and prosperity. But, as can readily be imagined, the Athenians, profoundly attached to the Acropolis, a site so ancient and revered, refused. The
harbor settlement rapidly grew in importance, and was
largely settled by traders and foreigners. As it was an
essential part of the city it was fortified and included
in the circuit of the Long Walls, which united and protected both Athens and its port.

Outside the harbor, not many miles distant and
plainly visible, lies Aegina, an island some twenty-five
miles in circumference, and a powerful Dorian state
in the sixth century. Rivalry and collision with the
growing power of Ionian Athens were inevitable, and
this " eyesore of the Piraeus," as Pericles called it, was
subjugated by Athens.

Off the western coast of Attica is the island Salamis,
noted for the momentous sea-fight in 480 B.C., between Greeks and Persians, where the invading host
of Xerxes was decisively defeated by the Greek fleet
under Themistocles.

Just north of Salamis on the bay of Eleusis is the
town of the same name, about fourteen miles from
Athens, the seat of the cult of Demeter and Persephone and the place for centuries of the celebration
of the Eleusinian Mysteries. Eleusis has been thoroughly excavated and the foundations of the Hall of
Initiation and other architectural and sculptural remains revealed.

Journeying to Athens from Eleusis over the Sacred
Way, the traveler crosses the Athenian plain and the
river Cephisus, which waters the Attic olive orchards.
The Cephisus ran through the gardens of Plato's gym-
nasium (the Academy) and fertilized the groves of
Colonus, birthplace of Sophocles and last refuge of
Oedipus of Thebes. The hill of Colonus, called
Colonus Hippius or Horse Knoll, was a lovely wooded
spot in ancient days and inspired Sophocles in his
play, *Oedipus at Colonus,* to celebrate its beauties

FIG. 11. THE CERAMICUS: OLD ATHENIAN CEMETERY

FIG. 12. THE AREOPAGUS AT ATHENS

in one of the finest lyrics in Greek tragedy (668 ff.).
The Sacred Way then took its course through the
outer *Ceramicus,* or Potters' Quarter, a district which
furnished suitable clay for the makers of vases. Here,
too, is the Street of Tombs, marking the ancient
burial-place. Many of the old tombstones have been
removed to the Museum in Athens, but some fine examples of Athenian sepulchral monuments remain *in*

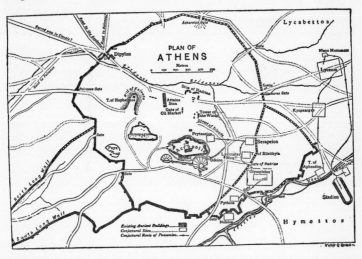

FIG. 13. PLAN OF ANCIENT ATHENS

situ (Fig. 11). The road then passed through a gate,
the *Dipylon,* into the *Inner Ceramicus,* and then into
the town proper and into the *Agora,* the market or
meeting-place, the center of the city's social, commercial, and political life.

A splendid view of all Athens and its environs is
obtained from the conspicuous conical hill of Mt.
Lycabettus, over 900 feet in height, at the northeastern extremity of the city. This prominent feature of the Athenian landscape is rarely mentioned
by the Athenian writers and evidently was not of great
religious significance. A little chapel of St. George
now caps its summit, while at its base to the southeast

are located the American School of Classical Studies and the British School.

The center of dominating interest and importance in both ancient and modern Athens is, of course, the *Acropolis* or Citadel, where the Athenians in early times first settled. The hill of the Acropolis is a flat-topped rocky plateau about 1000 feet long, 450 feet wide, and 500 feet high. It is precipitous on all sides except the western and was made more inaccessible by walls of masonry (See *Frontispiece*).

Some 300 feet northwest of the Acropolis lies the *Areopagus,* a rough hill of considerable surface area, 377 feet in height. The familiar Biblical name of the Areopagus is Mars' Hill (Hill of Ares), where Saint Paul delivered his message to the Athenians (Fig. 12).

To the west of the Acropolis lies the hill called the *Pnyx,* where the meetings of the *Ecclesia* (Assembly) were early held, while on the southeastern slope was the sacred precinct of the god Dionysus, with his temple and theater.

CHAPTER IV

ARCHITECTURE AND THE MONUMENTS OF ATHENS

"The lesson of the Parthenon is the lesson of a steadfast vision of beauty, held high above individual effort and failure, realizing itself not in complex detail or calculated eccentricity, but in a serene and exquisite simplicity of form. It teaches us that in the arts there are no short cuts, and that anarchy, the destruction of what has been won for us in the past, is not advance but the straight road to the bottomless pit of barbarism." — R. BLOMFIELD.

IT seems necessary to present a few of the most important facts relative to Greek architecture, in order that the nature, appearance, and purpose of the buildings and monuments of Athens may be more clearly understood.

In building materials the Athenians were fortunate. Limestone, both hard and soft (the latter mostly coming from Piraeus and called *poros*), was abundant, and marble, as we have seen, was quarried from Mt. Pentelicus and in later times from Mt. Hymettus. From the island of Paros a marble of coarser but glistening grain was obtained which was used extensively in sculpture; the Pentelic marble was employed for the great Periclean buildings of the fifth century B.C. Rubble construction was often used, the binding material being a mortar of clay: lime mortar is of Roman origin. The ordinary house or wall was built of sun-dried brick, which might be covered with stucco, resting on a course or foundation of stone-work. Burnt brick when found in buildings in Greek lands is of Roman date, as it was not used by the Greeks, although burnt tiles were employed for roofing. The chief woods were pine, fir, oak, and ash, but timber was never abundant and was used economically.

The Greek temple was not a house of assembly for the purpose of worship, but originated as a place of residence for the image of a deity and for the protection of religious offerings. The earliest Greek temples may have been made of wood and when stone was used as a substitute certain architectural forms seem to have been retained. For example, many scholars think that originally the stone columns were tree-trunks, the architraves were wooden beams, the triglyphs were the ends of the horizontal beams, the regulae were wooden cleats, and the guttae were wooden dowels. In the construction of the temple the structure rested on a foundation of stone, bed-rock if possible. Then came a series of three steps of which the top-step was called the *stylobate* or pillar-step, which supported the columns.

In Greek architecture we find three orders, the *Doric,* the *Ionic,* and the *Corinthian,* the last-named being a variation of the Ionic.

In the Doric order the rather sturdy pillar rests directly without a base on the stylobate. The shaft of the pillar is generally constructed of a series of sections or *drums* and is channeled usually with twenty channels or flutes which intersect at sharp angles. The diameter is somewhat less at the top than at the bottom, but there is a slightly swelling or curving outline of the shaft, called the *entasis.* The Doric capital consists of two parts — a lower curved portion or cushion, the *echinus,* and, on top of this, a square block, the *abacus,* completing the capital. Upon the capital rests a super-structure, the *entablature,* which consists of *architrave, frieze,* and *cornice.* The architrave is composed of the squared blocks, which reach from column to column. The frieze is made up of alternating *triglyphs* and *metopes,* the former thus called because of their division into three bands by two vertical channels; the latter being the interstices or holes between the triglyphs. The metopes were usually filled by stone blocks, sometimes decorated by sculp-

ture. Generally there is one triglyph over each column
and over each intercolumniation. Below each triglyph
is a small cleat, the *regula*, and under the regula are

Doric (Parthenon)   Ionic (Erechtheum)   Corinthian
(Monument of Lysicrates)

FIG. 14. THE THREE ORDERS OF GREEK ARCHITECTURE
(From Statham's *Short Critical History of Architecture*)

six *guttae* (drops). The function of the projecting
cornice above the frieze was to throw off rain-water.
The *cella*, or chamber of the temple, had a roof of

wood and rafters covered with tiles of terra-cotta or marble. The triangular *gable* or *pediment* thus formed at either end might contain sculpture.

The Ionic order differs from the Doric in that the Ionic column has a base consisting generally of an upper and lower convex *torus* separated by a concave *trochilus*. The shaft is more slender than the Doric and the *twenty-four* channels do not intersect, but each channel is separated from the other by a narrow flat surface. The capital has a *volute* or roll on either side and between these is a pattern, the so-called *egg-and-dart* ornament. Above the Ionic capital is an entablature, having an architrave which may be divided into two or three slightly projecting bands (*fasciae*). Above this the frieze is continuous (i.e., without metopes and triglyphs) and may be ornamented above with carved members. Characteristic of the Ionic order are the *dentils*, a row of projecting tooth-like ornaments, just below the cornice. In the Attic-Ionic style the frieze may be decorated with a continuous band of sculpture in relief and, in this event, there are no dentils.

The Corinthian order is the same as the Ionic except that its capital is composed of an ornamental design of *acanthus* leaves. Vitruvius, the Roman architect, says that the Corinthian capital was suggested to Callimachus when he observed an acanthus plant entwined about a basket of sepulchral offerings. In general it may be said that the Doric order gives an impression of simplicity, strength, and solidity, particularly in its earlier examples; the Ionic, of slenderness and grace; the Corinthian, of richness and ornamentation. The Corinthian was of comparatively late origin; the earliest example of its use in Athens is in the Monument of Lysicrates 335 B.C. Later, as taste declined, it became very popular and was a favorite of the Romans.

It still comes as a surprise to many persons to learn that color was extensively used on Greek marble temples and sculpture. The exact extent of the application of this *polychromy* is uncertain, but certainly red and dark-blue and occasionally yellow, green, and gilt were employed. Triglyphs and regulae were blue, guttae red. Likewise the background of sculptured metopes was red and moldings tinted. In the pediments, backgrounds of sculpture were painted red or blue. The statues might be colored as to borders of draperies, eyes, lips, and hair. Several statues unearthed in excavations on the Acropolis still show the colors bright and fresh. In the brilliant sunshine and clear atmosphere of Greece some touches of color on the milk-white marbles were doubtless highly effective. At any rate we may be sure that the beauty of these works of art was only enhanced and in no wise diminished by the use of color as applied by the original artists.

The *cella*, or interior of the temple, was lighted usually only by the large eastern entrance doors. Bright illumination of the interior was not needed or desired. Lamps, of course, could be used when necessary. The Erechtheum, however, had windows.

Athens before the Persian Wars was a town of plain appearance. It is true that the tyrant Pisistratus and his family, even in the sixth century B.C., began to adorn the city. The temple of Olympian Zeus was begun by Pisistratus, who also introduced the water supply from Hymettus for the Fountain of Nine Spouts, the *Enneacrunus*. The Acropolis was not neglected by the sons of Pisistratus, who added to its walls and constructed upon it buildings ornamented with sculptures. The early embellishment of the city, however, was rudely halted and in fact entirely destroyed by the Persian occupation of the city and Acropolis in 480 B.C., when the army of Xerxes brutally demolished and burned temples, walls, houses, and statues. Immediately after the departure of the invaders, who had suffered defeat at Salamis, the Athenians devoted themselves with great energy to

the work of rebuilding. This work, begun under
Themistocles, made progress under Cimon, but
reached a glorious climax under Pericles in the latter
half of the fifth century B.C., when numerous marble
temples adorned with sculptures were constructed.
The enormous expense of these building operations
was largely defrayed from the funds of the Delian
Confederacy, that confederation of states which had
been formed after the Persian Wars, with Athens at
its head, to insure protection against future attacks
from the barbarians. Earthquakes, vandalism, shell-
fire and explosions of gun-powder have wrought during the centuries grave injury to these wonderful
examples of architecture, but there remain still in
existence today ruined buildings of impressive beauty
and perfection. These monuments of Athena's city
we shall now describe, first, those outside the Acropolis; next, the buildings on the sacred citadel.

Northwest of the Acropolis and bounding the Agora
on the west stands one of the two best preserved Greek
temples in existence, the so-called *Theseum* (temple of
Theseus) (Fig. 15). Scholars generally believe that
this temple was built in honor of Hephaestus and should
therefore be called the *Hephaesteum*. It is a Doric
temple, 45 feet wide and 104 feet long, built mostly of
Pentelic marble. It is *hexastyle* (i.e., it has six pillars
at either end) and *peripteral* (i.e., has a continuous
colonnade or *peristyle* on all four sides). Thirteen
columns are on either side. The pedimental groups
have disappeared. A few sculptured metopes badly
damaged remain; these represent the labors of Heracles
and the deeds of Theseus. The date of the temple is
uncertain, although undoubtedly it is but little later
than the Parthenon. Its excellent preservation is partly
to be accounted for by the fact that in Byzantine times
it was used as a Christian church dedicated to St.
George.

Southeast of the Acropolis the visitor today in Athens
observes a group of colossal Corinthian columns, the

FIG. 15. THE THESEUM (so-called) AT ATHENS

FIG. 16. THE MONUMENT OF LYSICRATES, ATHENS

FIG. 17. THE TEMPLE OF "WINGLESS VICTORY," ATHENS

FIG. 18. THE PROPYLAEA (ENTRANCE PORTAL), FROM THE E.

ruins of the temple of Olympian Zeus, the *Olympieum* (Fig. 19), the largest of all Greek temples. As the case with some of the Gothic cathedrals this temple was under intermittent construction for centuries. It was begun by Pisistratus about 530 B.C., and was probably intended to be of the Doric order of architecture. Remaining incomplete at the death of the tyrant it apparently was untouched until about 174 B.C. when Antiochus Epiphanes, king of Syria, advanced the work, but increased the proportions of the building and changed the order of architecture to the Corinthian, the prevailing mode in his day. We learn that in 86 B.C. Sulla carried off some of the columns, perhaps these of the cella, to Rome for the Capitoline temple to Jupiter. It remained for the emperor Hadrian, a lover and benefactor of Athens, to finish the temple in 130 A.D. The proportions of the Olympieum were enormous. It measured 354 by 135 feet and was over 90 feet in height, having eight Corinthian columns at either end and twenty columns along the sides. The temple was dipteral, i.e., a double row of columns entirely surrounded the cella. The great size of the columns (56.6 feet) may be judged by comparing them with those of the Parthenon (34¼ feet). Nothing is known of the sculptures of the temple, except that in the cella there seems to have been a great gold and ivory statue of Zeus.

A short distance to the east of the Olympieum, in a dip between two hills, lies the *Stadium*, where the Panathenaic Games were held. The Stadium in its finished form is of the time of the orator Lycurgus who, in 330 B.C., supervised its construction. Originally there were no seats, the spectators sitting on the sloping hillsides. In 140 A.D. the Stadium was clothed in Pentelic marble at the expense of the wealthy Herodes Atticus, benefactor of Athens, who likewise built the Odeum, still an imposing Roman structure at the southwestern corner of the Acropolis. More than 50,000 spectators could be seated in the Stadium. The course proper was 600 Greek feet long. In recent years the Stadium has been built in Pentelic marble and appropriately served as the scene of the first celebration of the revived Olympian Games (Fig. 20).

Around the southeastern and eastern slopes of the Acropolis, beginning at the theater of Dionysus, ran a road called the *Street of Tripods,* so called because of a series of small supports of tripods which were erected along the thoroughfare. One of these structures has been preserved in the attractive little *Monument of Lysicrates* (Fig. 16), erected in 335 B.C. by Lysicrates, a wealthy Athenian citizen, who had been a victorious *choregus* in a contest of dithyrambic choruses. This well-preserved Monument, which served as a basis for the prize awarded him, a bronze tripod, is itself of great interest and charm and is likewise of importance as being the earliest example of the Corinthian order in Athens. On a base of *poros* about thirteen feet high rests a circular shrine of Pentelic marble, some twenty feet in height and about seven feet in diameter. This is constructed of six fluted columns and between these are curved marble slabs. On the columns is an architrave, and a frieze some ten inches high, which portrays the punishment of the pirates who were metamorphosed into dolphins by Dionysus — a theme which finds literary expression in the charming *Hymn to Dionysus.* The roof represents a thatch of laurel leaves and from its center arose a floral ornament, which supported the bronze tripod. This little building was formerly called the Lantern of Demosthenes and an absurd story related that the great orator used it as a study! An excellent reproduction of the Monument of Lysicrates is on exhibition at the Metropolitan Museum in New York City. The structure itself has served as inspiration for many monuments.

The Theater of Dionysus (Fig. 46) on the southeastern slope of the Acropolis will be discussed in the chapter devoted to the Greek theater.

The impressive monuments on the Acropolis now

FIG. 19. THE OLYMPIEUM (TEMPLE OF OLYMPIAN ZEUS)

FIG. 20. THE ANCIENT STADIUM (restored), AT ATHENS

claim our attention. These magnificent marble buildings of the latter part of the fifth century B.C. all owe
their existence to the initiative of the statesman Pericles and were erected in honor of the protecting
deities of Athens and for the glory and adornment
of Athens. As has been said, their great cost in large
measure was defrayed from the funds in the treasury
of the Delian Confederacy, that naval league or rather
empire of which Athens had become the dominating
mistress and Athena the patron goddess. The successful construction of these noble monuments, however,

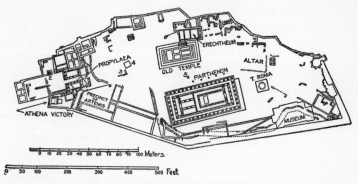

Fig. 21. PLAN OF THE ACROPOLIS
(From Weller, *Athens and Its Monuments*)

was due to the genius of such great architects as Ictinus,
Mnesicles, and Callicrates, the sculptor Phidias, and
the painter Polygnotus. But the lofty conceptions of
these artists were brought to glorious materialization
by the intelligent and conscientious labor of the Athenian workman, both freeman and slave. The materials
used and the workers employed are vividly described
by Plutarch (*Life of Pericles*, ch. 12, trans. by B.
Perrin): " The materials to be used were stone,
bronze, ivory, gold, ebony, and cypress-wood; the arts
which should elaborate and work up these materials
were those of carpenter, moulder, bronze-smith, stonecutter, dyer, worker in gold and ivory, painter, em-

broiderer, embosser, to say nothing of the forwarders and furnishers of the material, such as factors, sailors and pilots by sea, and, by land, wagon-makers, trainers of yoked beasts and drivers. There were also rope-makers, weavers, leather-workers, road-builders, and miners."

As one ascends the western slope of the Citadel and before he enters the Propylaea he sees on the right a beautiful little building, the temple of *Nike Apteros* or *Wingless Victory,* thus called as it was built in honor of Athena as goddess of Victory, whereas Victory was usually personified as a winged figure, e.g., the famous Victory of Samothrace. The temple of Wingless Victory, of about the same date as the Parthenon, is of small proportions, the dimensions of the cella being only some twelve by fourteen feet and the columns not quite thirteen and a half feet in height. It is built of Pentelic marble, of the Ionic order, with four columns at front and four at back. A sculptured frieze, eighteen inches high, somewhat damaged, runs around the building. The space in front and about the temple was enclosed by a sculptured marble balustrade or parapet; slabs from this balustrade representing winged Victories are preserved and are especially admired because of the beauty of the figures and the execution of the drapery. The story of the disappearance and the resurrection of this charming little temple is indeed interesting. In 1676 it was still standing, as a traveler reports. A little later the building was pulled down by the Turks and was used by them to build an emplacement for cannon. This battery was removed in 1835 and the little temple was rebuilt on the spot from its *disjecta membra* (Fig 17).

The entrance proper to the Citadel or Acropolis was guarded and adorned by a splendid structure of Pentelic marble, the *Propylaea,* or Entrance Gates (Fig. 18), which was built under Pericles by the architect Mnesicles. This building was begun in 437 B.C. and construction ended in 432 B.C. after the sum of 2012 talents (over $2,000,000) had been expended. The Propylaea consisted of a portal with five doorways, and porticoes in front and behind, and the plans called for two wings. In the western portico a combination of Doric and Ionic columns was effectively employed. The northwest wing, a chamber lighted by a door and two windows, fronted by three Doric columns, is designated the *Pinakotheke* (picture-gallery), as here paintings (described by Pausanias) were exhibited. The southwest wing of the Propylaea as originally planned was never built, as its construction would have encroached upon the precinct of the temple of Wingless Victory.

The visitor, having passed through the Propylaea, stands upon the flat top of the Acropolis and beholds two temples, on his right the Parthenon and on the left the Erechtheum. The foreground is littered with a wilderness of prostrate stones, blocks, and bases which testify to the numerous statues and shrines that once stood there. It was halfway between the Propylaea and the Erechtheum that the huge bronze statue of Athena *Promachos* (the Champion) by Phidias stood. With shield, spear, and crested helmet it stood some twenty-five or thirty feet in height, and Pausanias tells us that " the head of the spear and the crest of the helmet of this Athena are visible as you sail up from the direction of Sunium."

The *Erechtheum* (Fig. 24) is an Ionic temple of great beauty and interest. Its unique design is probably due to the fact that it was built over sacred shrines and tokens of Erechtheus (mythical hero of Athens), Athena, and Poseidon. Its dimensions are some 74 by 37 feet. There are three porticoes or porches, one at the eastern end fronted by six Ionic columns, one at the northwest corner with beautiful coffered ceiling and ornamented doorway, and, on the south, the famous *Porch of the Maidens* or *Caryatids*. This last porch has, instead of columns, six statues of maidens who support on their heads the roof of the portico. The figures

DOMINICAN COLLEGE
LIBRARY
SAN RAFAEL, CALIF.

stand on a parapet about six feet high and are in their proportions one half larger than life size. A remarkable effect of grace and dignity is given and there is no impression of strain because of the success of the sculptor in arranging the pose, with bent knee, the drapery columnar in effect, and the arrangement of masses of hair on the neck. Furthermore, the superstructure seems of light weight, as no frieze rests upon the architrave. One of the Caryatids is now in the Lord Elgin collection of Greek marbles from the Acropolis in the British Museum and for this missing figure there has been substituted a replica of terracotta. The Erechtheum was not entirely complete in 409 B.C.

Our discussion of the most important monuments of Athens appropriately ends with a description of the chief architectural glory of Athens and the world's most famous building, the *Parthenon* (Fig. 22). This temple was built in honor of Athena *Parthenos* (the Virgin Athena, hence the name, Parthenon) and took the place of an earlier temple destroyed by the Persians in 480 B.C. It was begun by Pericles in 447 B.C. and completed in 432 B.C. The architects were Ictinus and Callicrates, and the superintendent of sculptures, Phidias. This peripteral temple of Pentelic marble is a perfect example of the Doric order and has eight columns at the ends and seventeen on each side. The columns are a little over 34 feet in height and are built up of twelve drums. One entering the temple first passed through the east portico or vestibule, the *Pronaos,* then the great east room or cella proper, which was called, because of its length, the *Hekatompedos Neōs* or Hundred-foot Temple. This room contained the celebrated chryselephantine (gold-and-ivory) cult statue of Athena, the work of Phidias. Back of this room, but separated from it by a wall, was the Parthenon proper, which was used as a store-house for the treasures of the goddess. Finally there was the west portico, designated the *Opisthodomos,* or Rear-chamber.

The Parthenon is not merely admirable for its impressive and perfect proportions and its architectural beauty and finish, but is no less remarkable for the wealth of its sculptural adornment. The eastern pediment contained a group representing the birth of Athena; the western portrayed the contest between Athena and Poseidon for the land of Attica. A number of these splendid statues have been preserved and are in the British Museum. The metopes of the building, about four feet square, ninety-two in number, were sculptured; of these, fifteen are likewise in London. A beautiful feature of the decorative sculptures was the Ionic frieze, some 524 feet in length and three and a quarter feet in height, which was placed about forty feet above the floor of the outer corridor and ran entirely around the temple. This frieze, carved in relief, containing many hundreds of figures, represents the Panathenaic procession, which occurred every four years on the occasion of the great festival. Then it was that the *peplos,* or robe of Athena, which had been woven by chosen maidens of Athens, was carried to the Acropolis for presentation to the goddess. In the procession we see the young knights on their prancing steeds, chariots, lyre-players, worshippers with offerings, the animals destined for sacrifice, and the august deities themselves. About 247 feet of this wonderful frieze are among the Elgin treasures in the British Museum.

The later history of the Parthenon is of interest. Surviving the Hellenistic and Roman periods it was seen in the second century A.D. by the traveler Pausanias. In the fifth century A.D. it was used as a Christian church, first sacred to " Holy Wisdom," later to the " Mother of God." Certain alterations were effected, namely, an apse, a gallery, windows, and wall-paintings. When the Turks took Athens about 1456 the Parthenon became a mosque with a high minaret at the southwest corner! In 1687 the whole middle portion of the temple was blown out by an explosion of powder stored there by the Turks, who were being besieged by the Venetians. It was in 1801 that Lord Elgin, by the permission of the Turkish authorities, removed to London the sculptured treasures above described, thereby possibly saving them from further mutilation or even destruction and making them accessible to western Europe.

Plutarch (*Life of Pericles*, ch. 12, trans. by B. Perrin) gives us a striking account of the rapid construction of the Periclean buildings: ' So then the works arose, no less towering in their grandeur than inimitable in the grace of their outlines, since the workmen eagerly strove to surpass themselves in the beauty of their handicraft. And yet the most wonderful thing about them was the speed with which they rose. Each one of them, men thought, would require many successive generations to complete it, but all of them were fully completed in the heyday of a single administration."

What the Greeks accomplished in architecture has been always admired. It is true that Gothic art of the twelfth and thirteenth centuries, as perfected by the builders of the great cathedrals of Europe, is one of the most striking evidences of human achievement, when the feeble hand of man was given gigantic powers of accomplishment by the urge of the spirit and the will to create. The modern "sky-scraper" is a worthy product of modern needs and of practical commercial utility. And it is more than this. The Woolworth Building in New York City, for example, an impressive structure of awe-inspiring height and actual beauty of line, form, and mass, is worthy of comparison with the great architectural achievements of the past. But Greek architecture will ever remain as one of the chief sources of architectural inspiration by reason of its simplicity, its sincerity, its conscientious working out of legitimate detail, and its devotion to severe beauty of form.

FIG. 22. THE PARTHENON

FIG. 23. THE PARTHENON, RECONSTRUCTED AT NASHVILLE, TENN.
(From *Art and Archaeology*)

FIG. 24. THE ERECHTHEUM

Amphora   Hydria   Crater

FIG. 25   SHAPES OF ATHENIAN BLACK-FIGURED VASES (Metropolitan Museum)

CHAPTER V

HOUSE, FURNITURE, AND VASES

GREEK houses of the classical period were built of perishable materials and consequently excavations have failed to reveal to us much direct evidence relative to the private dwellings of Athenians of that time. Furthermore, the modern city of Athens is built on the ancient site and excavation is therefore difficult. It is true that in various parts of the Greek world, as at the island of Delos and Priene in Asia Minor and at Olynthus, Greek dwellings have been unearthed, but these are mostly of rather late date and show marked Roman influence. We are dependent, therefore, largely upon references in the literature. These acquaint us with the general characteristics of the Greek house but chance allusions naturally fail to give us detailed information. Although in Athenian houses a general plan of building and arrangement was followed, variations of course existed. The description given below must be prefaced with a few important considerations.

The private house was not so important to the Greek as it is to us, for the reason that he spent as little time as possible in it. A mild climate and keen interest in social and public life and happenings allowed and influenced him to spend most of his waking hours outdoors. At home the life of the family centered in and about the court-yard and early to bed and early rising were universal habits. In consequence of the comparative unimportance of the dwelling, the architecture of private houses was neglected. Expense and labor were lavished on the beautiful public buildings and temples, while the building of a pretentious house was considered bad taste in the extreme. Ancient writers tell us that the private houses of prominent and wealthy citizens were seldom more splendid than those of their neighbors and that most of the houses of Athens were so plain that the stranger could scarcely realize that he was in celebrated Athens.

As to the price of houses, we learn from the orator Isaeus that a house at Melite sold for half a talent (30 *minae,* about $540). A house at Eleusis was worth only five *minae* (about $90). Another city dwelling sold for fifty *minae* ($900). It was possible to rent a modest house for three *minae* ($54) a year. Socrates says that he could sell his house and all his other property for perhaps five *minae*. But Socrates was poor in the goods of this world. In estimating these sums allowance must be made for the great difference in purchasing power of money. We should, therefore, multiply the figures presented above by *at least* five. Even so, the modern tenant has good cause to envy the Athenian as a householder.

The foundation of the private house was of rough stone, while the walls were constructed of sun-dried brick. Such a wall was necessarily rather soft and we read that burglars might easily enter a house by digging their way through with a pick-axe; hence the Greek word for burglar signifies " wall-digger."

The wall of sun-dried brick was covered with a coating of stucco or plaster of lime, which might be tinted. The flat or sloping roof of the city house was covered with hardened clay or tiles. The house was built directly upon the street and the wall presented a blank surface except for the small windows which sometimes gave light to the second story.

The most essential feature of the Greek house was the rectangular, central, open court or *aulê (aula),* often with pillared cloister, surrounded by chambers. In the middle of the court were an altar of Zeus, protector of the family, and statues of Zeus and Apollo. The rooms (living-room, sleeping-room, store-closets, etc.) opening off the court might be few or many and were provided with doors or with portières. Besides the front street-door a second entrance at the back might be provided. A second story, often used for the women's apartments, was usual. The entrance was by simple stairs of wood.

Heating was little needed and was primitive: portable braziers for charcoal were common and an open hearth might find place in the living-room. Illumination at night was effected by lamps, with wick of flax and burning olive-oil, or by torches. By day the rooms were lighted from the court and those of the second story to some extent by the small windows which were protected by some sort of shutters, as window-glass was not used until Roman times.

The floors, originally of hard-packed earth, were later of cement and finally of mosaic. Mats and floor-coverings might be employed. The walls inside were whitewashed or stuccoed, and in finer homes of the later period decorated with wall paintings.

Some houses had cellars where huge jars containing wine, oil, and provisions were stored. Cisterns were general and necessary for collecting and storing rainwater. Fresh water was procured daily from springs. A common scene pictured on the vases is that of a woman getting water at the fountain and descriptions of this task are extremely frequent in the literature.

As we have seen, unostentation was the rule in the building of private houses. Gradually greater comfort was effected and even luxurious features were introduced by the wealthy. Demosthenes complains that private houses in his time are beginning to surpass public buildings in magnificence. Alcibiades had aroused adverse criticism by having the walls of his house decorated with paintings. This fashion, in later times, became prevalent. In the Greek house of the island of Delos (second century B.C.) and at Priene (third century B.C.) we find many magnificent details, such as elaborate mosaics, mural decorations, marble moldings and cornices, tinted stucco ornaments, and handsome columns.

Extreme simplicity likewise characterized the furniture and furnishings of the Athenian dwelling. As has been said, the Greeks lived out of doors as much as possible and the houses were not crowded with furniture as is the rule in the modern world. The list of furniture is short: chairs and stools, beds, tables, chests, rugs, utensils, and vases. The many illustrations on Greek vases give us a good idea of the actual appearance of these objects.

Beds were used not only for sleeping at night but also for use at meals, at banquets, and for rest and reading by day. The usual material was wood, the legs straight and upright, turned or square. Cords or leather thongs were stretched across the frame, which consisted of four strips of wood, and a thin mattress stuffed with wool or feathers was placed thereon. Woolen blankets, rugs, fleeces, and goat-skins were used as coverings and cushions and pillows were employed. Sometimes an inclined head-board was added to the equipment of the couch.

A variety of chairs was in common use. Of these the most comfortable was the *thronos* (throne) — a heavy chair with back, arms, and straight legs (turned or square). It was often so high that a foot-stool was needed. The *thronos* was the chair of honor and always, as in Homer, proffered to the guest. A variation of the chair just described was an easy chair with sloping back and curved legs, but without arms. This was called the *klismos*. It is constantly pictured on the vases. Also frequent is the simple stool, with either folding legs like our camp-stool, or with straight, rigid legs. A cushion was generally used with the stool. Benches, too, were common. The vase-paintings frequently show persons seated on chests which were in common use for storing clothes and valuables.

Tables were not used for so many purposes as with us. The dining and work tables were small, light, and usually rectangular; they had either three or four legs and these were straight or curved, and frequently ornamented. The table was in constant use by tradesmen, artisans and money-changers. In fact, the ancient and modern Greek word for bank is *trapeza* (table).

Wax candles were unknown before the Roman period. Torches made of pine, or dry sticks covered with pitch, might be carried at night in the streets and always appeared at festivals, weddings and funerals. Lamps of all sizes, of bronze or clay, were in common use. The latter were turned on the potters' wheel, although late Greek lamps were made on a mould. In them olive-oil was burned with wick of flax.

Rush mats as floor coverings were found in poorer houses, while imported rugs from Asia Minor could be afforded only by the rich.

Greek mirrors were often objects of beauty and works of art as well as things of practical utility. They were made of polished metal, generally copper, mixed with tin, zinc, etc., often silvered or gilded. Frequently they had ornamental handles and on the back a decoration usually portraying mythological subjects. To prevent scratching of the highly polished reflecting surface they were usually kept in special boxes and these might be elaborately and beautifully ornamented. Many interesting and artistic examples of Greek mirrors and cases may be seen in our museums.

Although glass was known, there was probably no glass at all in use in the Athenian home of the fifth and fourth centuries B.C. Household and kitchen dishes, utensils, and drinking vessels were made of pottery, bronze, or iron.

Vessels of pottery might be for practical use only and severely plain, those of larger size being intended for the storing or transportation of oil, wine, water, grain, and provisions generally, the smaller for manifold household use. In shape, however, they were always graceful. From earliest times vases and vessels of burnt clay were made in all parts of Greece and were fashioned in every size and shape and adorned and beautified in infinite variety. Not only are Greek vases, especially those of Athenian manufacture, extremely artistic in outline and fabrication, but they are worthy of special study and admiration because of the beauty of their decoration. Furthermore, since Greek painting is lost to us, the painted decorations on the vases are of particular interest. These vase-paintings portray scenes of every kind and contribute much to our information respecting Greek art, life, and mythology. They furnish us with contemporary evidence of manners and customs and illustrate daily life in all its aspects, as upon the vases were depicted scenes from the shop and the market, from the theater and the dance, from the school and the palaestra, from war and mythology. This testimony is of profound importance and interest to the student of Greek civilization. Fortunately, terra-cotta is an almost imperishable material and these vases have been excavated in countless numbers in all Greek lands. As they were generally buried with the dead they are commonly found in tombs, but almost every excavation of any kind yields its quota of vases. As the pottery again was fired after the application of the glaze and ornamentation the vases have been found wonderfully well preserved, frequently as perfect as on the day of manufacture. In the museums of Europe and America large and carefully chosen collections of Greek pottery are on exhibition and these may be studied at first-hand.

The manufacture of vases was an important industry as early as the Mycenaean Period, when Crete and the Aegean islands were the home of a flourishing civilization. In the decoration of the vases of this period *motifs* taken from sea-life, e.g., the cuttle-fish, nautilus, corals and shells, are common.

The succeeding period in vase making is called the *geometrical*, as the decoration on the pottery is geometric, the surface of the vase being covered with formal designs, horizontal and perpendicular lines and zigzag patterns. The most finished examples of this ware come mostly from Athens and are as late in date as the seventh century B.C.

Corinth and Athens became the two chief centers for the manufacture and exportation of artistic vases. In both cities clay of admirable quality for pottery was found. The clay of Corinth is extremely light in color. The early Corinthian ware (seventh and sixth centuries B.C.) shows marked Oriental influences and is characterized by strips of decoration in which appear animals, plants, and ornaments from the East, together with Hellenic subjects. In the sixth and fifth centuries B.C., however, Athens assumed the lead in the manufacture of pottery and exported her perfect ware to all parts of the Greek world. Many of the finest examples of Athenian vases have been found in Italy, especially in Etruria.

At Athens the clay found in the district Ceramicus (Potters' Quarter) was of excellent quality and here the workshops of the potters were located. In the process of manufacture the clay was washed and kneaded, red earth might be mixed in, and the body of the vase turned on the potters' wheel. The handles were made separately and joined to the body. After drying and polishing, the vase was then ready to receive its decoration, of which there were two styles, viz., (1) *black figures* on a light background; (2) *red figures* on a black background.

In the former system, which was in vogue to the latter part of the sixth century B.C., the figures and ornaments were applied in black silhouette on the surface of the vase, the background being the buff or reddish tone of the body of the vessel. The figures were painted on with solid black varnish and this, when fired, became a lustrous glaze. Previous to the final firing, however, additional fine details were incised in the figures with a sharp-pointed instrument.

In the red-figured style, a much superior system, which superseded the black-figured ware at the end of the sixth century and thereafter, the figure was sketched with details and the background was covered with black glaze.

Two kinds of vases peculiar to Athens were the black-figured Panathenaic *amphorae* and the white *lecythi*. The former were large two-handled vases, which were given as prizes to victors in the Panathenaic Games. These vases followed a set fashion and were always appropriately inscribed and decorated with a scene from the Games.

The lecythus, an oil-flask, was a slender graceful vase of great charm and beauty, with peculiar decoration in that the body was covered generally with a white slip or coating of paint. Upon this as background the figures were drawn in fine lines and filled in with washes of brown or red or other color which, in many cases, unfortunately have faded. These lecythi were intimately associated with mourning, burial, and the tomb; in fact, burial scenes are frequently depicted upon them. They have been found in large numbers in Attic graves.

Another circumstance of interest in connection with Greek pottery is the fact that maker and painter often signed their wares. Museums have many examples of these vases signed by such masters as Nicosthenes, Euphronius, Clitias, and Douris.

The most common kinds of Greek vases, classified according to their forms, are: the *pithus*, a large jar at least five feet high and used for storing provisions, the extremely common *amphora*, a large two-handled vase, in capacity from two to five gallons, employed for carrying and storing water, wine, and provisions, the *hydria*, a water-jar, with one large handle and two small ones on the sides, the *crater*, a mixing-bowl, with two handles, in shape like a big punch-bowl, the *stam-nus*, a variation of the amphora but of more squat form and wider mouth, the *oenochoe*, in shape very similar to our pitcher, the *cylix*, a drinking-cup, rather shallow, with two small handles, the *cantharus*, a two-handled

Scyphus   Cylix   Cylix

Oenochoe   Alabastrum   Stamnus   Lecythus   Olpe

FIG. 26. SHAPES OF ATHENIAN BLACK-FIGURED VASES (Metropolitan Museum)

cup, frequently seen in representations of Dionysus, the *rhytum*, a drinking-horn, often made in the likeness of an animal's head, the *aryballus*, a small round vase, with flat mouth and small orifice, used by athletes for rubbing oil on the person, and the *lecythus*, above described (See Figs. 25 and 26 for shapes).

To the Greeks the designing, manufacture, and decoration of pottery seem to have been considered merely a minor industry. To us, however, these vases are a fascinating study because of their symmetry of form and charm of ornamentation. And as previously said, they are all the more valuable because of their painted decoration in view of the inevitable loss of Greek mural and easel painting.

CHAPTER VI

SCULPTURE

"When we ask what is the debt of modern art to Greek art, there is no reply. We can point to this idea or that, and say this is Hellenic and that is non-Hellenic. We can say this is Pheidian, that Scopaic, or this is Pergamene and that Rhodian, but to say art is Greek is simply to say it is good. For Greek art comprises every genuine effort of the artist, every statue which is made with sincere love of beauty and unmixed desire for its attainment is Greek in spirit; every statue, however cunning and ingenious, which is merely frivolous or hypocritical or untrue, is a crime against Hellenism and a sin against the light. The Greek bequest to later artists is nothing tangible, it is the soul and spirit of the artist." — GUY DICKINS.

THE indebtedness of the world of today to the Greeks is perhaps even more strikingly shown in sculpture than in the other arts. Greek mural and easel paintings in the very nature of the case have largely perished. Although Greek architecture provides the inspiration and the actual details for many of our noblest buildings and monuments, as for example the beautiful memorial to Abraham Lincoln which has been recently erected at Washington, yet subsequent centuries evolved, as in the Gothic style, satisfying and beautiful architectural forms. In sculpture, on the other hand, the ancient Greeks still remain our best guides and teachers, so perfect are their works of art which have never been surpassed.

Greek sculpture was of gradual development, as the student may observe through a long series of surviving works of art. First, come the rather crude and primitive beginnings in the *Archaic Period*, before 500 B.C. Then, during the *Fifth and Fourth Centuries* B.C., the artist, having acquired mastery of his medium, produced works of superlative excellence. Next, during the *Hellenistic Period* (*ca.* 320–100 B.C.) the sculptor, still gifted with great technical skill, exercised greater freedom of choice and treatment of subject and turned more towards realism. Finally, in the *Graeco-Roman Age,* original inspiration was on the wane, Greek types served the Romans as patterns, and adaptations were the fashion.

We are indebted to recent excavations in Greek lands for many examples of archaic sculpture, and these are now chiefly in the museums of Greece. The British Museum in London has the Parthenon marbles; the Louvre, in Paris, the Aphrodite of Melos and the Victory of Samothrace; Berlin, the sculptures from Pergamum; Munich, the pediment statues from Aegina; Florence, Naples, and other European cities possess some excellent pieces. The Vatican Museum in Rome has almost countless Greek statues, although the majority are copies. The collections of original Greek art in the Metropolitan Museum of Art in New York and the Boston Museum of Fine Arts are not of great size, but they are choice and of great value to American students and lovers of art.

It is important to note at the outset that the Greek sculptor worked hand in hand with the architect. A shrine of a god always housed an appropriate cult statue and, as we have seen in the case of the Parthenon, the exterior of a temple might be richly adorned with works of sculpture. The pediments might contain statues in the round; the metopes were sometimes adorned with sculpture in relief, and a decorative frieze with carving in relief might even run around the entire building. This combination of architecture and decorative sculpture so happily achieved by the Greeks affords a striking lesson of successful artistic accomplishment — a lesson which should be taken to heart in modern times and followed more frequently than it is. Individual statues, conceived and executed without relation to the decoration of buildings — *substantive* or *free* sculpture, as the text-books designate this class — were, of course, common.

Another striking characteristic of Greek sculpture, in contrast with the general modern practice, was *polychromy* or the application of color. Numerous statues have been unearthed in recent years which still bear vivid traces of the colors originally used.

Many materials were employed by the Greeks for statuary. We read of primitive wooden images of the gods; these, of course, have not survived. Bronze was a popular metal for statuary in the open, as, for example, the statues of athletes. Some of these are extant, but most of them have disappeared, as many have been melted down for the metal they contained. In numerous cases they live again through extant marble copies. In the so-called *chryselephantine* (gold and ivory) statues — e.g., that of Athena Parthenos by Phidias — the framework was of wood. Terra-cotta (baked clay) was an extremely common material in the making of small images or statuettes, and was even employed occasionally for large statues in Cyprus and southern Italy. The Tanagra statuettes, and the little figures of painted terra-cotta found in many places — e.g., at Myrina in Asia Minor and Tarentum in southern Italy — are life-like, graceful, and appealing.

Various kinds and qualities of stone and marble were the materials out of which most surviving Greek statuary is fashioned. The islands of Naxos and Paros produced marble for the sculptor's needs, although the Parian marble, of finer grain, supplanted the Naxian. The marble of Mt. Pentelicus, so extensively used for Athenian building purposes, was a convenient and more accessible material. The Pentelic stone, however, contains iron and is subject to discoloration when it is long exposed to the elements.

Although the museums of the world are richly stocked with works of Greek art, these statues are, for the most part, copies of originals. Original specimens are by no means rare, yet masterpieces of the best period of Greek art are not numerous.

THE ARCHAIC PERIOD (down to 480 B.C.)

The excavations of recent years in Greek lands have brought to light numerous works of art of the archaic period. These statues in the round, of the sixth century B.C., in general admit of a triple classification. There are nude, standing, male figures — the so-called Apollos; draped, standing figures, generally female; and draped, seated figures. These early works of art are decidedly primitive. The pose is rigid, the outline angular, and the treatment of details, especially in the face, leaves much to be desired. The figure, severely frontal, is stiffly erect. The statues show promise, but the artist has many technical difficulties to surmount. The so-called Apollo of Tenea (now in Munich) is an excellent example of the nude male type of the archaic period. Numerous relief sculptures, too, of this early time have been found in many parts of the Greek world.

Specimens of early Attic sculpture were unearthed on the Acropolis in the excavations of the débris of the temples which were destroyed by the Persians in 480 B.C. Among these works are figures from pediment-reliefs of soft limestone, with details in color, a statue of a man carrying a bullock (*moschophorus*), and a number of draped female figures, which were made by sculptors of the school of the island of Chios and their Attic pupils, e.g., Antenor. The most beautiful of these early female statues from the Acropolis is that of a maiden, a work dedicated by Euthydicus. This figure is of great charm and the treatment of the head and features shows marked artistic advance (Fig. 27).

An interesting example of early Attic art is the gravestone (*stele*) of Aristion, by Aristocles, in which the warrior is shown, standing as in life, clad in armor and helmet, and with spear in hand. The details, although inaccurate in many respects, are carefully worked out by the sculptor. The figure reveals the exaggerated musculature which is a characteristic of the work of the early artists. Traces of pigment are still visible (Fig. 28).

Greek art of the pre-Persian period is further represented by the sculptures from the treasury of the Cnidians at Delphi, sculptured metopes from temples at Selinus in Sicily, the relief of the so-called Harpy Tomb from Lycia in the British Museum, and numerous other specimens of early schools. A little later than 480 B.C. probably are the life-like figures from the so-called temple of Aphaia on the island of Aegina. These well-known Aeginetan Marbles, with a few exceptions now in the Glyptothek at Munich, are from the two pediments of the temple. They represent fighting warriors (Fig. 29), with the goddess Athena in the center of each gable.

THE FIFTH CENTURY (480–400 B.C.)

The years 480–400 B.C., which witnessed so many momentous developments in Greek civilization, likewise produced masterpieces of art.

The excavations at Olympia revealed many examples of sculpture of a few years prior to 457 B.C., the approximate date of the completion of the temple of Zeus. From this temple were found a number of the figures from the pediment groups. These represent, as we are told by Pausanias, in the eastern gable, the preparation for the chariot race between Pelops and Oenomaus and, in the western, the fight of Lapiths and Centaurs at the wedding of Pirithous. Most striking of these statues is the figure of Apollo, which stood in the center of the western pediment. The metopes pictured the twelve labors of Heracles. Among other discoveries at Olympia is the Victory (Nike) of the sculptor Paeonius.

FIG. 27. ACROPOLIS MAIDEN (Athens)

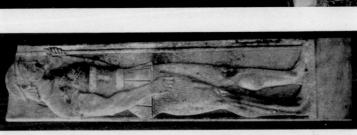

FIG. 28. STELE OF ARISTION

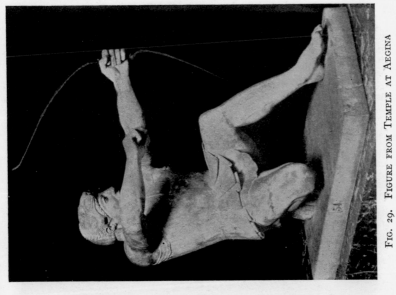

FIG. 29. FIGURE FROM TEMPLE AT AEGINA

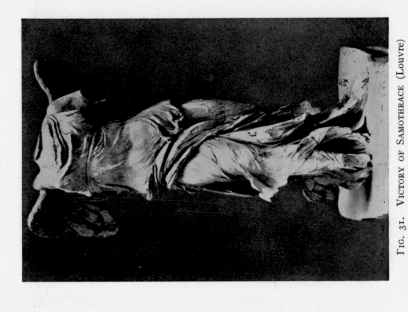

FIG. 31. VICTORY OF SAMOTHRACE (Louvre)

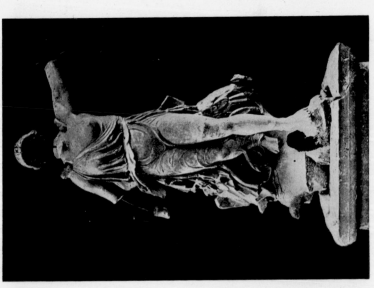

FIG. 30. VICTORY OF PAEONIUS (Olympia)

This statue (Fig. 30) was erected after the battle of Sphacteria in 425 B.C., and represents the winged goddess as if suspended in the air, with drapery and mantle clinging to the figure floating behind. It was a custom of the, Greeks to erect a statue of Victory as a goddess and we shall see another admirable example of the type in the Victory found at Samothrace, a fine specimen of the art of the Hellenistic Age (Fig. 31).

Also of the first half of the fifth century B.C. are the vigorous marble statues of Harmodius and Aristogiton, the tyrannicides, in the museum at Naples. This group is a copy by Critius and Nesiotes of originals by Antenor. Of this same period, but of uncertain date and authorship, is a statue of first-rate excellence — the bronze charioteer found at Delphi (Fig. 36). The chariot, steeds, and the goddess Victory, a group of which the charioteer was a part, have disappeared. The youthful driver, clad in a long chiton reaching almost to the ankles, stands erect, the right arm, holding the reins, outstretched. The details of the features, the hair which is bound with a fillet, and the drapery are reproduced with the utmost delicacy and charm.

The three greatest sculptors of the fifth century B.C. were Myron, Polyclitus, and Phidias.

Myron of Eleutherae, in northern Attica, was famous in antiquity for his statues of athletes. We are fortunate in having several marble copies of Roman date of his *Discobolus* or Discus Thrower (Fig. 41). This is the statue of a vigorous athlete who is shown, with body turned and with muscles at tension, at the moment before hurling the discus. Myron's technical skill as shown in this unusual study is remarkable, when his early date is considered. It should be observed further that Myron achieved fame by his figures of animals and especially by a life-like statue of a cow. This is noteworthy — as the representation of animals is generally thought to be of a later period only.

Polyclitus, of the Argive school, won renown through his bronze statues of athletes. Two of his works are known to us through marble copies. The *Doryphorus* (Fig. 39) represents a youth of rather massive physique, who carries, over his left shoulder, a spear. The *Diadumenus* is the figure of a youthful athlete who stands with both arms upraised to bind the fillet of victory about his head. Attributed also to Polyclitus is one type of the series of extant statues which represent the Amazons.

We have already surveyed (Chapter IV) the architectural monuments of the Athens of Pericles. In the description of the Acropolis in that chapter will be found a brief account of the sculptures which were an integral part of the adornment of the citadel — the Caryatides of the southern porch of the Erechtheum, the figures in relief of the Winged Victories from the balustrade of the temple of Wingless Victory and, most important of all, the numerous sculptures which were executed, or inspired and supervised, by Phidias. These works comprised the colossal statue of Athena Promachos (the Champion) which stood on the Acropolis, the chryselephantine (gold and ivory) image of Athena Parthenos in the Parthenon, and the pediment figures, sculptured metopes, and Panathenaic frieze of Athena's temple.

Phidias also executed a large statue of Zeus in the temple at Olympia, and Lucian admired as a beautiful example of the art of Phidias a statue of Lemnian Athena.

It may be said with little fear of contradiction that there are no finer or more perfect examples of sculptural art as employed in decoration than the marbles of the Parthenon.

For the most part the pediment statues, in so far as they have been preserved, are in the Lord Elgin collection of the British Museum. Impressive indeed are these figures, particularly the so-called Theseus (Fig. 32), and the three " Fates " (Fig. 33). Fifteen of the ninety-two sculptured metopes are also in the

Fig. 32. "Theseus" (E. pediment, Parthenon)

Fig. 33. "Three Fates" (E. pediment, Parthenon)

Fig 34. Horsemen from Parthenon Frieze

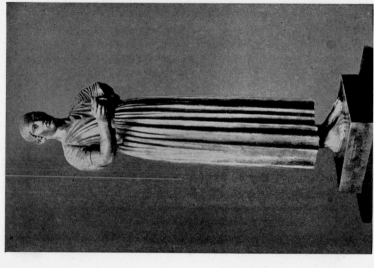

Fig. 36. Bronze Charioteer (Delphi)

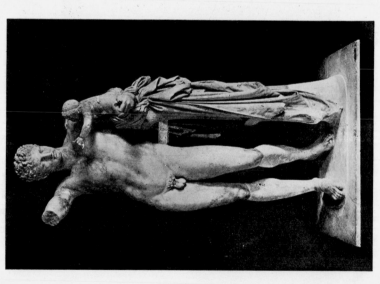

Fig. 35. Hermes of Praxiteles (Olympia)

British Museum. These portray combats of centaurs with Lapiths and vary considerably in style and merit.

This variation is to be explained by the fact that various hands must have executed the decorative sculptures of the Parthenon. The ornamentation of the temple with its very many figures and reliefs — a work accomplished in a comparatively few years — was far too onerous a task for the genius and industry of even such a master-artist as Phidias.

Of unique beauty are the graceful and life-like figures of the frieze of the Parthenon which ran around the outside of the cella, inside of the columns.

This frieze, high up on the cella wall, is only about 3 feet 4 inches high and is carved about an inch and a half in average depth. The upper portion of the frieze has greater depth than the lower and is carved in sharper outline, since the spectator looked at the figures from below. The lighting, too, came entirely from below. The scene pictured is the Panathenaic procession of the games, which were celebrated with peculiar magnificence every four years. Most of the extant slabs are in the British Museum; a few are still on the building or in the museum in Athens. The sacred procession, as seen on the temple, starts at the western end and proceeds on the northern and southern sides to the eastern front. The various celebrants are appropriately and graphically depicted. We see the young knights with their steeds (Fig. 34), chariots and charioteers and warriors, the animals — cows and sheep — for the sacrifice, the maidens carrying sacred vessels, and citizens and spectators. On the eastern front of the temple are the august seated figures of the twelve gods, a priest and priestess, two maidens and an attendant.

In these original and beautiful carvings Attic sculpture reached its zenith. The Parthenon marbles stand forth for all time as a glorious revelation of artistic achievement. The Athenian sculptor was proven to be the peer of the Athenian architect and builder.

The Fourth Century b.c.

There are indications of changing taste in Greek sculpture of the fourth century b.c. The classic reserve and the simplicity of the sculpture of the earlier period are not so conspicuous. The personality of the individual artist is now much more in evidence and emotion and sentiment find expression as, for example, in the beautiful and melancholy features of the statue of Demeter of Cnidus in the British Museum, and in the copy of the group by Cephisodotus — the goddess Peace, who looks with affection upon the infant god of Wealth on her arm.

Three sculptors of the fourth century, who enjoyed great reputation, were Scopas of Paros, Praxiteles of Athens, and Lysippus of Sicyon.

According to the ancient writers, Scopas produced many works of art and these were notable in that they expressed intense emotion. It is probable that he is known to us through four marble heads from the pediments of the temple of Athena Alea at Tegea. Conspicuous in these heads are the heavy brows, the parted lips, the deep-set eyes and the distant gaze directed upward. We know, too, that Scopas was one of the artists who were engaged in the execution of decorative sculpture for the Mausoleum at Halicarnassus. Many fine sculptural remains from this great memorial building are now in the British Museum. Conspicuous among them are two colossal figures of the ruler Mausolus and his wife, Artemisia.

Of original sculpture from the hand of Praxiteles, a sculptor of wide fame in ancient times, we are fortunate in having a genuine specimen. This is the well-known statue of Hermes (Fig. 35), which was found in the excavation of the temple of Hera at Olympia. The identification is certain, as Pausanias says that one of the statues in the Heraeum (temple of Hera) at Olympia was a marble Hermes, carrying the infant Dionysus, the work of Praxiteles. Although the lower part of the legs, with the exception of the right foot, and part of the right arm are missing, the remainder of the figure and the entire head are wonderfully preserved. The exquisite finish of the surface of the Parian marble is unmarred.

The Hermes is portrayed as an athletic, youthful figure, of more slender physique than the sturdy athletes of Polyclitus. He stands naturally and gracefully, with left leg slightly bent. The left arm which supports the child rests upon a tree-trunk, over which hangs his cloak. The folds of the garment are depicted with masterly skill. The uplifted right hand held some object, possibly a bunch of grapes, to attract the child's attention. The head is strikingly executed with strong nose, broad forehead which bulges slightly above the brows, and rather narrow eyes. The lower part of the face gradually narrows. The close-cropped locks of hair are only roughly blocked out, in impressionistic fashion. The infant was but sketchily represented as it was merely an accessory. The somewhat dreamy gaze of the god is not fixed upon the child.

Modern criticism pronounces this figure of the youthful god by Praxiteles a masterpiece. And yet it was but one of numerous statues of equal, or greater, merit which the Greeks created and enjoyed, but which unfortunately have not been preserved for us.

Several other works of Praxiteles are known to us from copies — e.g., the Aphrodite of Cnidus and his Satyr (the *Marble Faun* of Hawthorne). In Athens is a marble relief consisting of three slabs, from Mantinea, which shows the contest in music between Apollo and Marsyas. This was doubtless designed, if not carved, by Praxiteles.

Lysippus was the distinguished and prolific head of the school of sculpture which long flourished at Sicyon in the Peloponnesus. He worked in bronze almost exclusively, hence it is not surprising that no original statue by him has come down to us. For bronze statues, as has been observed, have been melted down for the most part for the metal they contained. It is

possible that in one of the marble statues found at
Delphi — that of Agias, a Thessalian athlete — we
have a copy of an original bronze work by Lysippus.
At any rate the Lysippic school of athletic sculpture,
as described by Pliny, seems to be exemplified in the
Apoxyomenus (Fig. 40) in the Vatican. This well-
known statue represents a slender, well-proportioned
athlete, who stands in an easy, graceful posture. The
left hand holds a *strigil,* and with this instrument he is
engaged in scraping from the under surface of the outstretched right arm the oil and sand of the exercise-
ground. The head and features are rather small, the
neck slender. Of particular merit is the natural and
careful treatment of the hair. The poise and finish
of this athletic figure is so remarkable that the observer
perforce is moved to inspect and admire the statue from
every angle. Among the works of Lysippus were
statues of Alexander, and extant portraits of the great
general seem to show Lysippic influence.

Other sculptured works of merit of the fourth century are fragments from the Artemisium at Ephesus,
a splendid bronze athlete with a strigil, also from
Ephesus (in Vienna), and the so-called Ariadne.

It is convenient to speak here of the marble sarcophagi discovered at Sidon and now in Constantinople.
These sarcophagi — one is perhaps of the fifth century
— are decorated with relief sculptures, which are re-
markably well preserved. The original colors — such
as red, light-blue, yellow and brown — are still clear and
bright upon the " Alexander Sarcophagus," so-called because the scenes depicted thereon represent the Macedonian general in battle and hunting.

A small relief of a horseman (Metropolitan Museum,
New York) is an admirable example of fourth-century
work. The modeling of the rider and of the prancing
steed are of great merit, while the composition as a
whole is reminiscent of the horsemen of the Parthenon
frieze.

An extremely beautiful bronze figure, perhaps a copy

of an original of possibly the fourth century, is the
statue of a handsome youth of athletic type, now in
Athens. It was found some years ago by sponge-divers
not far from the island of Cythera. The authorship is
unknown.

It remains to speak of an appealing type of sculpture,
mostly reliefs, the Attic tombstones. Our museums
possess many examples of these gravestones which are
of interest and of value to us in many ways. They are
in date mostly of the fourth century, although many of
them show fifth century influence. They are not the
product of great artists, but of the Athenian workshops.
Their merit, often considerable, and sometimes striking,
reveal the taste and skill of even the artisan. They frequently represent scenes from life and depict the dead
as in life, sometimes with singular refinement and
delicacy. Best known of these reliefs are the tombstones of Hegeso and of Dexileus. The former represents the deceased, a lady, handsome and dignified —
Hegeso, daughter of Proxenus, as the inscription
tells us — who is seated on a chair (a *klismos*). She
is engaged in selecting some article of adornment from
a jewel-casket, which is held by a maid, who stands
before her. On the latter monument an inscription informs us that the deceased Dexileus, who is shown on
a rearing steed striking down an enemy, was one of
five knights who were killed in the battle of Corinth,
394 B.C. The inscription reads: " Dexileus of Thoricus, son of Lysanias. Born in the archonship of Tisan-
der [414/3 B.C.]; died in the archonship of Eubulides
[394/3 B.C.] in Corinth, of the five knights."

HELLENISTIC SCULPTURE (*ca.* 320–100 B.C.)

As we have seen, the conquest of Asia and Egypt by
Alexander was followed by the rapid spread of the
Greek language and culture. Greek sculpture, likewise,
was no longer largely confined to limited spheres of
activity, but during the Hellenistic Age flourished at

numerous centers which were founded or fostered by the Macedonian conqueror. Athens no longer was paramount. It was not Alexandria, however, the center of the literary and scholarly activities of the new era, that assumed the leadership in sculpture. Pergamum, Ephesus, Tralles, and Rhodes were the most famous schools of the sculptural art.

The tendency of the sculptors of this period was to depart still further from the strict canons and types of the earlier time. We find, in general, the artist allowing himself far greater freedom in the selection of his subject and in the manner of its execution. The old-time self-restraint gives way to the expression of the individuality of the artist and the portrayal of his emotions. Realism, not idealism, is to the fore. Thus we have depicted, not idealized deities, not perfect youthful male and female types only, but old age and childhood, shepherds and satyrs. A good example of these realistic types is the old market-woman in the Metropolitan Museum. Humor now finds artistic expression and animal life is frequently represented. Especially does portraiture flourish in this later period, and Alexander of Macedon is a favorite subject.

It must not be inferred, however, that the Hellenistic Age is a period of decadence in art, when works of inferior merit and of dubious taste only were produced. Many splendid, vigorous, and beautiful statues are of this time.

We have already mentioned the magnificent Victory from Samothrace in the Louvre, one of the most prized statues of antiquity (Fig. 31). This winged figure of the goddess of Victory, standing on the prow of a ship, is thought to have been set up perhaps in 306 B.C. by Demetrius Poliorcetes to commemorate a naval victory. The pose is striking and the effect is expremely impressive.

The school of Pergamum, so important in this period, is known to us through copies of groups erected by Attalus I of the third century B.C., and by originals of the reign of Eumenes II of the second century. The former period is represented by the statue of the " Dying Gaul " — once called the Dying Gladiator — in the Capitoline Museum at Rome, and also by a series of figures of fighters fallen in combat, about three feet high. Sculpture of the later period was found in the German excavations at Pergamum and consists of fragments of friezes from the great altar of Zeus and Athena. The scene depicted on the larger is the battle of the gods and giants. The school of art of Pergamum is characterized by intense realism, dramatic power, successful and vigorous portrayal of emotion and pain, and skill in the rendering of anatomy.

The Apollo Belvedere of the Vatican and its counterpart, the Artemis of Versailles, are works of grace and refinement, but soon chill the observer's admiration by reason of their artificiality and theatricalism.

Other examples of this Age are the dramatic group of Niobe and her children — probably later than the fourth century, the realistic portrait-statue of Demosthenes, and the popular group of a little boy struggling with a goose — possibly a copy of a work by Boethus.

Of the Hellenistic Age, too, is the world's most famous statue, the Aphrodite of Melos (Venus of Milo), also in the Louvre (Fig. 37). The handsome head and features are worthy of the goddess of love and beauty. The nude upper part of the body is beautifully modeled. The whole figure is animate with dignity and loveliness. The date and authorship of the statue are unknown and have been much discussed. It may be of interest to quote the latest views of these questions as expressed by Mr. Guy Dickins in his book on *Hellenistic Sculpture* (p. 63): " The restoration of the figure is now easy. With her right hand the goddess held, or was about to hold, her drapery to prevent it from slipping, her left elbow rested on the pillar, and her left hand, palm upwards, held an apple, a frequent symbol of Aphrodite. The date is between 180–160 B.C. The pose is reminiscent of Lysippus. The head-type is Scopaic, but at second-hand, since the influence of

Pergamum is stronger. The twist of the body, the reason why she is half naked, the drapery — these are to be explained on the supposition that the statue is strongly influenced by the Venus of Capua (Fig. 38), who is represented as admiring her beauty in the mirror of the shield of Ares, the shield-edge holding up her drapery against her left hip. All examples of this type go back to an early Hellenistic or late fourth-century statue of the Armed Aphrodite. The Melian goddess was a second-century Hellenistic copy, or rather adaptation."

THE GRAECO-ROMAN PERIOD

The Hellenistic Age passed over into the Graeco-Roman Period with no appreciable line of demarcation. As in other realms of achievement originality in art also declined. Sculptors busied themselves largely in the making of copies of earlier masterpieces. Adaptations, too, are numerous. Greek sculptors, in great numbers, flocked to Rome where their services were in demand for the carving of copies and the making of portraits. In fact, Greek art was so much appreciated at Rome that Greek lands were mercilessly looted by Roman officials. Statues, by the shipload, were carried to Rome to embellish triumphal processions and to adorn Roman villas. Shipwrecked Roman galleys, with cargoes of Greek sculpture, have been discovered lying on the bottom of the sea south of the Peloponnesus and off the coast of northern Africa.

Two prominent Greek artists of the Graeco-Roman Period were Pasiteles and Arcesilaus. The former was the author of a work on Greek art which served as a source for Pliny. To Pasiteles is attributed the use of clay models for his statues of marble. This procedure made inevitable the practice of the making of numerous copies of a popular original by pupils and workmen and thus paved the way for commercialism.

Individual works of sculpture of the Graeco-Roman Period which are well-known to students of art are the

FIG. 37. APHRODITE OF MELOS (LOUVRE)

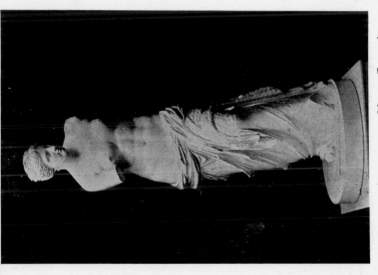

FIG. 38. APHRODITE (Venus) OF CAPUA

beautiful, but self-conscious, Venus dei Medici in Florence, the Capitoline Venus, the Venus Genetrix in the Louvre, the colossal Farnese Heracles, and the group of Orestes and Electra in Naples. This last group is a good example of the archaising tendency of the time.

It remains to make mention of two groups of the first century B.C., — the Farnese Bull in Naples, and the Laocoön group in the Vatican. Both of these works were by artists of Asia, the former group by sculptors of Tralles, the latter of the Rhodian school. In the choice of subjects and in the scenes of cruelty and anguish depicted, so alien to earlier art, we see the sculptor's desire to startle and to shock the onlooker.

The Laocoön group has world-wide fame. Vergil's description of the terrible death of Laocoön and his two sons in the coils of the serpents and, in modern times, Lessing's essay *Laocoön*, have made the theme familiar. Judged by the canons of classic Greek sculpture the Laocoön group is not deserving of its great reputation. The subject chosen, in its excessive realism, is repugnant, and unsuited to sculptural treatment. Great technical skill, however, is in evidence in the group.

Our brief survey may appropriately end here as we have now come to the period of Roman art proper. Roman art, it is true, can not be at any time disassociated from its Greek antecedents, but there came a time when Roman influences dictated the subjects chosen for treatment and the methods of their execution. These subjects were mostly portraits of famous contemporaries, reliefs which depicted historical events, and decorative reliefs of the Neo-Attic school.

We have now rapidly traced the course of Greek sculpture through the main periods of its history. In conclusion let us indicate two of its prominent characteristics.

The art of the Greeks was largely inspired by religion and this religion was polytheistic. Images of the gods in their various aspects and functions were desired as cult statues in temples, as embellishment for sacred edifices, and as patrons and protectors for public and private buildings and places. Greek humanism led the Hellenes to an anthropomorphic conception of their deities. Thus it is that the Greek sculptor embodied his vision of divinity in the human form. In Greek sculpture, therefore, during the fifth and fourth centuries we see, for the most part, the effort of the artist to mold the perfect human figure. The representation of children, of animals, of *genre* pictures and of the comic element, and the portrayal of extreme realism could not, and did not, find general expression at this time when the sculptor was dominated by religious motives and needs and by his belief in anthropomorphic deities. This helps to explain idealism in Greek art of the Age of Pericles. Phidias and his fellows in their idealized statues nobly materialized their conceptions of divine personages as lofty, benign, dignified and eternal. Later artists, however, especially those of the fourth century, humanized still further their embodiments and endowed them with human characteristics and emotions. Their figures are no longer types, they are personalities.

Another potent influence in Greek sculpture is athleticism. In the chapter on athletics we shall see the popularity and importance of athletics in Greek life and its connection with Greek religion. To the victors in the great athletic games at Olympia it was customary to dedicate statues. This custom created a great demand for athletic statues and from early times the Greek sculptor strove to express the athletic ideal. Athletic art is, therefore, an important chapter in the history of Greek sculpture. Of the most renowned of these sculptors — Myron, Polyclitus, and Lysippus — we have spoken above.

Later times saw different tendencies at work. Greek art is not perfect — nothing created by human hands can be. But in Hellenic sculpture at its best are those same eternal values which are conspicuous in the architecture and the literature of the Greeks — simplicity, proportion, and beauty.

FIG. 41. THE DISCOBOLUS, AFTER MYRON

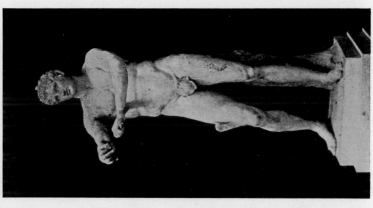

FIG. 40. THE APOXYOMENUS, AFTER LYSIPPUS

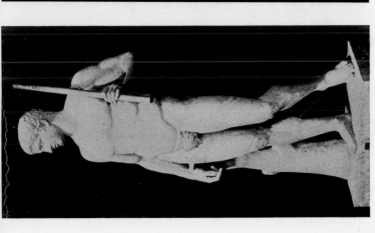

FIG. 39. THE DORYPHORUS, AFTER POLYCLITUS

CHAPTER VII

ATHLETIC SPORTS AND FESTIVALS

THE Greek love and practice of athletics are traits which bind the modern world to ancient Hellas in a sympathetic bond. The Greeks, and no other ancient people, have bequeathed to us the healthy tradition and the sound ideals of athleticism at its best.

From the earliest times in the Greek world we observe the importance attached to physical exercise and games. In the poetry of Homer there are numerous allusions to sports and descriptions of games. Wrestling and boxing are favorite pastimes; foot-racing, throwing the discus, hurling the spear, jumping, shooting the bow and chariot racing were commonly practiced. In Homer, too, ball-playing was a favorite game of both girls and boys, but this ball-playing was by no means the strenuous and recently developed game beloved by Americans of today; it was rather a form of calisthenics accompanied by singing and dancing. In the Sixth Book of the *Odyssey*, the princess Nausicaa and her maiden companions, after washing the garments of the royal household and refreshing themselves with bath and food, " fell to playing at ball, casting aside their head bands, and among these Nausicaa of the white arms began the song. . . . Then the princess threw the ball at one of her company; she missed the girl, and cast the ball into the deep eddying current, whereat they all raised a piercing cry." In Book Eight there is a detailed description of this graceful game as played by Nausicaa's brothers: " So when they had taken in their hands the goodly ball of purple hue, that cunning Polybus had wrought for them, the one would

63

bend backwards, and throw it towards the shadowy clouds; and the other would leap upwards from the earth and catch it lightly in his turn, before his feet touched the ground. Now after they had made trial of throwing the ball straight up, the twain set to dance upon the bounteous earth, tossing the ball from hand to hand, and the other youths stood by the lists and beat time, and a great din arose." (Butcher and Lang.)

The constant devotion of the Greeks in all periods to athletic exercises of all kinds may be attributed to their active nature and lively temperament, which urged them to the energetic use of body and mind. Furthermore, they admired exceedingly a sound body and good health with the physical grace and comeliness which accompany good physique. The athletic ideal can be observed everywhere in the masterpieces of Greek sculpture. The great sculptors, when they modeled their statues of youthful deities and ideal physical types, were inspired by the splendidly developed athletes who graced the palaestras. It has been well said that "without athletics Greek art cannot be conceived." The Greeks ever recognized, too, the value of athletics as a preparation for the activities of life and the duties of war. We find, therefore, that athletics were pursued not merely for recreation, but as an important and essential branch of education. Consequently, in the scheme of Greek education, gymnastics, or careful training of the body, and music, or training of the mind, received equal emphasis. Athletic exercises, too, were connected with Greek religion, as may be seen, for example, in the funeral games celebrated in honor of the dead hero, e.g., Patroclus in the Twenty-third Book of the *Iliad*. The great Panhellenic athletic festival games were founded in honor of gods and were celebrated regularly as a form of religious worship.

The essentially sane Greek conception of the pursuit of athletics should be noted and is surely worthy of modern imitation. Physical culture was not for a few specialists but for all. It was not a Greek custom to train highly a few youths so that hundreds and thousands of their fellows might sit idly by and admire and applaud their performance. Competition, it is true, was ever present, for competition was at the very bottom of every Greek pursuit. But it was a healthy competition and the resultant rivalry contributed to excellence and beneficial results. The fame of victory, or the breaking of a record, did not concern the Greek participant in athletics so much as the finish and grace of his performance and the perfection of his style.

While this wholesome pursuit of athletics was generally practiced, yet it is of interest to observe an exception which gradually grew and which was reprehended by several Greek thinkers. This was a tendency towards professionalism in connection with the great festivals, especially at Olympia, a professionalism which was inevitable in the nature of the case. The contestants became so numerous, the rivalry of the representatives of the various Greek states so keen, and the glory of a triumph so great, that only picked athletes after long training as for a profession had a chance of winning. While it is true that the victor in the great games, as at Olympia, officially received no immediate prize of intrinsic value, the reward being merely a crown of gray-green olive, celebrated by Ruskin, yet success brought in its train not merely the adulation of fellow citizens, but a shower of material blessings. For example, we hear not only of honorary statues and hymns of victory, but of actual purses of money. At Athens the Olympian victor might be given the right of free maintenance in the Prytaneum and the honor of *proedria,* or the privilege of a front seat at all public spectacles. Plato speaks of " that life full of bliss led by Olympian victors."

There are several very caustic protests of contemporary thinkers against this adulation and enrichment of athletic heroes of the Festival Games. Xenophanes of Colophon, who flourished about 500 B.C. and who, in old age, taught and wrote in Elea in southern Italy, in an extant elegiac poem thus makes protest:

" But if one should win the victory by swiftness of foot or in the pentathlon at Olympia where is the sacred precinct of Zeus by Pisa's waters, or in wrestling or in hardy boxing or in that formidable contest called the pankration, he would be more renowned in the eyes of his fellow citizens and would win a conspicuous front seat at the festivals and food from the city at public expense and a gift of lasting value; and if he should be victor in the chariot-race, he would win all these rewards although being less worthy than I; for my wisdom is of greater value than the strength of men and horses. Nay, these matters are not rightly regarded; to esteem physical strength more highly than excellent wisdom is not right. For, even if there should be among the people one who is good in boxing or in the pentathlon, or in wrestling, or in swiftness of foot (which is the most esteemed of all contests), not for this reason, in truth, would the city be better governed. Small joy would there be for a city, if a man win an athletic victory by Pisa's banks; this does not enrich the inmost parts of the city."

Even before Xenophanes, Tyrtaeus (frag. 10) at Sparta had disparaged athletic excellence if this were not accompanied by military prowess. When Socrates, on trial, is asked what penalty he thinks should be visited upon him he replies: " The reward of a poor man who is a benefactor of the state — free maintenance in the Prytaneum. For it is much more becoming that such a man receive this reward than the Olympian victor in horse-races. He confers upon you the semblance of happiness and I the reality. He does not need the support whereas I do."

Euripides in a certain fragment (*Autolycus,* 284) inveighs with great bitterness against the evil race of athletes who know not how to live, but are the mere slaves of their habits. He thinks that the training of the professional athlete does not fit him for war and concludes: " It is the wise and good man who should be crowned with leaves, the temperate and just ruler of the city who frees it from evils by putting an end to contention and factions — such deeds are beneficial to the city and to all Hellas."

The orator Isocrates (IV. 1–2) protests in the same strain thus:

" I have often wondered that those who assemble the great festivals and have established athletic contests have judged physical prowess worthy of such great gifts, yet reward with no honor those who individually toil for the public welfare and discipline their souls so as to be able to help others. Yet for the latter they properly should have had greater forethought. Should athletes acquire twice their normal strength no profit to others accrues, but if one man reveal wisdom all would profit thereby who desire to share in his understanding."

It should be noted, however, that these are but the protests of thinkers and writers who are not decrying the beneficial physical culture everywhere daily practiced as an essential part of education, but are raising their voices against the professionalism which was creeping into the Panhellenic Games.

The cultivation of athletic exercises was of great value in still another and very important way. The Greeks were an artistic people and were lovers of beauty. Now the worship of beauty and the pursuit of art if indulged to excess sometimes results in indolence, love of luxury, and enervation, and consequent effeminacy. From this weakening of moral fiber the Greeks were saved largely through their devotion to wholesome athletics.

The training school where gymnastics were practiced was called the _palaestra_, literally wrestling-ground, and was under the direction of a master, who is often represented on vases with his long forked stick. In Athens, a palaestra was connected with a gymnasium. A large and well-equipped gymnasium would contain a palaestra with porticoes, a stadium and baths, and lecture-rooms besides. Of these gymnasia there were three of importance at Athens — the Academy, Lyceum, and Cynosarges — all located in sacred groves near streams outside the walls of the city. Plato, with his school of philosophy, has made the Academy immortal, while Aristotle used the Lyceum for his school of the Peripatetics.

The large Stadium in Athens lay between two hills to the southeast of the Acropolis and was laid out by Lycurgus in the latter half of the fourth century B.C. Here Herodes Atticus, in the second century A.D., constructed seats of marble. The great structure again has been clothed in white Pentelic marble, so as to seat some 60,000 spectators, and was used for the revival of the Olympian games and is now employed for large assemblages.

THE FESTIVALS

The athletic festivals of the Greeks are of particular interest in Greek history because of their influence on the life and thought of the Hellenes as a whole. A striking moral characteristic was the tendency and practice of individual communities to stay by themselves. Segregation and isolation we find to have been largely the rule. Although the area of Greece proper is small and enemies from the outside were ever a menace, yet the Greeks never formed a stable federation of states for offense or defense. United action was seldom achieved. The reason for this is that the Greeks were intensely independent in their nature and jealously preserved their own individuality and complete freedom of action. Although the various peoples of Greece had certain prominent characteristics in common, yet they differed widely in dialects, in political ideals, and in social and religious practices. Boeotian, Spartan, and Athenian were all Greeks, but were poles apart in many respects. The physical character of their country — a succession of mountains, valleys, and gulfs of the sea — tended inevitably to separate and hold aloof the various settlements. Quarrels and wars from earliest times and rivalry for Hellenic hegemony fostered antipathy and chronic ill-feeling. Only two institutions, more or less general, made possible a national feeling, and both of these were primarily of religious origin — the Amphictyonic Council and the great national games. Of the former this is not the occasion to speak; we are here concerned with the festival games.

Besides the local games held at various cities, and of importance to them only, there were four great national festivals: The *Olympian*, celebrated every four years at Olympia in Elis, in honor of Zeus; the *Pythian*, every four years at Delphi in Phocis, in honor of Apollo; the *Isthmian*, every two years at the Isthmus of Corinth, in honor of Poseidon; and the *Nemean*, every two years at Nemea in the Peloponnesus, in honor of Zeus.

Of these games the Olympian were by far the most important and even Greek chronology is dated by Olympiads or intervals of four years. According to tradition they were founded by Heracles, as Pindar tells us, and were not abolished until 394 A.D. Regular and continuous lists of victors were kept from 776 B.C. and with this year the reckoning by Olympiads begins. Such was their vitality that they had a continued existence of nearly 1200 years, notwithstanding the profound political vicissitudes.

Olympia is in Elis in the northwestern part of the Peloponnesus near the village of Pisa, and here a precinct sacred to Zeus was laid out at the foot of the hill of Cronos by the river Alpheus. In this precinct, or *Altis*, as the Eleans called it, wooded with olives and poplars, were placed a Stadium and a Hippodrome, and buildings of all sorts were constructed, of which the most famous were the two temples dedicated to Zeus and Hera. Here, in the excavations conducted by the Germans in 1875–1881, was found a veritable wilderness of ruins of temples, treasuries, gymnasia and altars, together with such magnificent works of art as the Hermes of Praxiteles and the Apollo from the west pediment of the Temple of Zeus. The Alpheus river, and especially its tributary, the Cladeus, which flowed by the site, had covered the whole precinct with some fourteen feet of earth, which made the excavation so difficult that the Stadium was not entirely cleared.

The Olympian games, celebrated every four years, were held in midsummer and lasted probably about five days. Announcement of the approaching festival was given some weeks before its celebration by ambassadors from Elis, who visited the various states with invitations to participate accompanied by a proclamation of a truce. The truce bound all Greeks to keep the peace during a period of some three months, that all might attend without fear of molestation. Herein is seen another striking evidence of the religious nature of the festival. Contestants for the games, who qualified for entrance — they must be Greeks by blood, free born, and fit in every way for participation — trained at Olympia for a period of thirty days.

The attendance at Olympia was enormous. Visitors came from all parts of the Greek world, no matter how remote. Every station in life was represented and every calling. People came not only for religious reasons and to view the exciting contests, but the occasion afforded splendid opportunity for personal and political advertisement and display and for material gain and profit, but best of all for the exchange of ideas. Thus it was that this great Panhellenic festival served as an intellectual clearing-house, so to speak, where leading representatives from the various states could compare their achievements and plan for improvements. This meant much, especially for art and literature. The orator Isocrates (*Panegyricus,* 43ff.) is our authority on this subject: " The founders of the great festival are justly praised because they have handed down to us such a custom that after making truces and reconciling existing hostilities we assemble in the same place.

Here, after prayers and general sacrifices, we are reminded of our common and original relationship and
are thus more amicably disposed towards each other;
former friendships, too, are renewed and new ones con-
tracted. . . . Many blessings result from such assemblies, of which Athens is by no means deficient."

We know that the throngs at Olympia were addressed by the rhetorician Gorgias of Sicily, and by
the orator Lysias. Isocrates composed for the Olympic
festival his greatest speech, the *Panegyricus,* urging a
united Greece against Persia. Lucian affirms that
Herodotus read his history at Olympia.

The festival consisted of two parts: first, the religious
ceremonies with sacrifices, feasts, speeches, sacred em-
bassies and offerings to Zeus and, second, the contests.
In the fifth century B.C. the sports comprised foot-
races for men, e.g., the *dromos* or stade-race (600 feet),
the *diaulos* or double-stade run, the *dolichos,* or long
distance run, a distance of perhaps 24 stades, boxing,
wrestling, pankration, pentathlon, chariot and horse-
races, race in armor, and boys' events.

The judges who supervised the games as a whole,
and the separate contests as well, were natives of Elis,
originally two, and later, generally ten, and were called
Hellanodicae. The sports lasted for several days from
morning to night. A herald proclaimed each event
and later announced the victor, who was crowned with
the olive wreath by the chief judge.

A very brief account must suffice for the other national festivals. Many of their details were identical
with those of the celebration at Olympia; emphasis
therefore will be placed on divergences.

The Pythian festival was founded, as the story goes,
to commemorate the victory of Apollo over the python.
The first Pythiad dates from 582 B.C. when the festival
was finally reorganized. It was celebrated every fourth
year in the August of the third year of each Olympiad
and was under the control and supervision of the
Hieromnemones, officials of the Amphictyonic League.

The Pythian festival was originally devoted to musical competitions only, in which the Hymn to Apollo was a constant feature, and these were always of greater importance than the athletic events. Considerable portions of a hymn to Apollo with the original Greek music carved on the Treasury of the Athenians at Delphi have been preserved.[1]

Chariot and horse-races were very popular at the Pythian games and attracted many entrants. Forty chariots came to grief in one race as Pindar tells us in one of his Pythian Odes (*On the Victory of Arcesilas*). In the *Electra* of Sophocles we have a magnificent description of a chariot-race at Delphi, where Orestes, one of ten competitors from all Greece, is represented as having met a tragic death. The prize was a wreath of laurel leaves.

The Isthmian games, celebrated in the spring of the second and fourth year of each Olympiad, were of lesser importance, although extremely popular and well attended because of their central location. At the Nemean games athletics alone seem to have been practiced. The prize at both the Isthmian and Nemean games was a wreath of wild parsley.

The name of Pindar is eternally linked with the great Greek festivals. This Boeotian poet, perhaps the greatest lyricist of ancient Greece, celebrated in magnificent verse in his *Epinician Odes,* or Songs of Victory, the successful contenders in the four great Panhellenic games. Forty-four of these songs of praise are extant. They are characterized by lofty beauty, bold and poetic diction and splendid imagery. Unfortunately, we can never feel their real power as we lack the accompanying music, voices and dancing. Of the games and Pindar's genius, Professor Gildersleeve (Introduction to his edition of Pindar) well says: " It is only in accordance with the principle of the organic unity of Hellenism that the acme of Greek lyric art should have embodied

---

[1] See Smyth, *Greek Melic Poets,* Appendix, and Poulsen, *Delphi,* p. 165.

the acme of Greek festal life. The great games of
Greece are as thoroughly characteristic of her nation-
ality as the choral poetry which was the expression of
them and the crown of them." Simonides of Ceos and
his nephew Bacchylides were contemporaries and rivals
of Pindar in the writing of Epinician odes. Only scanty
fragments of this kind of poetry remain of the former;
of the latter, there were discovered in 1897 fourteen
odes of victory; they are of great interest, but of inferior poetic merit as compared with Pindar.

Local games were everywhere held throughout
Greece, and with these we are not here concerned.
Especial mention must be made, however, of the
Panathenaea, the festival in commemoration of the
union of Attica and in honor of *Athena Polias*. The
lesser Panathenaea were celebrated annually in July;
the greater every fourth year, in the third year of each
Olympiad. This festival occupied several days, nine
according to Mommsen, and comprised musical competitions, athletics, chariot and horse-races, military
competitions, torch-races, and boat-races at the Piraeus
on the last day. On the greatest day of the festival
(the 28th of the month) occurred the procession, so
admirably depicted on the frieze of the Parthenon, and
the sacrifices. At the Panathenaea, musical competitions were very important and consisted of contests in
singing and playing on the lyre and on the flute, for
which the prizes in the fourth century were numerous
and valuable. To the winners in the contest in singing
to the lyre were given a crown of gold of the value of
1000 drachmae (drachma = about 18 cents) and 500
drachmae of silver; other prizes were purses of silver
of the value of 1200, 600, 400, and 300 drachmae.
Lesser prizes were awarded to winners in the contest in
singing to the flute and to players on lyre and flute.

All the athletic events contested at Olympia found a
place on the program of the Panathenaea and special
contests were held for boys, youths and men. Two
prizes, consisting of a number of amphorae of olive oil

from the sacred trees belonging to the State, were awarded in the athletic contests and, in addition, there was given to the victor a large and beautifully painted amphora. A large number of these interesting Pana-thenaic amphorae have survived. They are in date from the middle of the sixth to the end of the fourth century. These vases are of the black-figured type and have as decoration, on one side an athletic scene and, on the other, Athena with aegis, shield and spear. On them is regularly an inscription, " Of the prizes of Athens," and sometimes the archon's name is added, in which case we learn the date.

Only at Sparta did girls participate freely in athletics and there they joined with the boys in athletic exercises of all kinds. At Athens systematic physical culture for girls was not practiced. Women attended the Delian festival at Delos and at Chios wrestled with boys. Women and maidens form part of the procession of the Panathenaea. At Olympia, however, they were not allowed to attend the festival, this rule apparently being due to some early religious taboo. Pausanias (v. 16) tells the story of a certain lady, Pherenice, who attended the games in the disguise of a trainer to see her son compete in boxing. Overjoyed by his victory, she jumped over the barrier and betrayed her sex. She was, however, pardoned because her father, brothers and son had all been Olympic victors.

Women might enter their horses in the chariot-race at Olympia and, if victorious, set up statues. There was, too, a special festival for women at Olympia, namely, the *Heraea*, with races for girls of various ages. The distance was 500 feet, one hundred feet less than the similar race for men. The girls ran with hair unbound, a short tunic not reaching the knee, and right shoulder bare. There is a statue of a running girl in the Vatican (Fig. 43), a copy of a fifth century origi-nal, which exactly corresponds to Pausanias' description. The prize in the girls' race was a crown of olive and a share of the ox sacrificed to Hera. Statues, too, they could set up in the Heraeum.   This festival Pausanias asserts to be of great antiquity, founded, indeed, by Hippodamia to commemorate her marriage with Pelops.

THE ATHLETIC CONTESTS

Even a brief description of the most popular and important athletic contests of the Greeks should be of great interest to the present outdoor-loving generation as athletic exercises were never more popular since the days of the ancient Greeks than they are today.   For a detailed account of the various contests, with illustrations from the monuments, the reader should consult E. N. Gardiner's book on *Greek Athletic Sports and Festivals*.

The *pentathlon* — the contest consisting of five events — comprised jumping, discus-throwing, throwing the javelin, running, and wrestling.

While the standing jump was practiced by the Greeks, the running long jump seems to have been the regular event in competition.   In this leap weights (*halteres*) of several pounds, of stone or lead, were held in the hands to increase the momentum of the jumper.   The leap had to be taken in good form, with feet together, and the contestant alighted upon freshly dug earth.

The Homeric discus was of stone, but that of later times of hammered bronze.   The discus varied in weight and size, there being different standards for the many games and for the competitions of men and boys. The average ancient discus seems to have weighed between four and five pounds and an ancient notice credits the athlete Phayllus with a throw of ninety-five feet.   In the celebrated statue of Myron, the *Discobolus*, we have a splendid illustration of the Greek athlete in this event (Fig. 41).

The javelin was about six feet in length.   It was without a point when used in the palaestra and sometimes had a blunt metal cap at the forward end.   Generally the object of the contest was for distance, although practice exercises for accuracy of throw were also held. The Greek javelin was always provided with a thong or loop of leather (Latin *amentum*) fixed about midway of the shaft into which the fingers of the thrower were inserted at the moment of hurling. The use of this loop makes it possible considerably to increase the distance of the throw. In the modern Olympian Games the *amentum* is not used. The Greek javelin-thrower is exemplified for all time by the *Doryphorus,* Polyclitus' statue of a sturdy athlete (Fig. 39).

Foot-races were of various lengths, e.g., of one, two, four, and up to twenty-four stadia. The stade-race (our sprint) was the length of the Stadium, i.e., about 200 yards; the *diaulos,* twice the distance. The long-distance race (*dolichos*) varied as to length. In the Olympian Games it was, perhaps, of 24 stadia, or about three miles. Races in armor, too, were a feature of various games. Of especial interest to us are the torch-races which were popular at various places throughout Greece, particularly at Athens. The torch-race naturally took place at night and might be a contest between individuals or between teams. From Plato's *Republic* we learn of a torch-race on horseback, a decided novelty. In the torch-race for individuals the contestants ran from the Academy into the city and victory was awarded to him who first arrived with torch still alight. In the team-race (our relay race) the runners were stationed at intervals and the torch was passed from one member of a team to his fellow.

That wrestling was early very popular is proved by the Greek word for an exercise-ground — *palaestra,* which means wrestling-place. The rules are uncertain, although there seem to have been both upright and ground-wrestling, with three falls necessary for victory. A fall on back, shoulders, or hip was a fair throw, and tripping was permitted.

No sport, however, is of greater antiquity and popularity than boxing. Were not Heracles and Polydeuces famous boxers? Bare fists sometimes were used, but generally a form of " gloves " was customary. In the classical period a soft, thin leather thong (the Latin *cestus*) was wound around each hand leaving the thumb free. Thus the effect of a blow was softened. But a more formidable " glove " came into use, a strip of thick hard leather which stood out, with sharp edges, from the hand. Finally, in Roman times, for bloody gladiatorial use, a barbarous " loaded " cestus was introduced, when a strip of metal was buried in the leather strap. In Greek boxing it would seem that blows were aimed at the head, and no formal rules, as in modern times, with ring and rounds, governed the combat. The fight was fought to a finish and the defeated boxer was " knocked out " or held up his hand in token of defeat.

The *pankration* (literally, *all-strength* contest) was a combination of wrestling and boxing, the cestus not being used. This contest, not known to Homer, was a feature of the Olympian games and victorious pankratiasts are eulogized in eight of the odes of Pindar. While the pankration seems to us the roughest of Greek athletic sports, yet it was regulated by definite rules. Hitting, wrestling, and kicking were permitted, as also the strangle hold. But such unfair tactics as biting or gouging (i.e., the digging of finger or hand into the eye or vulnerable part of the opponent's body) were forbidden. The combat started with the contestants facing each other standing; it ended on the ground with the vanquished, as in wrestling, holding up his hand in token of defeat.

In all these contests, as pictured on the vases, the rules were administered by an umpire, an older man, who is represented as standing by in an attitude of close attention, holding outstretched a long forked stick with which to punish infractions of the regulations.

Horse-races were, of course, of great popularity. Vase paintings and coins show single riders and two- and

four-horse chariots. We see jockeys guiding their gal-
loping mounts with bridles, but riding without saddle
or stirrups. The chariot-races in the hippodrome were
splendid and exciting events. The element of danger
was ever present as the competing chariots were generally numerous and the risk of upset and collision, particularly at the frequent turns around the terminal
pillars, was very great. Reference has already been
made to the magnificent description in Sophocles'
Electra of a tragic chariot-race.

Wrestlers, hockey-players, charioteers, and athletes
exercising are admirably depicted on sculptured bases
recently found in Athens.

CHAPTER VIII

POLITICAL, SOCIAL, AND ECONOMIC CONDITIONS OF THE ATHENIAN PEOPLE

" The first valuable contribution the Greeks made to political study was that they invented it." — A. E. ZIMMERN.

" The small city communities of Greece created the intellectual life of Europe. In their literature we find models of thought and expression, and meet the subtle and powerful personalities who originated for Europe all forms of poetry, history and philosophy, and even physical science itself, no less than the ideal of freedom and the conception of a self-governing democracy; while the student is introduced to the great problems of thought and life at their springs, before he follows them through the wider but more confused currents of the modern world." — *From a public statement signed by distinguished Englishmen.*

IN THIS chapter it is proposed to discuss the population of Attica, the various elements and classes constituting Athenian society, and the political, social, and economic status and life of the inhabitants in the latter half of the fifth century B.C.

It is impossible to ascertain the exact population of Attica, as there are no authoritative figures which include all the inhabitants. It is true that various official lists were kept. Each tribe, for example, entered in a register the names of all children born of citizen parents; there was, too, a list of all male citizens who were eligible to vote in the assembly; and, finally, citizens between the ages of eighteen and sixty who were liable to service in the cavalry or heavy-armed infantry were registered. No accurate census, how-ever, was ever taken of all the elements forming the population, which comprised the citizens, the for-eign population (the resident aliens, or *metics* as they were called), and the slaves. Furthermore, an estimate of the population is made more uncertain by reason of the fact that it was subject to severe fluctuation as to numbers, due to the sending out of colonies; the high death-rate which was normally perhaps double that of the United States; the great plague of 430 B.C. which killed almost one quarter of the inhabitants of Attica; the constant wars with their ravages, such as the steady drain on the Athenian fighting forces in the protracted Peloponnesian War; and the ill-starred Sicilian expedition of 413 B.C. On the basis of all the information available it has been estimated that the *total* population of Athens and Attica at about the year 431 B.C. was between 300,000 and 400,000 persons. These consisted of: *adult male citizens*, between 40,000 and 55,000, and with their wives and children far above 100,000; resident aliens or metics, 14,000 to 24,000, with their families perhaps 50,000; slaves, *adult males*, perhaps 50,000. To the citizen of a modern state which stretches across a continent and numbers its inhabitants by tens of millions it is indeed a revelation to learn what great and eternal achievements were won by a population so small and inhabiting a district so insignificant in area.

Under what conditions did this population live, politically, socially, and economically? The majority of the numerous books which deal with Athenian political and social life in the latter part of the fifth century B.C. convey to the reader the general, but emphatic, impression that Athens, while theoretically a democracy, was, generally speaking, an aristocracy. In fact, the traditional view of Athens under Pericles reveals a society brilliant in its achievements, but quite selfishly constituted, and gravely defective, save from the viewpoint of the favored few. Profound social distinctions, even among the citizens themselves, are insisted upon. The conception still is widely prevalent that the *élite* of Athenian society, few but fit, led a life of glorious, but intensely selfish, leisure, which was their prerogative as the result of the ruthless exploitation of all professional men, artists, producers, traders, artisans, workers, resident aliens, and slaves. Almost everywhere the time-honored assertion is made that in Athens all work was despised, labor was contemned, the workers were disdained, and, in fact, that any service for which financial remuneration was received was in disrepute and branded the doer with a humiliating social stigma. The free man is supposed to have done little or no work, for surely the aristocratic citizen must have had a completely independent and care-free existence for his manifold political, social, and religious duties.

It may well be asked, why is it that this view of Athenian society as intensely aristocratic, if erroneous, is generally held? The reasons are, it would seem, as follows: (1) Athens, like other Greek states, at an early period in its history, in fact, until after Solon and Clisthenes, was, in large measure, oligarchic and aristocratic, both politically and socially. It is mistakenly assumed that these early conditions, particularly in social life, continued. (2) Certain Greek states, e.g., Sparta, Thebes, and Crete, never experienced democratization. The strictly aristocratic conditions which were permanently characteristic of these states are sometimes thought of as necessarily existing also in Athens. (3) Modern writers have the tendency implicitly to follow Plato and Aristotle as authorities and imagine that actual fifth century Athenian conditions are accurately reflected in the pages of these philosophers, even when the latter are discussing theoretical polities and imaginary and ideal societies. And yet caution must always be observed in the case of these "Laconizing" theorizers who, furthermore, were aristocrats and in many respects distrusted democracy. (4) It is true that Athens was not a democracy in the complete sense of the word, inasmuch as the vote was denied to women, foreigners, and slaves. Slavery was, of course, a recognized institution from time immemorial throughout the ancient world and Athens as well.

I. The Citizens

So far as native males were concerned Athens was politically a perfect democracy. We are fortunate in having no less an authority than Pericles himself to testify for us — Pericles, the aristocrat, in the immortal *Funeral Oration,* as reported in the second book of the history of Thucydides, the aristocrat. " Our government is not copied from those of our neighbors; we are an example to them rather than they to us. Our constitution is named a democracy, because it is in the hands not of the few but of the many. Our laws secure equal justice for all in their private disputes, and our public opinion welcomes and honors talent in every branch of achievement, not for any sectional reason, but on grounds of excellence alone. And as we give free play to all in our public life, so we carry the same spirit into our daily relations with one another. We are obedient to whomsoever is set in authority, and to the laws, more especially to those which offer protection to the oppressed and those unwritten ordinances whose transgression brings admitted shame. Wealth to us is not mere material for vainglory, but an opportunity for achievement, and poverty we think is no disgrace to acknowledge, but a real degradation to make no effort to overcome. Our citizens attend both to public and private duties, and do not allow absorption in their own various affairs to interfere with their knowledge of the city's. We differ from other states in regarding the man who holds aloof from public life, not as quiet but as useless. In a word, I claim that our city as a whole is an education to Greece, and that her members yield to none, man by man, for independence of spirit, many-sidedness of attainment and complete self-reliance in limbs and brain." (See A. E. Zimmern, *The Greek Commonwealth,* Part II., chapter VIII).

From this speech it is seen that in Athens, if not in Sparta and Plato's *Republic,* the State existed for the

individual and not the individual for the State.   The
actual facts as we definitely know them clearly reveal
Athens as a political democracy to a degree greater even
than is possible for us today.   Athens was a small community and allowed all citizens directly to participate
in the government, whereas in our great modern democratic states authority must be delegated by government through representatives.   All citizens over eighteen years of age were members of the Athenian Assembly; all citizens over thirty were eligible to mem-
bership in the Council of Five Hundred, the members
of which were elected annually by lot; and all citizens
over thirty were eligible to election by lot to serve as
jurymen in the Heliastic law-courts.   The practice of
filling offices by election by lot may not commend itself
as the best means to secure efficient officers, but it is
eloquent proof of political equality, showing that class
distinction of any kind was not prejudicially operative.
Furthermore, that lack of means might not prevent
participation in public service, Pericles introduced the
system of a small financial remuneration for office-
holders.

   The Athenian ASSEMBLY, or ECCLESIA as it was
called, was composed, as has been said, of all citizens
over eighteen years of age.   The attendance was voluntary and there was no compensation during the fifth century; pay was introduced in the fourth century.   The
sessions were originally held in the *agora* or market
place, but the regular place of meeting was the hill
called the *Pnyx;* later the theater of Dionysus built by
Lycurgus afforded a more comfortable location.   The
Assembly convened only once in a *prytany* or tenth
of the year period, but met more frequently as time
went on, as often as four times in each prytany.
The legislative powers of the Assembly were great
and determined matters of policy and administration,
involving questions of war and peace, treaties and
alliances, the raising of military forces and their
dispersal, and finances.   The election of generals

and some others of the most important public officers devolved upon the Assembly. In the regular order of business of the Assembly there was first a consideration of the *program* provided by the Council, i.e., those preliminary decrees or proposals recommended by that body. Voting was by a show of hands. In cases of ostracism the voting took the form of inscribing the name of the proposed victim on *ostraka* or potsherds. The decrees passed by the Assembly which had been recommended by the Senate were inscribed on stone or bronze and were exposed to public view. Any member of the Assembly was at liberty to speak, although custom and modesty prescribed that precedence should depend upon age, older citizens speaking first. As in all popular assemblies a few men did most of the speaking, assuming leadership through their oratorical gifts, special knowledge, or interest. Professional orators (*rhetors*) held sway over the populace for better or worse.

The COUNCIL OF FIVE HUNDRED was made up of citizens over thirty years of age who had been chosen by lot, fifty from each of the ten tribes. Members were elected annually and could serve not more than twice. The qualifications of each new elected councillor were passed upon (the *dokimasia*) by the outgoing Council. Pay of three obols a day (nine cents) was awarded members since their duties demanded all their time, the Council meeting daily in the Council-chamber except during the festivals. For the expedition of business the fifty members from each tribe in turn constituted a committee which was responsible for the preparation of business and was always available for the immediate handling of affairs. These were called the *prytanes* or presidents and held office for the tenth part of the year, meeting in a special building, the circular *Tholos*, where they took their meals. The chief duty of the Council was to prepare business for the Assembly and thereafter to execute, if requested, the decrees favorably acted by that body. It had also numerous powers of administration, control of magistrates, and certain religious and judicial functions.

The COUNCIL OF THE AREOPAGUS, composed of ex-archons holding office for life, originally had enjoyed great political powers, but these were curtailed by the reforms of Ephialtes and Pericles. It became thereafter merely a court supervising certain matters of religion and law, cases of homicide, in particular, being frequently tried before it.

Of great importance in Athenian government were the MAGISTRATES. These officials were of three classes according to their duties, administrative, military, and financial. The chief administrative officers were the *Nine Archons,* consisting of the Chief Archon (*Archon Eponymus*), who in records gave his name to the year; the King Archon (*Archon Basileus*), who had general charge of religious matters; the *Polemarch,* who was originally Commander-in-chief, but later, being superseded by the ten generals, he was given various judicial duties, especially jurisdiction over the resident aliens or metics; and finally the six Junior Archons, the *Thesmothetae,* who recommended revision of laws and served as presiding officers of the law-courts.

The TEN GENERALS were the most influential officers in Athens. Originally each of the ten tribes appointed a general; later all ten were elected by the citizens at large. They were in charge of all military and naval administration and operations and of foreign affairs generally. Of equal powers and responsibilities in the beginning, they were eventually assigned specific duties. They influenced legislation in Council and Assembly and could submit motions. Under them were subordinate infantry and cavalry officers. Special and extraordinary powers might be granted to a particular general, who would thus become virtual ruler of Athens. This was true in the case of Pericles, a general, appointed year after year, and nominally subject constitutionally to higher authority, and yet in effect beneficent tyrant of Athens for many years because of the enormous power and influence which he exerted as general.

FINANCIAL OFFICERS consisted of various boards of treasurers, tax officials, and stewards of funds.

The LAW-COURTS in Athens are of peculiar interest, as the Athenian legal system differed widely from our own. These courts, called *Heliastic,* drew their *dicasts* (jurors) for jury service from a list of six thousand citizens. These men, usually of advanced years, had volunteered for such service and were chosen by lot, 600 from each tribe. The size of juries was extraordinarily large, ranging from 201 to a possible 6000, depending upon the importance of the case. The pay of jurymen for service was three obols (nine cents) a day.

The established facts concerning the government of Athens and the relations of the citizens thereto show the essential democracy of Athenian political institutions in the period under consideration. There was complete political equality among the citizens regardless of poverty, wealth, family, occupation, and prestige. Citizenship was enjoyed by all of Athenian birth and might be extended, as it was in some cases, to metic, or to slave. The Assembly was composed, as Xenophon and Plato tell us, largely of fullers, cobblers, carpenters, smiths, farmers, and wholesale and retail dealers. Offices were, for the most part, filled by lot, and payment for public service made it possible for the poorer classes to serve. Naturally, the superior virtues, abilities and qualifications of a Pericles or a Demosthenes made him conspicuous in the affairs of government and gave him great power for the good of Athens. On the other hand, a democratic form of government has in its very nature inherent weaknesses and potential dangers, since it is always possible for men of great ability but of dishonest character to pursue their selfish ends. These dangers Athens did not wholly escape. Just as in modern democracies, especially in municipal government, demagogues, bosses, and venal professional politicians often came into power to the despair and hurt of honest citizens, so in Athens there inevitably arose unscrupulous demagogues such as Cleon, venal statesmen, like Aeschines, professional politicians, like certain *rhetors,* informers and black-mailers, like the *sycophants,* and oligarchical cliques in successive generations, e.g., the pro-Medes, the pro-Lacedaemonians, and the pro-Macedonians. Some of the great Athenian thinkers, even Plato and Aristotle, seeing these defects and fearing that the democracy with all its advantages might degenerate into an ochlocracy (mob-rule), disparage a democratic polity and eulogize the aristocracy or the benevolent monarchy. But they were on the wrong track. The political salvation and personal independence of mankind is to be achieved, as the majority of thinking men today believe, only through " a government of the people, by the people, and for the people." The Athenian ideal of 2300 years ago is our ideal. It was not completely realized by them and it has not been perfectly achieved by us today. But their ideals are ours. Their successes we should emulate; their failures we should avoid. In both respects Athens remains our teacher and our benefactor.

We are now ready to examine the social and economic status of citizens in Athenian life and to scrutinize it particularly for evidences of caste, snobbery, inequality and injustice.

In the city the house of the rich man and that of the poor man differed little in appearance. Private unostentation as contrasted with public magnificence was the rule. In fact, it was considered a breach of good taste to build and occupy a house of conspicuous cost or size. In the next place, simplicity in dress was general. Only the young (and, in particular, the Knights) dared to provoke possible derision or to invite popular prejudice by foppery of attire or appearance. Young Mantitheus, in an oration of Lysias, apologizes to the Senate for his long hair, and Strepsiades, the old farmer in Aristophanes' *Clouds,* is disgusted with his son's "dandyism." Wearing the hair long might arouse suspicion of Spartan or aristocratic sympathies. An ancient witness testifies that "the Athenian people are not better clothed than the slave or alien, nor in personal appearance is there any superiority." Of course the nature of the employment might influence the quality and nature of the costume.

In all forms of social activity all the citizens participated on a parity. All could attend the theater; all joined in the public festivals and in religious sacrifices and observances. The poor and lowly enjoyed great advantages and privileges. Listen to the testimony of that unregenerate old Aristocrat (just quoted) who is bitterly opposed to Democracy as an institution but admits that it really exists in Athens. He says that if you *must* have Democracy, Athens is a perfect example of it: "I do not praise the Polity of the Athenians, because the very choice involves the welfare of the *baser* folk as opposed to that of the *better* class. The poorer classes and the people of Athens should have the advantage over the men of birth and wealth because it is the people who row the vessels, and put around the city her girdle of power. Everywhere greater consideration is shown to the base, to poor people, and to common folk, than to persons of good quality — this should not surprise us, this is the keystone of the preservation of the democracy. It is these poor people, this common folk, this riff-raff, whose prosperity, combined with growth of their numbers, enhance the democracy. All the world over the cream of society is in opposition to the democracy. The objection may be raised that it was a mistake to allow the universal right of speech and a seat in council; privileges which should have been reserved for the cleverest, the flower of the community. But if only the better people sat in council, blessings would fall only to that class and the baser folk would get nothing. Whereas it is the other way round. The people desire to be free and to be masters and their bad legislation is the very source of the people's strength and freedom." The happy lot of the common people in ancient Athens is further described by this contemporary witness: "The rich man trains the chorus; it is the people for whom the chorus is trained. The rich man is trierarch or gymnasiarch and the people profit by their labors. The whole state sacrifices at public cost a large number of victims; the Attic Democracy keeps holiday. They build at public cost a number of palaestras, dressing-rooms, bathing establishments; the mob gets the benefit of the majority of these luxuries rather than the select few or the well-to-do. In the theater the people do not like to be caricatured in comedy; it is the wealthy or well-born or influential man who is lampooned."[1]

The essential simplicity and sufficiency of life in Athens is in striking and refreshing contrast with the extremes of luxury and poverty which characterize Rome of the first century A.D. and the world today. In Athens, the rich did not grow richer while the poor grew poorer. Great fortunes, as we know them and as the Romans knew them, were not, and could not be, accumulated. It is true that some men were wealthier than others and enjoyed certain superior advantages as a result, but there was no overwhelming disparity between rich and poor in matters of dress and house, food and drink, and in physical, mental and spiritual joys and relaxations. Surplus wealth was not at the disposal of the few, but was expended for the good of all. Funds from the public treasury provided the marble temples, buildings and the theater and likewise supported war-orphans and pensioned invalids.

Individuals who acquired greater means than their fellows were expected to use it for the good of the city as a whole. This was accomplished through the *liturgies* or public services, which may be compared with modern income taxes. This interesting financial in-

[1] *Polity of the Athenians* (translated by Dakyns), composed about 425 B.C., falsely attributed to Xenophon.

stitution peculiar to ancient Greece merits attention. The revenue which accrued from the Athenian system of indirect taxation was quite insufficient to defray the expense of government; this taxation took the form of certain customs duties, income from public lands and mines, fines, confiscations, dues and licenses and personal taxes on metics, all of which were largely collected by tax-farmers. In place of direct taxation as a means of obtaining public revenue — a method which was rejected by the Athenians as they regarded it as an infringement upon personal liberty — through the liturgies, wealthy citizens were called upon to support by money and personal service various public activities. Some of these liturgies were: the *trierarchia,* the equipment of the naval fleet; the *choregia,* or the equipment and payment of all expenses of a chorus in the dramatic and religious festivals; and the *gymnasiarchia,* or service through which races of all kinds were provided. There were numerous other minor liturgies and special occasions and taxes which made demands upon the wealthy. The amount of some of these contributions is of interest. For example, the expense of a choregus in tragedy might be 3000 drachmas (drachma = about 18 cents); in comedy, 1600 drachmas. Lysias tells of a man who spent during the years 411–403 B.C. some 63,000 drachmas on the performance of liturgies, or an average of over 7000 drachmas a year.

While liturgies were imposed by the state upon the wealthier citizens, these tax burdens were often voluntarily assumed out of term for many years in succession by the more generous and public-spirited who contributed also to special funds at times of public need. This interest in public welfare in ancient Athens and private generosity may be compared with the frequent large gifts made by public-spirited men in the modern world, especially in America.

But what was the social and economic position of Athenian citizen workers of various kinds? As has been stated, it is generally asserted that all work was regarded as degrading, that every activity for which one was paid was condemned, and that producers, artisans, and all workers were branded by a humiliating social stigma. No adequate proof of such a condition of affairs is forthcoming. Why, then, is there this general mistaken notion? It is probably because of certain pronouncements in Plato and Aristotle. In the *Laws* and in the *Republic* Plato insists upon the gulf that should separate the citizen from the mechanic or trader. His ideal state rests upon agriculture and all the citizens are landed gentry forbidden to engage in trade. In this ideal *polis* trade and commerce are to be insignificant and the productive class is actually debarred from all political rights. A caste system is presupposed. Governors and governed are sharply differentiated and each class is trained for its predestined position in the state. Aristotle, too, in his ideal state, divides the population, on the one hand, into a ruling class of soldiers and judges and, on the other, into a subject class consisting of artisans and producers. As a mechanical trade renders the body and soul and intellect of free persons unfit for the exercise and practice of virtue, Aristotle denies to the artisan the proper excellence of man on the ground that his occupation and status are unnatural. In an extreme Democracy the mechanic and hired laborer must needs be citizens; this is impossible in an Aristocracy in which virtue and desert constitute the sole claim to the honors of state. Other radical statements of Aristotle are that the producer only differs from a slave in being subject to all instead of to one man, and that the sedentary and within-door nature of the crafts unfits the man who exercises them for war and the chase, the most dignified employments. Physical labor is condemned by him in that it is cheapening to work for another for pay or material profit, as this reduces one to the rank of a slave (*Politics* 5. 1337 b. 8). That Aristotle did not represent Athenian opinion is conclusively shown by his condemnation of agriculture as preventing leisure

which is at the basis of virtue. But no one doubts that
agriculture was generally and highly esteemed by the
Athenians. In Xenophon, in a passage which is represented as spoken by Socrates, those base mechanic arts
are condemned which ruin the bodies of all those engaged in them, as those, for example, who are forced
to remain in sitting postures and hug the gloom or
crouch whole days confronting a furnace. This results
in physical enervation and enfeebling of the soul, and
the victims have no desire to devote to the claims of
friendship and the state. Such will be sorry friends
and ill-defenders of the fatherland.

One makes a grievous mistake who accepts the passages summarized above as conclusively proving that
the Athenians regarded work as degrading and workers
as social outcasts. These writers do not claim to be
describing actual Athenian conditions. They have in
mind an " ideal " society of a Spartan complexion.
They are thinking, too, of soul-destroying drudgery, not
of reasonable labor and skilled work; of corrupt and
petty business, not of necessary and honest trade and
affairs. Frequently they were contrasting the philoso-
pher-statesmen set apart for ruling with the defective
yokel. We can, indeed, if we wish, invoke the above-
quoted writers in defense of work and the dignity of
producing. Plato says in the *Laws* (xi, 918) " Retail
trade in a city is not intended by nature to do any harm,
but quite the contrary; for is not he a benefactor who
reduces the inequalities and incommensurabilities of
goods to equality and common measure? And this is
what the power of money accomplishes, and the mer-
chant may be said to be appointed for this purpose."
Plato goes on to observe that many occupations have
suffered ill-repute because of the inordinate love of
gain and consequent corrupt practices on the part of
the unscrupulous. He concludes: " If . . . we were
to compel the best men everywhere to keep taverns for
a time, or carry on retail trade, or do anything of that
sort: or if, in consequence of some fate or necessity,

the best women were compelled to follow similar call-
ings, then we should know how agreeable and pleasant
all these things are; and if all such occupations were
managed on incorrupt principles, they would be
honored as we honor a mother or nurse." Aristotle
in the *Politics* condemns agriculture, as we have seen,
yet elsewhere (*Rhetoric*, 2. 1381 a) he declares: "We
honor the generous and brave and just. Such we conceive to be those who do not live upon others; and
such are they who live by labor . . . chiefly agriculturists, and chief among the agriculturists, the small
farmers." Now these small farmers tilled their own
fields; in the remote districts of Attica slavery had
scarcely penetrated. Xenophon tells the story of
Eutherus, an old friend of Socrates, who, in poverty,
as his property had been lost in the war, was gaining
a livelihood by bodily toil. Socrates warns him that
such employment in his case can be only temporary
because of lack of necessary physical strength and
urges him to secure a position as assistant to a large
proprietor as manager of an estate. Eutherus fears
that the work may be servile. Socrates replies that
heads of departments in a state who manage property
are regarded not as performing undignified work but
as having attained a higher dignity of freedom.
Eutherus still demurs on the ground that he does not
like to be accountable to anyone. Socrates replies
that it is difficult to find work that is devoid of liability
to account. It is difficult to avoid mistakes or un-
friendly criticism. "Avoid captious critics," he says,
"attach yourself to the considerate. Whatever you
can do, do it heart and soul and make it your finest
work." Another interesting and significant opinion of
Socrates on this subject is reported by Xenophon. It
was expressed in a conversation between the philosopher
and Aristarchus. The time was during the régime of
the Thirty when economic and political conditions were
very bad. Aristarchus' house was full of his indigent
female relatives, fourteen in all. As these ladies were all

expert needlewomen, skilled in the making of garments, Socrates advises his friend to put them to work; Ceramon, for example, with a few slaves, is very prosperous. Aristarchus objects to this proposal; the situations are not comparable; the members of his large household are not barbarian slaves but are kinswomen and free-born. Socrates replies: " Then, on the ground that they are free-born and relatives you think they ought to do nothing but eat and sleep? Or is it your opinion that free-born people who live in this way lead happier lives and are more to be congratulated than those who devote themselves to such useful arts of life as they are skilled in? Are work and study of no value? Did your relatives learn what they know merely for useless information or as a future asset? Is the well-tempered life and a juster one attained rather through idleness or the practice of the useful? If they were called upon to do some shameful work, let them choose death rather than that; but it is otherwise. It is suitable work for women. The things which we know are those we can best perform; it is a joy to do them, and the result is fair."

Plenty of evidence is available to show that work was esteemed not only in the times portrayed by Homer in the *Iliad* and the *Odyssey* and Hesiod in his *Works and Days,* but in Athens of the fifth century B.C. In Athens there was actually a law directed against idleness. That it was long in force is shown by the fact that Lysias wrote a speech in connection with a prosecution in such a case for which the penalty on conviction was a fine of one hundred drachmas and disfranchisement if the accused were thrice convicted. Plutarch tells us that a son who had not been taught a trade by his father was thereby released from the obligation to support his parent in old age. We have already quoted Pericles to the effect that not poverty but indolence is degrading.

Now the old-fashioned assumption that the Athenians found abundant leisure and opportunity for the *real life* (i.e., art, literature, politics, and philosophy) only because slaves and women did everything for them and the state treasury liberally supported them in *dolce far niente* is ridiculous.   One thing is certain from all we know of the Athenians: they were not indolent; they were energetic in mind and body.   Certainly in any State the wealthy are but a minority of the total population and even upon these rests the duty to manage their property and care for investments.   Participation in public life and fulfilment of the demands and duties of good citizenship did not exact from the average Athenian anything like the major part of his waking hours.   The Assembly met four times in each prytany (or tenth of a year period), i.e., about once in eight days.   The attendance was voluntary and only a fraction of all who were entitled to attend were ever present, as convenience or interest dictated.   The Council was limited to five hundred citizens and no one might serve more than twice; furthermore, fifty only of the Council (the Presidents, the Standing Committee) were continuously on duty, so that the majority thus were free to attend to their private affairs.   The *Heliaea*, or Courts of Justice, drew their dicasts (jurors) for service from a list of six thousand citizens.   These jurors were usually men of advanced years who had volunteered for such service. Universal military service at this time was not obligatory.   Festivals and contests were generally attended, but they occurred probably not oftener than once a week on the average.   It has been estimated that a total of from two to three years of every citizen's life were required for deliberative and administrative duties.   Many writers have emphasized the huge number of citizens who were supposedly pensioners luxuriously supported, apparently permanently and completely, by largess from the Periclean treasury.   But we have seen that public duties were not constant.   As for the compensation, it must be remembered that the daily living wage for the workman was from one drachma (about eighteen cents) to one and a half drachmas. Now, at the time under consideration, Assemblymen received no compensation; jurymen received three obols (about nine cents) daily for service; members of the Council of Five Hundred, elected annually by lot, were paid at most five obols (about fifteen cents). In the light of these facts, how can it be claimed that " Pericles *corrupted* the citizens generally by gifts of money, making them idle, cowardly, and greedy," or to assume that these citizens were all dependent on public pay and could entirely support their households on these meager stipends? Only a minority of the some fifty thousand adult male citizens received any State pay. The remuneration given was not a living wage; it was merely a contribution to support by which Pericles provided that *all*, and not merely the well-to-do, might participate, in turn, in civic affairs and obtain that benefit and culture from active personal public service to which he eloquently refers in the *Funeral Oration*. Nor was the remuneration intended as a sop to placate the discontented and starving proletariat. As Professor Ferguson says: " Pericles did not intend to create a class of salaried officials; nor yet to make an advance toward communism. His ideal was political, not economic, equality to enable all, irrespective of wealth or station, to use the opportunities and face the obligations which democracy brought in its train. Like all the great democratic leaders who preceded him, he was a nobleman by birth and breeding, and, like them, he did not doubt for a moment that the culture that ennobled the life of his class would dignify and uplift that of the masses also. His aim was to unite the whole people in a community of high ideas and emotions. It was to make them a nation of noblemen." If this were not the case, Pericles' noble speech, which stands in history by the side of Lincoln's Gettysburg address, is the most hypocritical document preserved to us from the past.

Since the number of wealthy citizens was small, how

did the ordinary citizen gain his livelihood?   It was by means of agriculture, handicrafts, trades, wholesale and retail business, and daily labor.   No occupation was more respected and admired than agriculture. Farms were small, tenancy almost unknown.   The small farmer tilled his fields with his own hands.   In the arts and crafts and in labor no one needed to be idle, for the state policies of Pericles and the great building operations not only gave employment to all the residents of Athens, whether free men or slaves, but attracted workers from far and near.   Thousands of citizens, perhaps a third of the whole, gained a livelihood by labor.   While commerce was largely in the hands of the resident aliens, and the heaviest drudgery was performed by slaves, the mass of the skilled workers were free citizens.   Stone-cutters, masons, and sculptors had their shops or yards where they worked privately with their apprentices, or they might be engaged in public work, such as the building operations on the Acropolis, working side by side with other citizens, with metics, and with slaves.[1]

Modest means was the rule in Athens and was no bar to achievement and distinction.   Life and its needs were simple, and money in itself as an accumulation was not desired.   A uniform wage was paid practically to all skilled workmen alike.   Everyone who had skill or art was an *artist*, a term applied to sculptors, painters, physicians, and cobblers.   Plato, to be sure, who was wealthy, speaks harshly of those sophists and teachers who were compelled to take money for teaching.   There were, indeed, some charlatans in this profession, but we may be certain that such sophists as Gorgias, Protagoras, Isocrates, and Alcidamas (all of whom were professors who accepted tuition-fees from countless students who were only too glad to pay it) were held in esteem in Athens.   So were lawyers and speech-writers for pay, such as Antiphon, Lysias, and Isaeus. Literary men who accepted pay, poets who received

[1] See Chapter IV for Plutarch's description of these activities.

purses for prizes, and actors who profited financially
by their labors were in good social repute. The prestige
of physicians depended on their skill and personality.
The ignoramus and the charlatan were contemned;
the skilled and public-spirited surgeon might be richly
rewarded and given an honorary crown and public
thanks. The elementary-school teacher, the music and
gymnastic instructor, were not highly regarded, not
because they received money for their services, but
because most of them were ignorant men and often
of inferior breeding. As for the great artists, sculptors,
and painters, it is impossible to believe, as we have
been told, that they fell under public contempt simply
because they earned money. Could this be true of a
Phidias, a Polygnotus, an Ictinus, or a Mnesicles? But
we know that Phidias was a warm and extremely intimate personal friend of Pericles. In fact, the statesman admired the sculptor so highly that the latter was
entrusted with the greatest powers in superintending
the ornamentation of the great temples. As for Polygnotus, a native of Thasos, he was the personal friend
of Cimon, and was actually honored by the Athenians
with citizenship. Expert potters and vase-painters
were very numerous. While some of these were resident aliens (e.g., Amasis and Brygus), very many were
citizens. Thus we find such names of prominent vase-
makers as Clitias, Ergotimus, Nicosthenes, Epictetus,
Pamphaeus, Euphronius, Hieron, and Megacles. A
typical vase-making establishment would engage the
services of some twelve persons, who might be citizens,
metics, and slaves, all working side by side in equality.
Citizen artists and artisans proclaim with pride, and
do not conceal in shame, their occupations. Vase-
painters and makers signed their wares. A scene (The
Workshop of a Greek Vase-Painter) on a vase shows
two Victories and Athena herself crowning the workmen, as Pottier says, " a poetic symbol to glorify the
fame of Athenian industry." Indeed, artisans regarded
themselves as under the special protection of Hephaes-

tus, the smith, and of Athena, mistress of the arts and crafts, and proudly claimed descent from these deities. Euphronius, when making an offering to Athena, calls himself in his dedication a potter, and the same procedure is followed by the fuller Simon, the tanner Smicrus, and the potters Mnesiades and Nearchus. On a funereal bas-relief a cobbler was represented in a heroic attitude holding the insignia of his trade. In the neighborhood of the Agora shops were especially numerous. These places served as centers of gossip and of news for Athenians generally, as we are told in a graphic passage in an informative speech of Lysias (*On the Cripple*): " My accuser says that many unprincipled men gather at my shop. But you (the large jury) all know that this accusation is not directed at me more than at other artisans, nor at those who frequent my place more than those who go to other shops. Each of you is accustomed to visit the establishment of the perfumer, or the barber, or the leatherworker, etc. If any of you shall condemn my visitors, then he must condemn the frequenters of other places; and if these, then *all the Athenians.* Certainly *all* of you are accustomed to frequent these shops and spend time somewhere or other." It was among these craftsmen that Socrates, who had himself started in life as a stonecutter, spent much time in conversation. When he was, on an occasion, in search of a gentleman, he did not hesitate to go the round of various good carpenters, bronzeworkers, painters, and sculptors.

The comedies of Aristophanes are sometimes taken as proof of great social distinctions and inequalities existing among the citizens of Athens; e.g., the passage in the *Knights* where the sausage-seller is assured that his crass ignorance, boorish vulgarity, and dense stupidity are the strongest possible recommendations and assets for the highest political distinction. We are apparently to infer that Aristophanes was himself a deep-dyed aristocrat who despised the people and their rule and that he was the spokesman for a large aristo-

cratic section of Athenian society which was extremely
hostile to democratic government. These views are
unwarranted and, indeed, have been discredited. Aristophanes was not a partisan; he was a conservative.
He was not an opponent of democracy, nor yet an aristocrat. It is true that he was a well-educated man of
keen discernment, a friend of the Knights, and was
doubtless on good terms with members of the aristocratic element in Athens. But he was friendly to the
cause of democracy and sincerely wished to do it a
favor by fearlessly revealing those defects to which a
democratic form of government is especially liable and
to give warning of possible dangers. This he constantly
does in his plays with that exaggeration and caricature
which are characteristic of the Old Comedy. In the
opinion of the poet grave danger to the democracy
might arise from unscrupulous demagogy as represented by such knaves as Cleon. In the case of Cleon,
who is lampooned in the *Knights,* Aristophanes is actu-
ated by intense animus as a result of previous personal
encounters. Thus Cleon is excoriated as a vulgar,
coarse, and despicable individual, and the dramatist tries
to discredit his influence and popularity. It is a great
mistake, however, to take Aristophanes' savage attacks
on vulgar demagogues and his criticisms of weaknesses
in democratic government as proof that the playwright
was an aristocrat who condemned and arraigned the
people as a whole for vulgarity and incompetency.
That he did not despair of the democracy and that he
sympathized and fraternized with the " lower classes "
is shown by those plays in which the chief personages,
although of low degree, are " sympathetic " characters,
e.g., Dicaeopolis, the charcoal-burner of the *Acharnians,* and Strepsiades, the rough countryman of the
Clouds.

In the opinion of Croiset, " the best Athenian society
was the most open-hearted, most variously constituted,
and most liberal society that has ever existed. The
Athens that Plato shows us is a sort of talking place,

where everybody is supposed to know everybody else, and where each person has a perfect right to make acquaintance with those he meets." As typical illustrations of this social democracy he refers to two social gatherings of which we have admirable accounts. In Xenophon's *Symposium* there is a description of a banquet held in 421 B.C., in the house of the wealthy Callias, son of Hipponicus, of a great and rich Athenian family. The guests include all sorts of people, rich, poor, philosophers and ignoramuses, and all converse familiarly on terms of equality and intimacy. In the same way, Plato, in his *Symposium*, an account of a dinner held at the house of Agathon in 416 B.C., reveals the same intermixture of classes and professions.

We have now completed our discussion of the essentially democratic political and social status of Athenian citizens. We shall next consider the other classes of the inhabitants of Attica who are commonly regarded, along with the poorer citizens, as the victims of the Athenian aristocracy.

II. The Metics

The rapid commercial growth and naval expansion of Athens early caused a shortage of workers and helpers of all kinds. The citizen population was numerically inadequate to assume these new duties in addition to the performance of their regular occupations and the prosecution of agriculture. This demand was met by extending a welcome to foreigners and this policy was continued and encouraged by Pericles. Their exact number in the year 431 B.C. is unknown and various estimates have been made. There may have been one adult male metic for every two citizens.

What was the lot of the metics? Pericles says: " We open our city to all and never drive out foreigners." The scene of Plato's dialogue, *The Republic*, is the house of Cephalus, a prominent and influential man, but a metic who had been invited to Attica by Pericles

himself. Another contemporary speaks of " the equality between the metics and the full citizens, because
the city stands in need of her resident aliens to meet
the requirements of such a multiplicity of arts and for
the purposes of her navy."   Thucydides has Nicias
say to metic sailors that they and not any friends or
allies outside were the " only free partners with the
Athenians in the Empire."   The metics participated
fully in the social and religious life of the city. Neither
in dress nor in appearance could they be distinguished
from the citizens. They attended the theater, they had
a prominent place and dress in the Panathenaic procession, and worshipped the same deities as the citizens.
With the citizens they defrayed the expenses of the
liturgies and served in the navy. When any list of
Athenian inhabitants is given the metics are always
named as an essential element of the population. They
worked in large numbers side by side for equal pay with
the citizens in all kinds of work, as, for example, in
the construction of the Erechtheum. They are found
engaged in all the occupations as workers and artisans
in manufacture and in the shipping, fishing, and im-
porting industries.   At Athens not only were they
retailers and petty tradesmen but they occupied the
highest places and gained the greatest repute in large
business affairs as well as in the realms of art and intellect, the " higher professions " as we should designate
them. To give some examples of these prominent metics
will be illuminating. Sosias of Thrace was the employer
of a thousand slaves at Laurium.   Pasion, who possessed a fortune of sixty talents, and Phormion were
the greatest bankers of the fourth century B.C.   In the
arts Nesiotes (probably an Ionian), Agoracritus, and
Cresilas were great sculptors; Polygnotus of Thasos,
Zeuxis of Heraclea, Parrhasius of Ephesus were painters of renown; Hippodamus of Miletus, the architect,
was the designer of the city Piraeus. Hippocrates of
Cos, the physician, enjoyed great popularity. Many of
the greatest philosophers, sophists, and teachers were

metics.   Such were Anaxagoras of Clazomenae, Protagoras of Abdera, Gorgias of Sicily, Prodicus of Ceos, Hippias of Elis, Polus the Sicilian, Aristotle the Stagirite (of Thrace), Theophrastus of Eresus, Antisthenes (a half-Athenian), and Zeno.

The annual fee of twelve drachmas (about $2.16) required of metics was a legal formality of registration and license and not a very serious tax burden. The liability to taxes beyond those required of citizens was not great.   Perhaps the most serious limitation imposed upon metics was the inability legally to own real property.   But metics might be placed on equal terms as to taxation and the owning of property and even full citizenship might be conferred by vote of the Assembly.   For example, an inscription is preserved which records the grant of full citizenship on those metics who participated in the return of the democrats from Phyle (in 404–3 B.C.) and helped in the restoration.   In the list occur some strangely sounding foreign names and the occupations of these persons, as given, are decidedly humble, such as cook, gardener, carpenter, fuller, etc.

The Athenians have been harshly criticized for not freely and generally granting citizenship to the metics.   At first thought the criticism may seem valid and Athens may appear illiberal.   Doubtless selfish considerations, such as an unwillingness to share with others the material benefits of citizenship, played a part in this policy.   But to the Athenian, citizenship was not merely a political privilege; it was a sacred and usually an *inherited* possession.   Loss of citizenship was to be feared more than death itself.   Athens was a small and homogeneous community and the Athenians regarded themselves as autochthonous, like their favorite and symbolic cicada, sprung from the very soil of Attica itself.   There is danger to a state in a too rapid influx of aliens who are given the powers of citizenship before real political and social assimilation has taken place.   Even free America requires a term of years of

probation before naturalization, and one of our greatest
problems surely is this very one of the assimilation of
the large number of our resident aliens. As Aristotle
says: "Another cause for revolution is difference of
races which do not acquire a common spirit; for the
state is not the growth of a day, neither is it a multitude brought together by accident. Hence the reception of strangers in colonies has generally produced
revolution." It is true that the metics of Athens were
not on full terms of political equality with the citizens,
but it has been shown that the social and economic gulf
postulated by modern writers as existing between
citizen and resident foreigner did not really exist.

III. The Slaves

The institution of slavery existed throughout the
ancient world from the earliest times. The Athenians,
with but few exceptions, regarded slavery as natural
and justifiable. It is again Aristotle, the fourth-century
theorist and philosopher, who is made the starting-point
for most modern discussions of slavery among the
Greeks and of the iniquity of the institution as maintained even by the cultured Athenians of the time of
Pericles. In his treatment of this subject Aristotle
characterizes in cold-blooded legal fashion the slave
as being merely " a breathing machine or tool, a piece
of animated property," and asserts that some men are
so inferior that they may be regarded as slaves by
nature. It is interesting to note, however, that Aristotle in another passage admits that there were some
who protested against such a view. He says: " Others
regard slave owning as doing violence to nature on the
ground that the distinction between slave and free man
is wholly conventional and has no place in nature, and
therefore is void of justice, as resting on mere force."
Plato (*Republic* 5.469), too, regards slavery as natural
and justifiable, but would forbid the enslavement of
Greeks (*Laws* 777b); he admits (*Republic* 563b), how-

ever, that " a slave is an embarrassing possession, the distinction between man and slave being a difficult one and slaves should be well-treated and not abused or insulted." Aristotle (*Politics* 1255b), also, advises good treatment for the slave.

Whence came the slaves owned by the Athenians? Who were they? A few were born in servitude of slave parents, but the majority were captives of war. Barbarian captives were generally sold into slavery and sometimes even prisoners of Greek blood suffered the same fate. Most of the slaves in Athens were from Thrace and Scythia and Illyria, from Asia Minor and from Syria. At Athens there was a flourishing slave market. The price varied according to age, sex, origin and abilities. At a household auction at Athens in 415 B.C. male slaves sold at an average price of 166 drachmas (= francs); women, 170. Mine-slaves sold for somewhat less. An Athenian family of moderate means might have perhaps three slaves; a richer household would own more.

Some writers have been very severe in their strictures on the Athenians for tolerating slavery. When we consider that slavery, which has not even yet disappeared from the earth, is of great antiquity and that it was an integral part of all ancient social institutions, it is not surprising that Athens was not free of this blemish. As it has been well said, we should not ask, How could Athens tolerate slavery? but, How did the Athenians treat her slaves? And the answer is, " with humanity and on the whole, with kindness and liberality." It is true that a minority of slaves in Attica must have had an unenviable existence. These were the men of the lowest type who worked in the silver mines at Laurium. Elsewhere occasionally, no doubt, an individual slave suffered at the hands of a cruel master. But what was the lot of the majority of the slaves in Attica? A contemporary testifies: " An extraordinary amount of license is granted to slaves . . . where a blow is illegal, and a slave will not step aside to let you pass him on the street. . . . The Athenian people is not better clothed than the slave or the alien, nor in personal appearance is there any superiority. . . . Slaves in Athens are allowed to indulge in luxury, and indeed in some cases to live magnificently. . . . We have established an equality between our slaves and free men." Newly acquired slaves were received into the household with showers of confetti. They participated as members of the family in religious rites and sacrifices. They might attend the theater. They worked side by side with their masters in the workshop or might even be permitted to work on their own account exercising an independent profession either paying a commission to their masters or actually purchasing their freedom and gaining thereby the status of metics. The law protected a slave from being the victim of insolent violence and the aggressor was subject to fine. The slave might not be put to death; a free man who had killed a slave was subject to prosecution for manslaughter. Refuge from a cruel master was afforded by flight to a temple as sanctuary, especially to the Theseum, to the Sanctuary of the Erinyes, and to the altar of Athena Polias. Freedom might be granted outright by the master, while the state at times enfranchised slaves who had fought for Athens. In case of illness a slave might be affectionately cared for and at death mourned as a relative.

On the whole, then, Athenian slaves were treated with consideration. They were not sweated and worked under the lash of a slave-driver, but were given a place in the household or participated in friendly relations in the work of shop and factory. The work they did, with the exception of mining, had variety and was of a nature to arouse their interest and demand skill and it was performed under agreeable and healthy conditions. Can this be said of the toilers today in the sweat-shops and factories of our congested industrial centers?

Finally, the almost universal assumption that Athenian achievements were possible *only through slavery,* and that slavery was the *dominant* factor in Athenian economic life, is a gross exaggeration. On the contrary, the slaves were in the minority in the total population in the latter half of the fifth century B.C. and the prosperity and greatness of the city-state was due not to the exploitation of slave labor, but to the industry, the initiative, and the efficiency of citizen and metic, in whose hands the political, the intellectual, the artistic, and the commercial fortunes rested. In the flourishing period of Athenian greatness the slaves were not a source of political discontent as at Rome. We hear of no serious servile uprisings or servile wars at Athens. They were not a social and economical menace, nor was there competition in labor between slave and free man, for there was no unemployment in Athens in the age of Pericles, but there was a demand for labor, immigration was encouraged, and there was a living wage for all. Nor was it the case at this time that all hand-labor became associated with slavery and hence became incompatible with the dignity of the free man. It is undoubtedly true, however, that in the fourth century and later the competition of slave with free labor gave rise to economic distress at a time when the citizens had decreased in number and the slaves had enormously increased.

IV. The Women of Athens

When we survey the position of women in Athenian life we are disappointed to discover how small and unimportant a rôle they seem to have played. In an era of greatness and freedom, at a time and in a community when the flower of mighty achievement and the attainment of individual liberty came to magnificent bloom, the influence of women was largely negligible in the larger life of the city-state. Plato in his *Republic* would grant women complete intellectual and spiritual development and equality, but this ideal was not realized in Athens. This condition of affairs would strike us as deplorable and would be well-nigh inexplicable were it not for the fact that in modern times the emancipation of women has been of slow attainment and even to-day awaits full realization. Athenian women did not enjoy the political privileges of the vote and of participation in affairs of government; nor did American women until very recently. Athenian girls did not receive the systematic schooling and higher education which their brothers might enjoy; higher education for American girls dates from the last few decades and even now some doors, as those of certain professional schools, are closed to them. Athenian young women of good family did not, and could not, leave the protection of their male relatives and embark upon any independent life or career: this, too, is a phenomenon of very recent appearance in a modern society which accounted itself respectable. There was no economic pressure to bring about economic independence. Modern emancipation of woman has largely come about through excess of women over men, late marriage, spinsterhood, and the influence of the World War which drew women into active life.

The marriage of an Athenian girl was a matter which was arranged by her parents and a dowry must be provided, as is the case today in many lands. The mental education of an Athenian girl was limited to elementary instruction obtained from mother or nurse in the home. Regular schooling was denied her. She might at best acquire a knowledge of reading, writing, and dancing and music. Emphasis was placed on the acquisition of domestic arts, weaving, cooking, and household management. She did not enjoy the privilege of participation in athletics, a prerogative of Spartan girls. From the protecting care of her parents she passed at an early age to the home of her husband to put in practice the domestic accomplishments previously acquired. There her life was largely passed and having had little education and not enjoying the intellectual advantages which Athens so richly furnished to men, she gave little pleasure to her husband as an intellectual companion. Nor did he seek to improve her mind and give her opportunities, since nearly all his time was spent away from home, at his work or pleasure or devoted to public service. And when he brought home friends or guests it was not customary for his wife or daughters to appear.

There are two passages which are always quoted to show the position of women in Athens. The first one is found in Xenophon's *Economist* (vii. 5, translated by Dakyns), where Ischomachus relates to Socrates the training and virtues of his young wife, not quite fifteen when she was wedded. The second quotation, from the speech of Pericles, will be given later. Ischomachus says: " Socrates, when after a time she had become accustomed to my hand, that is, was tamed sufficiently to play her part in a discussion, I put to her this question: ' Did it ever strike you to consider, dear wife, what led me to choose you as my wife among all women, and your parents to entrust you to me of all men? . . . It was with deliberate intent to discover, I for myself and your parents in behalf of you, the best partner of house and children we could find. If at some future time God grant us to have children born to us, we will take counsel together how best to bring them up, for that too will be a common interest, and a common blessing if haply they shall live to fight our battles and we find in them hereafter support and succour when ourselves are old. But at present there is our house here, which belongs alike to both. It is common property, for all that I possess goes by my will into the common fund, and in the same way all that you deposited was placed by you to the common fund. We need not stop to calculate in figures which of us contributed most, but rather let us lay to heart this fact that whichever of us proves the better partner, he or she at once contributes what is most worth having.' " The gist of Ischomachus' homily to his young wife is that by divine dispensation woman's nature was shaped for indoor and man's for outdoor occupations; man and woman alike need and must use memory, carefulness and self-control. But the wife, like the queen-bee of the hive, will order the home, apportion and assign the work, spinning, weaving, preparation of food and the nursing of the sick, and teach the young servants their tasks. The young couple then proceed carefully to arrange furniture and all belongings where they may be found and used when needed. The young wife, we are told, was a willing pupil and obediently agreed to the carrying out of these suggestions to the best of her ability and even assented to her husband's suggestion that she discontinue the use of rouge, face-powder and high-heeled shoes on the ground that "beauty unadorned is adorned the most!"

The sentiment of romantic love in a highly developed and idealistic form is of modern origin. Here, Greek realism largely reigned. To the Greek, marriage was primarily natural and indeed inevitable since only thus was the family perpetuated. It was in itself a political and economic institution: political, as only the offspring of Athenian parents on both sides were citizens; economic, as the husband was provided with a home and housekeeper and the wife with a protector and a livelihood. The sons would be defenders of the state and a support and solace to their parents in their advancing years. Athenian literature is almost silent with regard to women. It is true that Homer has noble feminine types, Penelope, Andromache, Arete and Nausicaa, and that tragedy abounds with such women as sublimely courageous Antigone, intrepid Electra, self-sacrificing Alcestis, loving Deianira and many others, but these are women of heroic times and heroic mold.

It must not be thought, however, that, because the Greek marital union was a *mariage de convenance,* tenderness and affection were lacking in Athenian marriages. Scattered references in the literature, the inscriptions and the evidence of the graves and the grave monuments attest the presence of natural human ties of love and devotion. The high ideals of womanhood found in the poets were doubtless inspired by women of Athens. Monogamy prevailed as a legal institution, showing the regard for the integrity of the family and the tribe, and respect for woman. The seclusion of the Athenian women was not the Oriental seclusion of the harem. Women participated in public festivals and religious rites, in the celebration of the *Panathenaea* with the sacred procession to the Acropolis, and they could attend the theater. The fact remains, however, that the native Athenian woman of the well-to-do classes was carefully protected and largely secluded according to the old tribal feeling. Pericles doubtless gave utterance to the common sentiment with regard to women of the most highly respected class when he said: " Great is your glory if you fall not below the standard which nature has set for your sex, and great also is hers concerning whom there is least talk among men whether in praise or blame." These Athenian conventions did not bind the foreign-born women in Athens, who enjoyed freedom of action and opportunities for mutual improvement together with association with men. These women, called *hetaerae* (companions), are represented at their best by the beautiful, clever, and high-born Aspasia, the mistress of Pericles. The women of the poorer classes, too, naturally had more freedom of action and probably engaged in outdoor work and in trade to a certain extent.

Although Athenian women generally led happy and contented lives, their segregation was unfortunate in its consequences. It was unjust to the women themselves and it reacted unfavorably upon the young men, who, in some cases, were driven to the society of courtesans or formed sentimental attachments with youths.

Conclusion

In summing up conditions of Athenian life in the Age of Pericles as we have above attempted to do, the following considerations, which are unfortunately often forgotten or ignored, must be kept in mind. The place is democratic Athens and not aristocratic Sparta or Thebes; evidence which is pertinent for the latter cities must not be adduced for the former. The time is the latter part of the fifth century and not the sixth or late fourth century B.C., when, to be sure, social, political, and economic conditions were very different.

The ideas and theories of Plato and Aristotle on these questions are of the greatest interest and value — but they are ideal and aristocratic conceptions relative to hypothetical communities and must not, and cannot, be taken literally to reflect actual Athenian conditions, nor are they truly representative of contemporary popular belief.

With regard to work, it is true that in Athens, as with us, some occupations were thought less desirable and less dignified than others. In no land and at no time is the day-laborer esteemed as highly as the statesman. Drudgery and menial employment the Athenians disliked and avoided; so do we. But the citizen who earned his living in some honest way and accepted money for his services was the rule and not the exception, nor was he as a result a social outcast, but he was a member, in good political and social standing, of the commonwealth. We may compare, perhaps, Athenian social conditions with those existing today in an American village where socially the blacksmith or the grocer may be on a par with the doctor or lawyer.

While the metics, or resident aliens, did not have full participation in political duties and privileges, nor yet complete legal freedom, they did share in large measure the life of the citizens. The door of opportunity and of material and social well-being lay open to them.

Athenian civilization of the Age of Pericles was not

dominated by the institution of slavery. But slavery was, of course, a constant and very important factor and influence in Athenian life. The right of owning slaves was hardly questioned. It is clear that as a rule slaves were treated by their masters with humaneness, with the exception perhaps of the lowest grade of public slaves who were employed in the mines.

The position of women in Athens was not what it was even in Homeric times, and, from the point of view of the most advanced modern society of the last few years, their lives were unfortunately restricted. The wives and the daughters of Athenian citizens were respected, protected, and no doubt genuinely loved in most cases, and were generally happy and contented, but the fact remains that they had only a minor share in the intellectual freedom and opportunities of that great period.

Athens, then, was a city-state with many imperfections. Her escutcheon is by no means free from blots, and some of these are deplorable. She was vexed by innumerable problems which she could not solve completely and many of these still await solution in our world today which is torn by dissensions and evils. But in her civilization, her achievements, and strivings for a genuine democracy and a better social order she has much of value to contribute to us.

CHAPTER IX

GREEK WRITING AND BOOKS

"The ancient classical writings furnish perpetual delight as models of style; they touch imagination, stimulate thought, and enlarge our view of man and nature. They enter into and have done much to instill what is best in modern literature and are the common heritage of civilized peoples, the permanent foundation on which the republic of letters has been built."—LORD BRYCE.

FOR the purpose of writing many materials served primitive society. The leaves of trees, as the palm, were used; the bark of trees, or the inner rind (hence *liber*, in Latin, came to mean book); and linen cloth was employed by the ancient Egyptians, and occasionally by the Romans, for books in ritual. The favorite medium of the Babylonians and the Assyrians was pottery or clay, such as sun-dried or fire-burnt bricks. In early Greece we hear of inscribed potsherds, or *ostraka* (hence the word *ostracism*, since the name of the person condemned to exile was written on vase fragments). Charms, prayers, and especially curses were frequently inscribed on lead tablets. Stone was extensively used by the Greeks for inscriptions of all kinds such as laws, epitaphs, and dedications.

In the classical period in Greece the common medium for writing was the waxed tablet, which was employed for letters, memoranda, accounts, etc. This tablet was a smooth wooden surface about seven by four inches covered with black wax and with a raised frame at the edges. Thus two tablets (a *diptych*) or three (a *triptych*) could be fastened together, the surfaces protected and held apart. For writing on the waxed surface an instrument, sharp at one end and with the other blunt for erasing, made of bronze, bone, or ivory was used.

Three materials for permanent written records have been in general use, namely, papyrus, vellum (skin), and paper. Of these, papyrus was the common medium for the writing of books among the Greeks. Vellum was employed largely in the second century B.C. and thereafter. Paper was not used by the Greeks.

Papyrus was used in Egypt from great antiquity and was an article of manufacture and commerce until the tenth century A.D. As it was customary to bury the dead as mummies wrapped in layers of papyrus, and since the dry soil and climate of Egypt are wonderful preservatives, we have obtained, and are still finding, many papyrus documents of greater or lesser value and interest in Egyptian excavations.

Papyrus (*papyros* or *biblos,* hence the Greek word for book, *biblos,* English *bible*) was made from the reedy plant grown in the delta region of the Nile in Egypt. Strips from the pith of the stem of the reed were taken and wetted, placed some vertically and others transversely, rolled and flattened, smoothed into sheets and then glued together to form a roll.

These rolls, in the fifth and fourth centuries, were of great length, as much as 150 feet so as to contain, for example, the whole *Iliad* or *Odyssey.* But such manuscripts were very unwieldy and the protest of Callimachus, the Alexandrian scholar-poet of the third century B.C., is famous, for he said that a " big book (i.e., a long roll) was a big evil." After his time we find that for convenience classical works were marked off into divisions, each portion of such length so as to fill a standard roll (*biblion*), which was some twenty to thirty feet in length and nine to ten inches in width. Thus, in the Alexandrian period, the *Iliad* was divided into twenty-four books or rolls designated by the capital letters of the Greek alphabet; the *Odyssey* likewise into twenty-four books indicated by the small letters of the alphabet; Herodotus into nine books, each named for a Muse; Thucydides into eight books; Plato's *Republic* into ten books, etc. A single roll (*volumen*) would suffice for a short work or poem. The roll was rolled on a stick and kept in a cylindrical box for preservation. A vellum strip with title or index was attached to the roll for identification. This might easily be torn off or lost and thus the authorship of the work be uncertain as the document itself might not indicate the writer's name or the exact title of the work. For writing on the papyrus a sharp reed (*calamus*) was at first used, the quill of a feather much later. Black ink, made of lamp-black in the classical period, was employed, which might be erased, when still fresh, with a sponge. Writing was on one side only of the papyrus and in columns the lines of which ran parallel with the length of the roll. The lines of the columns were the average length of the hexameter verse, that is, 16 syllables or 34 to 38 letters. A roll containing poetry comprised 700 to 1100 verses, iambic and dactylic verses being written line by line, lyric and dramatic meters sometimes as verse and sometimes as prose. The prose book-roll contained 2000 to 3000 lines. These lines, on one side of the papyrus only, were written as continuous script, generally without separation of words, without punctuation or paragraphs, and with no numbering of columns or lines. Exact references to writers, therefore, were difficult to make or to find and this, together with the scarcity of copies of books, led to much quoting from memory by classical authors. Signs of punctuation were few and rarely used. Lateral strokes might show a pause or change of speaker or indicate strophe or antistrophe. The early script was in Greek capital letters, as in inscriptions. For ease and rapidity of writing the capitals came to be written as curved capitals, i.e., *uncials*. A further stage was the use of small letters somewhat run together, i.e., *cursive* script. The marks of accent and breathing were invented by the Alexandrian scholar Aristophanes of Byzantium, in the third century B.C., for the purpose of teaching Greek pronunciation to foreigners. Such marks are not found in general and constant use before the seventh century A.D.

Skins were early employed for writing purposes, but were not commonly used because of the expense of manufacture. There is an Egyptian skin-roll in the British Museum dating from about 2000 B.C. Pergamum was the ancient center of the trade in vellum. In fact, the word *parchment* comes from the proper name Pergamum. The story is told by Pliny that the Ptolemies forbade the exportation of papyrus to prevent Eumenes II (B.C. 197–158) from founding at Pergamum a library which might rival that at Alexandria and that the manufacture and use of vellum were thereby greatly stimulated. The advantages of vellum are great as the material is extremely durable and permits the *codex,* or book form (a development of the early tablets), and also makes possible erasure and re-writing and the use of color and dyeing. As skin allows writing on both sides, a large work may be accommodated in small space; references, too, are easy. The codex, or folded book, however, was not common before the fourth century A.D.

Paper was not used by the Greeks, although it was known to the Chinese from early times. Europe became acquainted with its use in the eighth century A.D. through the Arabs, but it was not employed to any great extent before the thirteenth century. In the fourteenth and fifteenth centuries, with the invention of printing, paper superseded the use of vellum.

There was no reading public in Greece before the fifth century B.C. The early literature was exclusively poetical and intended for recitation and singing. For centuries the Homeric poetry was declaimed or recited by rhapsodes; lyric poetry was, of course, sung to the accompaniment of the lyre; elegy was originally recited to the accompaniment of the flute. Written records of this great body of verse were not numerous and memory was the vehicle of its transmission. Lovers of literature enjoyed this poetry through the medium of the ear and not through the eye. In the fifth century, Attic tragedy became very popular and this, together with more wide-spread education of the people generally, led to the making of books, the establishment of a book-market in the market-place at Athens and, in some cases, the accumulation of private libraries. Aristophanes refers to Euripides' large library and Socrates mentions the published works of Anaxagoras and also says that his friend Euthydemus has a complete copy of Homer. Xenophon relates that a part of a cargo of a wrecked ship consisted of books. It is evident that there was a considerable business in books in Athens at the close of the fifth century B.C. Publication of a work was, of course, entirely a private matter. The author had no protection or copyright; he made, or caused to be made, a number of copies of his work and these were sold by a bookseller. Thereafter, any one could copy and dispose of the book. We do not know much with regard to the details of Athenian book-making, selling, and copying. No doubt dictation by a reader to a number of copyists facilitated manufacture. Constant copying early and inevitably caused many errors and corruptions in texts and this was particularly true of the plays where interpolations, changes and additions by actors and trainers crept into the text. Because of this growing evil official texts of Homer and the tragedians were compiled to insure their integrity.

The first large public library seems to have been that of Alexandria.[1] The city of Alexandria was founded in 332 B.C. by Alexander the Great. In the next century Ptolemy Soter with the Peripatetic philosopher-statesman Demetrius of Phalerum founded the famous Library and Museum (temple of the Muses) and these educational and scientific institutions were fostered by Ptolemy Philadelphus. It is said that the

---

[1] On the history of scholarship at Alexandria and the great library, consult the Introduction to J. W. White's *The Scholia on the Aves of Aristophanes;* also, G. Murray, *The Tradition of Greek Literature.*

great Library eventually contained 700,000 volumes. In charge of this great collection were librarians whose names are famous in classical scholarship, and in Homeric criticism particularly, e.g., Aristophanes of Byzantium, Aristarchus, Eratosthenes, and Callimachus. These men catalogued and published editions of the books in the Library and compiled commentaries upon the classical writers. Lists or " Canons " of the best of the authors of the past were established, as, for example, the Canon of the Ten Attic Orators, the Nine Lyric Poets, and others. Texts were purged of errors and much was done to interpret and to elucidate the literature of an earlier age. Another great library of 200,000 volumes was established by the first century B.C. at Pergamum. At Antioch, Cos, and Rhodes were other collections of manuscripts.

An interesting but melancholy subject is that of the losses which Greek literature has sustained. The extent of the writings of the great Greek authors which we possess is fortunately very considerable and sufficiently ample to give us a splendid conception of the beauty, merit, and genius of the literature and an excellent knowledge of Greek civilization. But we know that the losses have been enormous. For example, there were numerous epic poems besides those of Homer. Literary losses before the Alexandrian Age were great, but they were tremendous thereafter. The Alexandrians had a great body of lyric poetry — many books of the poetry of Alcman, Alcaeus, Sappho, Stesichorus, and Simonides — whereas we have scanty fragments only of these poets. They had seventeen books of Pindar which Plutarch (80 A.D.) read; we have four. It has been estimated that over nine hundred tragedies were produced in Athens by the prolific and original dramatists; only thirty-three remain to us today. Of Aeschylus the Alexandrians had seventy-two plays; we have seven. Sophocles wrote over a hundred plays; seven are extant. Euripides wrote more than ninety tragedies and of these the Alexandrians had seventy-eight; we have nineteen. As late as 200 A.D. plays of Euripides, now lost, were extant.

How can this great shrinkage be explained? There are many reasons that may be assigned. First and foremost, doubtless, is that gradual loss of interest in the fine literary masterpieces which inevitably accompanied the decline in general and higher education, and the worship of the purely practical. Learning decreased. The Greek language, i.e., the pure Attic and literary dialect, suffered corruptions and inevitable change in foreign lands since Athens was no longer " the eye of Greece." As the centuries passed the classical authors could no longer be easily understood and came to be neglected because of their difficulty. So the student of English today needs help in reading even Shakespeare. The student in the modern University of Athens translates his ancient writers into modern Greek. In Greek poetry, accent gradually took the place of quantity as the basis for verse. The short-cut to knowledge was preferred; hence there sprang up a veritable crop of Anthologies, Scrap-books, and Collections of all kinds with explanatory notes and commentaries. For example, since the *Epinician Odes* of Pindar were the most popular of his works, some unknown person in the second century A.D. published with notes this part only, and the other books were lost. Certain plays of the trio of Attic tragedians, seven of Aeschylus and seven of Sophocles, were chosen and annotated for the use of schools and intelligent readers. Many copies were probably made of these plays and the others were lost.

It is probable, however, that the chief losses of Greek literature occurred at the time when vellum was substituted for papyrus as a medium of writing. Vellum was much the more expensive material and consequently only works of great interest or importance or popularity were chosen to be transmitted to the rarer material. As papyrus is very perishable when neglected, the earlier manuscript decayed. Long works were often copied only in part, hence many writings were subjected to mutilation. Libraries, as the Alexandrian, suffered from theft or fire. Finally, the coming of the Turk, which put an end to the Byzantine Empire, brought about the destruction of the surviving Greek literature, with the exception of those literary remains which were carried to Italy by Greek refugees. Many agencies, we see, operated to reduce the extensive mass of the original Greek literature.

Is there hope of recovering any of these lost writings? There is little chance of finding in the libraries of Europe many more vellum manuscripts, but the sands of Egypt annually yield Greek papyri. In Egyptian excavations many important works have been found, such as the *Constitution of Athens* of Aristotle, the *Odes* of Bacchylides, the *Mimes* of Herondas, several speeches of the Athenian orator Hyperides, a few poems of Sappho and Pindar, a large part of a Sophoclean satyr play, and large portions of several comedies of Menander.

CHAPTER X

GREEK LITERATURE

"Greek poetry springs out of life, remains always in touch with life, sees life steadily and sees it whole, and therefore presents to the imaginative reason the broadest, sanest, truest poetic criticism of life. . . .

"We cannot recover the habitual temper of mind that created Greek poetry. But we can make of it an incomparable educational instrument in youth, and in our riper years a possession of beauty that will keep, amid the turmoil and distractions of our fevered modern life, 'a bower quiet for us and a sleep full of sweet dreams and health and quiet breathing.'"—PAUL SHOREY.

WHY should persons today, other than scholars, be concerned with Greek literature? Our own English literature is an overflowing treasury of prose and verse. Consider, too, the extensive literature in French, Italian, Spanish, German, and the other modern languages. Must we take time, then, amid our many modern and pressing interests and duties to read Greek literature produced hundreds, nay, even thousands of years ago? Shall we find interest and derive profit in its study commensurate with our labors? To these questions an emphatic yes is the answer given by all discerning and competent readers, who appreciate Greek literature not merely as a mirror which reflects the life and thought of a gifted people, but who enjoy it as a thing of beauty and a revelation of truth. Because, too, of the pervasive and all important influence which Greek literature has exerted on all subsequent literature no student can afford to neglect its study. The literature of Greece, as all literature of intrinsic excellence, should be read in the original. However, for those who do not enjoy the privilege of a first-hand acquaintance there are now available many excellent translations. The titles of these are found in the bibliographical list for this chapter.

Ancient Greek literature falls into five great periods or ages: I. The Age of Epic Poetry (from the beginning, to the seventh or the beginning of the sixth century B.C.). II. The Age of Lyric Poetry (the seventh, sixth, and part of the fifth centuries B.C.). III. The Attic Period (about 475–300 B.C.). IV. The Alexandrian Age (from about 300 B.C. until the Roman Conquest of Greece in 146 B.C.). V. The Graeco-Roman Age (146 B.C. to Justinian, 526 A.D.).

I. THE EPIC AGE

It is a remarkable phenomenon in Greek literature that its earliest manifestations, the Homeric poetry, is likewise a very great, if not its greatest, literary achievement. This is not the time or the place for a discussion of the much vexed Homeric question, which has produced a vast literature in itself on the problem of the origin, date, and authorship of the Homeric Poems. The *Iliad* and the *Odyssey*, the two great epics, handed down in the Epic-Ionic dialect and composed in dactylic hexameters, undoubtedly are the culmination of a long period of literary activity which was concerned with early legends, hymns, and folk-songs. In particular these songs dealt with heroes and celebrated their glorious deeds. The hero of the *Iliad* is brave, " swift-footed " Achilles, and its 24 " books," or divisions, vividly relate the fighting of Greeks and Trojans at Ilium, the wrath of the hero, and its consequences. The *Odyssey*, also divided by the Alexandrians for convenience into 24 books, narrates the exciting adventures of the intrepid and resourceful Odysseus on his long and much-delayed journey home to Ithaca. These two great epic poems *may* have originated in Asia Minor, between Aeolis and Ionia. They seem to have come from the same poetic school and to have been largely perfected in the ninth or by the end of the eighth century B.C., and many scholars today maintain that they were composed by *one* great mind, the traditional poet Homer, whose genius re-created the subject-matter of tradition. He who wishes to enjoy great poetry, however, must not trouble his peace of mind and waste his time in reading books about Homer. Let him turn to the immortal poems themselves. Their stories are simple and the thought is plain, but the observation is profound. The characters are vividly portrayed. The style is noble and dignified. The Homeric Poems are the greatest of the world's epic poems. Without them Greek literature can hardly be imagined; through them the world has been inestimably enriched.

Other epics, too, now lost, the Greeks possessed, e.g., the *Cyclic Poems*, the epic cycle of poems, such as the *Little Iliad*, the *Cypria*, the *Sack of Ilium*, the *Nostoi*, the *Oedipodeia*, etc.

The second great name in Greek literature is that of Hesiod, of Ascra in Boeotia, the author of two important poems, the *Works and Days* and the *Theogony*. Hesiod's poetry is didactic and gnomic rather than epic, although he borrows freely from Homer in his use of the dactylic hexameter, and in his diction and phraseology. The *Works and Days* is a sort of *Farmers' Almanac*, treating of agriculture and its conduct and specifying lucky and unlucky days for the husbandman. With navigation, too, the poem deals. The necessity and the dignity of labor and thrift are constantly preached, together with exhortations to good behavior and justice. The *Theogony* is largely concerned with the creation and origin of the universe and the descent and relationship of the gods. Another long poem, the *Shield of Heracles*, was anciently, though falsely, attributed to Hesiod. Although the poems of Hesiod reveal at times passages of poetic excellence, yet, in general, the Muses of Helicon granted him no great inspiration. But as early Greek documents, treating of cosmogony and theogony, these poems are of great interest and are of value in the study of Greek religion, while the *Works and Days* to some extent influenced the *Georgics* of Vergil.

The *Homeric Hymns,* thirty-four in number, may conveniently be included in the discussion of Epic poetry although they are much later than this period, as they date from the end of the eighth to the beginning of the fifth century B.C. They are Homeric only insofar as they are written in the dactylic hexameter, employ epic narration, and borrow freely the diction and the phraseology of the Homeric poems. The shorter Hymns, as we have them, are merely preludes to longer compositions sung by rhapsodes at festivals in praise of the gods. Several are of considerable length and great excellence and charm, for example, the *Hymn to the Delian and Pythian Apollo* (546 lines) and the Hymns to *Dionysus, Aphrodite, Demeter,* and *Hermes.* The long hymn to Demeter is of moving beauty. It tells the familiar tale of the rape of Persephone by Pluto, of the sad wanderings of the bereaved mother, Demeter, in search of her lost daughter, of Demeter's stay at Eleusis where she takes the disguise of an aged nurse, the founding of the sacred Eleusinian Mysteries, of Persephone's restoration to her mother for part of the year, and of the reconciliation of Demeter with the gods. The appeal of this Hymn is potent and the myth is of unusual beauty symbolizing the death and rebirth of vegetation. Very different, but extremely delightful, is the serio-comic *Hymn to Hermes,* which describes in detail the mischievous adventures of the rascally infant Hermes:

> The babe was born at the first peep of day;
> He began playing on the lyre at noon;
> And the same evening did he steal away
> Apollo's herds.

The reader is strongly urged to read Shelley's successful rendering of the Hymns, from which a few lines are quoted above.

II. Lyric Poetry

Lyric Poetry should strictly mean only poetry sung to the lyre, but the term is loosely, although conveniently, used to designate the Elegiac, Iambic, and Melic poetry of the Greeks. Lyric poetry followed Epic and flourished particularly during the seventh, sixth, and first part of the fifth centuries B.C. It was the natural result of profound social and political changes throughout Greek lands when monarchies were being succeeded by oligarchies, tyrannies, and democracies, and when colonies were being sent out, commerce was being extended, and, most important of all, education became more general and men began to think for themselves. Lyric poetry is reflective poetry. The Epic bard narrates; the Lyric poet sings of his own moods, thoughts, or reflections.

The remains of Greek lyric poetry are extremely scanty and tantalizing in their fragmentary character. We possess manuscripts of the poetry of Theognis, Pindar, and Bacchylides, but most of these singers so famous in antiquity are now represented by mere snatches, the chance quotations of later writers. How disappointing this is in the case of a Sappho or an Archilochus, an Alcaeus or a Stesichorus!

Lyric poetry was composed by poets in the three chief dialects (Aeolic, Doric, and Ionic), but elegy originated in Ionia. The term *elegy*, which seems to have been a non-Greek word applied to a plaintive song accompanied by the flute, is used of reflective poetry composed in the elegiac couplet. This couplet, or distich, consists of a dactylic hexameter followed by a shorter line, the so-called dactylic pentameter. The effect is striking; as Puttenham in his *Arte of English Poesie* (15) says, it is " a pitious manner of meetre, placing a limping Pentameter after a lusty Exameter, which made it go dolourously more than any other meetre." Readers of Catullus are familiar with his beautiful ode

in elegiac verse written at his brother's tomb, beginning:

> Multas per gentes et multa per aequora vectus
> Advenio has miseras, frater, ad inferias.

Elegy was first used by Callinus of Ephesus (beginning of the seventh century B.C.) in martial verses
whose aim was to arouse his sluggish fellow-citizens
against the invaders, and also by Tyrtaeus (seventh
century) at Sparta. The apocryphal story is told that
Tyrtaeus was an Athenian, a lame school-master, sent
to Lacedaemon as a joke when the Spartans asked for
aid against their powerful neighbors, the Messenians.
But his stirring lines put new life in the soldiers, who
speedily won the victory. Here are the first lines of
one of his poems, as translated by Thomas Campbell:

> How glorious fall the valiant, sword in hand
> In front of battle for their native land!
> But oh! What ills await the wretch that yields,
> A recreant outcast from his country's fields!
> The mother whom he loves shall quit her home,
> An aged father at his side shall roam;
> His little ones shall weeping with him go,
> And a young wife participate his woe;
> While scorned and scowled upon by every face,
> They pine for food, and beg from place to place.

Elegy was first used for the expression of love by
the Ionian Mimnermus (seventh century), who thus
was the father of the erotic elegy, a literary form much
used by the Greek poets of the Alexandrian age and
popular among the Romans, e.g., Catullus, Ovid, Pro-
pertius, and Tibullus. The verse of Mimnermus is
smooth and facile, but his character as revealed by
poetical fragments which we possess is more Asiatic
than Greek. He is a poet of pleasure and of indolence
continually obsessed by the fear of sickness, old age,
and death:

> What's life or pleasure wanting Aphrodite?
>   When to the gold-haired goddess cold am I,
> When love and love's soft gifts no more delight me,
>   Nor stolen dalliance, then I fain would die!

> Ah! fair and lovely bloom the flowers of youth;
>   On men and maids they beautifully smile:
> But soon comes doleful eld, who, void of ruth,
>   Indifferently afflicts the fair and vile:
> Then cares wear out the heart; old eyes forlorn
>   Scarce reck the very sunshine to behold —
> Unloved by youths, of every maid the scorn,
>   So hard a lot God lays upon the old.
>
> — J. A. SYMONDS, Sr.

Mimnermus' prayer was to die at the age of sixty, free from disease and grievous pains. For this wish he was rebuked by the wise Solon (author of the famous saying: " I grow old always learning many things ") who substituted eighty for sixty.

Solon (600 B.C.), the Athenian law-giver, used the elegiac couplet for his political moralizing, and Xenophanes employed it for philosophical and ethical pronouncements. Xenophanes is discussed more fully in the chapters on Philosophy and Religion.

Moral or Gnomic Elegy, the aim of which was primarily to instruct, to advise, or to admonish, embellished with many proverbs or sententious sayings, is best represented by Theognis of Megara (sixth century B.C.). Some 1400 lines of his poetry are extant. Much of this was addressed to a young friend named Cyrnus. In the following lines Theognis celebrates the immortality which his songs will confer on Cyrnus:

> Lo, I have given thee plumes wherewith to skim
> The unfathomed deep, and lightly hover around
> Earth's huge circumference. Thou shalt be found
> At banquets on the breath of paean and hymn:
> To shrill-voiced pipes with lips of seraphim
> Lovely young men thy rapturous fame shall sound:
> Yea, when thou liest lapped in the noiseless ground,
> Thy name shall live, nor shall oblivion dim
> Thy dawn of splendour. For these lands, these isles,
> These multitudinous waves of refluent seas,
> Shall be thy pleasure-ground wherethrough to roam,
> Borne by no steed, but wafted by the smiles
> Of Muses violet-crowned, whose melodies,
> While earth endures, shall make all earth thy home.
>
> — SYMONDS.

Iambic poetry was " invented," as the Greeks said, or perfected, as we should express it, by Archilochus of Paros (seventh century B.C.). The iambic line consists of six iambic feet or their equivalent, and became the standard line for the dialogue parts of the Greek drama. Little is left to us of the poetry of Archilochus, whose fame in antiquity was very great. Unhappy in love and poor in purse he was a soldier of fortune, meeting death in war. How he lost his shield in battle he playfully relates in a few lines translated thus by Professor Shorey:

> Some Thracian strutteth with my shield,
> For, being somewhat flurried,
> I left it by a wayside bush
> As from the field I hurried;
> A right good targe, but I got off;
> The deuce may take my shield;
> I'll get another just as good
> When next I go afield.

This humorous confession that discretion is the better part of valor was imitated by Alcaeus and Anacreon and even by Horace (*Odes*, 2.7.) in his " little shield ingloriously left behind " (*relicta non bene parmula*) at Philippi.

Archilochus wrote also in elegiac and trochaic measures. It is surprising to find in a Greek poet of this early date these subjective verses, an apostrophe to his own soul:

> Tossed on a sea of troubles, Soul, my Soul,
> Thyself do thou control;
> And to the weapons of advancing foes
> A stubborn breast oppose;
> Undaunted 'mid the hostile might
> Of squadrons burning for the fight.
> Thine be no boasting when the victor's crown
> Wins the deserved renown;
> Thine no dejected sorrow when defeat
> Would urge a base retreat!
> Rejoice in joyous things — nor overmuch
> Let grief thy bosom touch
> 'Midst evil, and still bear in mind,
> How changeful are the ways of human kind.
> — WILLIAM HAY.

Iambic and elegiac poetry might be merely recited or declaimed, but melic verse (lyric poetry proper) of necessity was sung to the accompaniment of the lyre. Melic poetry was of two forms, *monodic* (composed for one voice), a favorite of the Aeolians and *choral*, developed by the Dorians. Choral poetry was composed for a chorus, and dancing accompanied the singing and the music.

The Aeolian isle of Lesbos was the home of a great school of singers represented by Terpander, Alcaeus, and Sappho. Tradition attributed the invention of the seven-stringed lyre to Terpander (seventh century B.C.) of whose poetry only a few lines have come down to us.

The renown of Alcaeus (end of seventh century B.C.) was great. He was of the nobility and led a life of peril in struggling against the tyrants, Pittacus and Myrsilus, in his native city of Mytilene. His hardships in war, exile, and travel by land and sea, reflected in his poems, are aptly referred to by Horace (*Odes*, 2. 13), *dura navis, dura fugae mala, dura belli*. Famous is the allegory of Alcaeus of the Ship of State with reference to the distress of Mytilene under the tyrant, Myrsilus, a poem which served Horace (1.14) as model: *O Navis, referent in mare te novi fluctus!*

An example of a drinking-song by Alcaeus may be given:

> The rain of Zeus descends, and from high heaven
>   A storm is driven:
> And on the running water-brooks the cold
>   Lays icy hold:
> Then up! beat down the winter; make the fire
>   Blaze high and higher;
> Mix wine as sweet as honey of the bee
>   Abundantly;
> Then drink with comfortable wool around
>   Your temples bound.
> We must not yield our hearts to woe, or wear
>   With wasting care;
> For grief will profit us no whit, my friend,
>   Nor nothing mend;
> But this is our best medicine, with wine fraught
>   To cast out thought.
>   — SYMONDS.

With this must be compared Horace (1.9): *Vides ut alta stet nive candidum Soracte,* etc.

Too little remains, however, of the verse of Alcaeus to reveal to us that magnificence, grace, and force which, as ancient critics assert, were characteristics of his style.

Sappho was also of Lesbos and lived at the beginning of the sixth century B.C. Of her life we know little. Comedy and late tradition made her the target for unwarranted scandal and contumely. It is not surprising that because of her great fame legends and fanciful tales gathered about her name. Not only Alcaeus, but, regardless of chronological possibilities, Archilochus, Hipponax, and Anacreon were said to have been her lovers. We are told that when her love for a youth Phaon was spurned she threw herself from the Leucadian rock — hundreds of miles from Lesbos, it may be observed!

Sappho seems to have been married, to have had a daughter, and, even to have suffered exile in the political disturbances of the time. From her poetry it would seem that she taught girls of Lesbos in poetry and music and that she felt for them the greatest interest and affection. The poetic genius of Sappho has been acclaimed by all critics ancient and modern. Plato called her " the tenth muse," and Strabo speaks of her as " a marvel — in all history you will find no woman who can challenge comparison with her even in the slightest degree." The loss of Sappho's poems is one of the most cruel disappointments in literature. Antiquity possessed no less than nine books of her verse; we have but a few poems, largely fragmentary. In these scanty remains, however, it is possible to discern her remarkable gifts. Her poems are of profound emotional intensity; her verse is graceful, polished, and melodious and the meters are varied. The stanza perfected by her, the Sapphic, is a favorite of Horace. The themes of her Muse are love and beauty, odes to Aphrodite, and *epithalamia* or wedding-songs. Translation, never wholly satisfactory, lamentably fails to do justice to Sappho's verse. That the reader may get some idea of her poetry several versions are appended:

PRAYER TO APHRODITE

Glittering-throned, undying Aphrodite,
Wile-weaving daughter of high Zeus, I pray thee,
Tame not my soul with heavy woe, dread mistress,
 Nay, nor with anguish!

But hither come, if ever erst of old time
Thou didst incline, and, listenedst to my crying,
And from thy father's palace down descending,
 Camest with golden

Chariot yoked: thee fair swift-flying sparrows
Over dark earth with multitudinous fluttering,
Pinion on pinion, thorough middle ether
 Down from heaven hurried.

Quickly they came like light, and thou, best lady,
Smiling with clear undying eyes didst ask me
What was the woe that troubled me, and wherefore
 I had cried to thee:

What thing I longed for to appease my frantic
Soul; and whom now must I persuade, thou askedst,
Whom must entangle to thy love, and who now,
 Sappho, hath wronged thee?

Yea, for if now he shun, he soon shall choose thee;
Yea, if he take not gifts, he soon shall give them;
Yea, if he love not, soon shall he begin to
 Love thee, unwilling.

Come to me now too, and from tyrannous sorrow
Free me, and all things that my soul desires to
Have done, do for me, queen, and let thyself too
 Be my great ally.

        — SYMONDS.

THE MOON

The stars about the lovely moon
Fade back and vanish very soon,
When, round and full, her silver face
Swims into sight, and lights all space.

       — EDWIN ARNOLD.

ATTHIS

I loved thee once, Atthis, long ago.
    — Cp. SWINBURNE, *Songs of the Springtides*.

NEGLECT OF THE MUSES

Yea, thou shalt die,
And lie
    Dumb in the silent tomb;
Nor of thy name
Shall there be any fame
    In ages yet to be or years to come:
For of the flowering Rose,
Which on Pieria blows,
    Thou hast no share:
But in sad Hades' house,
Unknown, inglorious,
    'Mid the dim shades that wander there
Shalt thou flit forth and haunt the filmy air.
                                        — SYMONDS.

A COMBINATION FROM SAPPHO

I

Like the sweet apple which reddens upon the topmost bough,
A-top on the topmost twig, — which the pluckers forgot, somehow, —
Forgot it not, nay, but got it not, for none could get it till now.

II

Like the wild hyacinth flower which on the hill is found,
Which the passing feet of the shepherds for ever tear and wound,
Until the purple blossom is trodden into the ground.
                                        — D. G. ROSSETTI.

Anacreon of Teos (latter part of the sixth century B.C.), an Ionian, was a poet of pleasure. The remains of his graceful and elegant verse are scanty. His fame among English readers rests upon the popularity of the *Anacreontics* as translated by Thomas Moore and Cowley. But these pretty Alexandrian verses were composed centuries after the real Anacreon.

The Dorian school of choral poets is represented by Alcman and Stesichorus. Alcman was born at Sardes in Lydia, but his literary activity centered at Sparta. He was famous for his *Partheneia* or choral dance-songs for maidens. It is probable that to Alcman we owe the full development of the choral ode into the division of strophe, antistrophe, and epode.

The poetic remains of Stesichorus of Sicily are extremely slight. For his real name, Tisias, the designation Stesichorus — " Marshal of the chorus " — was substituted. The poetry of this " lyric Homer " was extremely popular and greatly influenced tragedy and art. Famous in antiquity was his *Palinode* or Recantation to Helen. Threatened with blindness because of his verses blaming Helen, now deified, he recanted in verses beginning thus:

" This story is not true. Thou didst not go in the well-benched ships, nor didst thou come to the citadel of Troy."

The very existence of Arion of Corinth, a Lesbian by birth, has been doubted, although ancient testimony attributed to him the elaboration of the dithyramb, the choral hymn to Dionysus, from which tragedy developed.

The lyric poetry of Simonides of Ceos, a contemporary of the Persian wars and long a resident of Athens, achieved perfection of form and great variety. His epitaphs, or elegies in praise of the Greek heroes who fell in the Persian wars, are of remarkable beauty and power. Familiar is the couplet on the Spartans who fell at Thermopylae:

> Go, tell the Spartans, thou that passest by,
> That here obedient to their laws we lie.
>   — BOWLES.

Cicero's translation (*Tusc. Disp*. 1. 101) is of interest:

> Dic, hospes, Spartae, nos te hic vidisse iacentes,
> dum sanctis patriae legibus obsequimur.

Admirable is an encomium by Simonides on the same theme:

Of those who died at Thermopylae glorious is the fate and fair the doom; their grave is an altar; instead of lamentation, they have endless fame; their dirge is a chant of praise. Such winding-sheet as theirs no rust, no, nor all-conquering time, shall bring to nought. But this sepulchre of brave men hath taken for its habitant the glory of Hellas. Leonidas is witness, Sparta's king, who hath left a mighty crown of valour and undying fame. — SYMONDS.

The versatility of Simonides' genius is shown in one of the most beautiful lyrics in Greek poetry, the Lament of Danaë. The young mother Danaë, with her infant son Perseus, has been set afloat upon the sea to die:

> When, in the carven chest,
> The winds that blew and waves in wild unrest
> Smote her with fear, she, not with cheeks unwet
> Her arms of love round Perseus set,
> And said, O child, what grief is mine!
> But thou dost slumber, and thy baby breast
> Is sunk in rest,
> Here in the cheerless brass-bound bark,
> Tossed amid starless night and pitchy dark.
> Nor dost thou heed the scudding brine
> Of waves that wash above thy curls so deep,
> Nor the shrill winds that sweep, —
> Wrapped in thy purple robe's embrace,
> Fair little face!
> But if this dread were dreadful too to thee,
> Then wouldst thou lend thy listening ear to me;
> Therefore I cry, Sleep, babe, and sea, be still,
> And slumber our unmeasured ill!
> Oh, may some change of fate, sire Zeus, from thee
> Descend, our woes to end!
> But if this prayer, too overbold, offend
> Thy justice, yet be merciful to me!
>
> — SYMONDS.

The beauty and pathos of these lines enable us to understand Horace's reference (*Odes* II. 1. 38) *Ceae munera neniae;* Catullus (38. 8) *maestius lacrimis Simonideis;* and Wordsworth's " or unroll/One precious tender-hearted scroll/Of pure Simonides."

Bacchylides was the nephew of Simonides, and achieved fame in the province of Pindar, in the writing of odes in praise of victors in the athletic games. In 1897 some twenty of his poems were discovered in Egypt and these reveal Bacchylides as a poet of merit, although inferior both to Simonides and to Pindar.

Pindar, of Thebes, who flourished during the first half of the fifth century B.C., was regarded by antiquity as the greatest Greek lyric poet. To this place of pre-eminence his claims are legitimate, yet a few modern critics are disposed without good reason to question it. Although he won fame in the composition of choral lyrics of every type, we possess entire the *Epinicia* only, triumphal odes written to commemorate victors and victories in the four great Hellenic festival games. These poems are magnificent. They are original in invention, architectonic in structure, and brilliant in execution. Pindar's diction is vivid, rich, and varied, his epithets and figures striking. His verse is not easy reading and it is at times somewhat obscure. In some respects he may be called a poet's poet, and he may be aptly characterized by his own words, " to the many he needs interpreters." To appreciate Pindar at his real worth is impossible for us today. We lack the accompanying music and the choral dance, we miss the voices of the singers and their costumes, nor can we envisage the festal scene on the occasion of the celebration of the victory for which Pindar had composed the song. Even the best English translation, therefore, does injustice to the Theban lyricist, Horace's " Dircaean swan."

III. The Attic Period

The genius of the Athenians came to rich literary fruition in the fifth and fourth centuries B.C. The Epic poetry of the minstrels had flourished throughout Greek lands, a form of expression suited to the social conditions of that early age. A different political, social, and religious background inspired lyric poetry. At Athens in the period subsequent to the Persian Wars, when a mighty effort had prevailed against the great peril from Asia, the rise of the democracy and the spread of general education stimulated remarkable literary activity in varied forms. The literary and other artistic achievements of this era cause the Attic

Period to rank with the few outstanding periods in the history of human civilization. In poetry, the drama — both tragedy and comedy — flourished. In prose, early and comparatively crude efforts were quickly succeeded by mastery in the writing of history, rhetoric and oratory, and philosophy.

Athenian dramatic and philosophical literature are discussed elsewhere in this volume. It remains to treat of history, rhetoric and oratory.

HISTORY

As compared with verse Greek prose was of slow development. If we disregard early Ionian chroniclers and compilers whose writings are largely lost, the first important name is that of Herodotus of the fifth century B.C., the " Father of History." Although Herodotus was born at Halicarnassus, a city of Asia Minor, he spent much time in Athens. Herodotus laid a foundation for the writing of his great history of the growth of Persia and her wars with Greece by extensive travel to Babylon and Egypt, to the Euxine, through Greece and the islands, and to Magna Graecia. The nine books of his chronicle, written in the Ionic dialect, are composed in a style which has great charm and lucidity, although it is loose in structure and parenthetical. Herodotus is not a critical or scientific historian in the modern sense, but his work, properly estimated, is of the greatest value. He is, too, a veritable prince of story-tellers and his pages are enlivened by many entertaining anecdotes, such as the Ring of Polycrates, the tale of Hippoclides, and the story of the minstrel Arion. The many pages descriptive of the customs of Lydians, Babylonians, and Egyptians are of absorbing interest. In his writings there is to be observed a religious feeling akin to that of Aeschylus. The downfall of the Persians Herodotus ascribes to Nemesis, the righteous wrath of Heaven, which justly brings ruin upon those of overweening ambition who wax fat and insolent; verily, pride goeth before a fall.

Thucydides, in his *History of the Peloponnesian War* in eight books, has a different conception of the historian's task. He was a participant as one of the Athenian generals in the long struggle between Athens and Sparta (431–404 B.C.), but lost his command in 424 B.C. and lived in exile for the remainder of the war. For his history he engaged in long and careful study and travel and strove to give not only an accurate account of the actual events of the war but also their causes. He therefore used documents and treaties as evidence, and, as he wrote with remarkable freedom from prejudice and bias, his work stands as the first critical history. If Herodotus is the Father of History, Thucydides is the first philosophical historian. The style of Thucydides is somewhat austere, at times obscure, and reflects the rhetorical tendencies of the time. Prominent in his work are the speeches which he attributes to the chief personages who find place in his history. One who wishes to gain some idea of the skill of Thucydides as a narrator and of his merit as a historian should read, after the introductory paragraphs, the whole of the splendid funeral oration of Pericles (2. 41–43), pronounced over the Athenian dead of the first campaign of the war, next, the graphic description (2. 49–53) of the dreadful plague which caused such cruel havoc in Athens in the second year of the war, and finally the account of the unfortunate Sicilian Expedition of the Athenians.

The third and last historian of the Attic Period is Xenophon, (born about 431 B.C.) the author of the *Hellenica* and the *Anabasis*. Although Xenophon was born in Attica and was a pupil and admirer of Socrates, long absence from Athens, admiration for the Spartan government, and military service in the Spartan army caused him to reside near Olympia. In the *Hellenica,* a work of no great inspiration, the narration of Hellenic affairs is continued from the conclusion of Thucydides' history down to the battle of Mantinea, in 362 B.C. The *Anabasis* is a composition of permanent value by reason of the interest of the subject matter and the attractiveness of the style. It tells the story of the march inland into Asia of the 10,000 Greek mercenaries under Cyrus, the young Persian Prince in search of a throne, of the death of Cyrus in battle, of the resourceful leadership of Xenophon himself, who had accompanied the expedition, and the adventurous and successful trip home of the Greek soldiers. Xenophon's *Memorabilia,* or Recollections of Socrates, picture the Master on the personal side and is an effort to defend his character and teachings. Minor essays of Xenophon are also extant, such as the *Cyropaedia* (*Education of Cyrus*) and the treatise *On Hunting*.

Rhetoric and Oratory

We come now to the consideration of Rhetoric and Oratory in the Attic Period. It is difficult to overestimate the importance of rhetoric and oratory in Greek life and thought. An account is given in the chapter on Education of rhetoric as an important part of higher education. In the Greek sense of the term rhetoric has a much broader connotation than its modern derivative. We think of rhetoric as merely written composition; to the Greek, rhetoric comprised oral as well as written discourse. It was oratory in a broad sense. The pursuit of rhetoric led to the study of grammar, the exact meaning of words, argumentation, figures of speech, the development of style, and the presentation of a cause. Rhetoric was, to Aristotle, *persuasion,* or the manner and the methods whereby an audience is won over. Its field was that of knowledge itself and as an instrument of instruction it was of paramount importance. The works of the rhetoricians or orators, such as Isocrates and Demosthenes, are highly significant to us, not merely because of their stylistic influence on subsequent prose, but also because of the light they throw upon every aspect of Athenian civilization. In the discourses of the Attic orators we obtain contemporaneous authentic evidence of law and government, ethics and religion, manners and customs.

Two factors contributed to the development of oratory and stylistic Greek prose: the Sicilian rhetoric from the west, as taught by Corax, Tisias, and Gorgias, and the influence of the teachings of the Sophists from the east. The former influence is discussed in the chapter on Education, while the Sophists play a prominent rôle in both education and philosophy and are treated under those captions.

Athens of the latter half of the fifth century B.C., and in the fourth, took the keenest interest in public speaking and rhetoric. For this, there were many reasons. The spoken, not the written word, influenced the minds of men and brought fame to successful speakers. Effective speaking was the desideratum in the Assembly, the Senate, and in the Law Courts. In fact, in the courts, litigants were compelled by law to plead in person their causes. All men are not thus gifted by nature. Hence arose the profession of *logographos,* or one who writes speeches for others to deliver, a profession practiced by a number of the Attic orators.

Any history of Greek oratory must begin with Homer. Speeches comprise over half of the Homeric Poems. Eloquence characterizes the utterances of Achilles, of Nestor, and of Odysseus.

The effective discourses of the Attic orators, however, are the result of native ability schooled by study and discipline. Of the many orators of this period a list of the ten greatest was drawn up by Alexandrian critics, the famous Canon of the Ten Attic Orators.

Antiphon, the earliest, and the first speech-writer, is represented by three important speeches and twelve rhetorical exercises; all are concerned with homicide. The style of Antiphon is effective, but rugged and austere.

Andocides, " an amateur," is revealed to us by three extant speeches, of which the best and most interesting, *On the Mysteries*, deals with the scandal connected with the profanation of the Eleusinian Mysteries and the mutilation of the statues of Hermes in 415 B.C.

Lysias was a resident alien at Athens, a wealthy young man of excellent education. When the Thirty Tyrants came to power at the close of the Peloponnesian War, Lysias' family property was confiscated, his brother executed, and he himself narrowly escaped death. On his return from exile after the democracy was restored, Lysias adopted the profession of writer of speeches for litigants. Thirty-four speeches are extant under his name; of these the longest and greatest, *Against Eratosthenes*, was spoken by Lysias himself on the occasion of the trial of one of the Thirty Tyrants for the murder of his brother. Lysias is regarded as a master of the Attic idiom. His style is conspicuous for simplicity, lucidity, purity of diction, and vividness. Lysias is most famous, however, for the skill and success with which he adapted his material and style to the characters and the situations of the speakers for whom he composed speeches.

As Isocrates (436–338) occupies a prominent place in Athenian education he is discussed fully in the chapter devoted to that subject. He was a Sophist in the best sense of that term and conducted an influential and popular school for over fifty years. Because of temperamental defects he was not a public speaker, but devoted himself to teaching and to the composition of pamphlets or discourses, in which he aimed to make contributions of permanent value. Of especial interest are the *Panegyricus* — his masterpiece (380 B.C.) in which he expounds his cherished political idea, *viz.*, the subjugation of Asia by a united Hellas — and the discourses called *Panathenaicus* and *Philip*. His theory of culture is elucidated in the pamphlets *Against the Sophists* and *On the Antidosis*. In style, Isocrates is smooth and polished and his periods are lengthy and flowing. Of the three classes of rhetoric —namely, forensic, deliberative, and epideictic — Isocrates'

preference was for the last named. The influence of
Isocrates' style was very great upon subsequent Greek
prose and upon Cicero, and, through Cicero, upon
modern literary prose.

Isaeus specialized in the writing of speeches in will-
cases and of these discourses eleven are extant.

Demosthenes (384–322) is the greatest of all the
ancient orators. Ancient and modern critics alike unite
in praise of his oratorical powers. Other orators in the
Canon possessed special virtues, but Demosthenes was
master in every province of oratory.

Demosthenes, having lost his patrimony through the
dishonesty of his guardians, turned to professional
speech-writing. After great success had attended him
in this pursuit he assumed an active part in public life
and as a patriotic statesman strove to save Athens from
the Macedonian peril. In the three *Olynthiacs* and the
three *Philippics* Demosthenes vigorously opposed Philip
and urged his fellow-citizens to more active resistance.
But his efforts were largely in vain. The battle-field of
Chaeronea (338 B.C.) witnessed the triumph of Philip
and Alexander. Demosthenes' masterpiece is his
famous speech *On the Crown,* in which the orator-
statesman successfully defended his whole public
career and convincingly showed himself deserving of
the golden wreath of honor which his envious rival,
Aeschines, strove to have withheld. Translation fails
to do justice to the virtues of the style of Demosthenes.
A few short passages from the Oration *On the Crown*
may suggest the intensity and fire of the great orator:

" Having by these means brought the cities into
such dispositions towards each other, Philip, encouraged by these decrees and these replies, came in
his strength, and seized Elatea, sure that, happen what
would, we and the Thebans could never more conspire.
Enough — you all know what a storm then awoke in
the city. Yet listen to me for a moment, suffer me to
give you the barest outline.

" It was evening when a courier came to the presidents with the news that Elatea had been seized. The presidents instantly rose from table — they were supping at the moment: some of them hastened to clear the market-place of the shopmen, and to burn the wickerwork of the booths: others, to send for the Generals and order the sounding of the call to the Asembly. The city was in a tumult. At dawn next day the presidents convoked the Senate, you hurried to the Ecclesia, and before the Senate could go through its forms or could report, the whole people were in assembly on the hill. Then, when the Senate had come in, when the presidents had reported the news that they had received and had introduced the messenger, who told his tale, the herald repeatedly asked, *Who wishes to speak?* But no one came forward. Again and again he put the question — in vain. No one would rise, though all the generals, though all the public speakers were present, though our Country was crying aloud, with the voice that comes home to all, for a champion of the commonwealth. Yet, if they should have come forward who wished Athens safe, every man in this court, ay, every man in Athens, would have risen and moved towards the platform. Every man of you, I know well, wished the city to be saved. . . . But no — it seems that that crisis, that hour, demanded not merely a patriot, but a man who had followed the train of events from the beginning, who had accurately reasoned out why and wherefore Philip was acting thus. A man who did not know this, who had not made it the subject of long and thorough research, might be ever so loyal, might be ever so rich, but he was not the man to see what should be done or to direct your course. Such a man that day was found in me. . . .

" Thus, or to this effect, I spoke, and left the platform. Everyone approved — there was not a dissentient; and what then? I did not make a speech and leave others to move a resolution. I did not move a resolu-

tion and leave others to go on an embassy. I did not
go on an embassy, and leave others to persuade the
Thebans. No. I went through with the business from
the beginning to the end; I gave myself to you without
reservation in face of the perils that encompassed the
city. . . .

" These were the first steps towards the adjustment
of our relations to Thebes, at a time when enmity,
hatred and distrust had been sown between our cities by
yonder men. The people gave their voice, and the
danger that hung upon our borders went by like a
cloud. . . .

" But never, Athenians, never can it be said that you
erred when you took upon you that peril for the freedom and safety of all!" No, by our fathers who met
the danger at Marathon, no, by our fathers who stood
in the ranks at Plataea, no, by our fathers who did
battle on the waters of Salamis and Artemisium, no,
by all the brave who sleep in tombs at which their
country paid those last honours which she had awarded,
Aeschines, to all of them alike, not alone to the successful or the victorious! And her award was just. The
part of brave men had been done by all. The fortune
experienced by the individual among them had been
allotted by a Power above men. . . . "

Finally, we quote the eloquent peroration and the
noble prayer which closes the speech:

" Here is the proof. Not when my extradition was
demanded, not when they sought to arraign me before
the Amphictyonic Council, not for all their menaces or
their offers, not when they set these villains like wild
beasts upon me, have I ever been untrue to the loyalty
I bear you. From the outset, I chose the path of a
straightforward and righteous statesmanship, to cherish the dignities, the prerogatives, the glories of my
country, to exalt them, to stand by their cause. I do
not go about the market-place radiant with joy at my
country's disasters, holding out my hand and telling

my good news to anyone who, I think, is likely to report it in Macedon; I do not hear of my country's successes with a groan and a shudder and a head bent to earth, like the bad men who pull Athens to pieces, as if, in so doing, they were not tearing their own reputations to shreds, who turn their faces to foreign lands, and, when an alien has triumphed by the ruin of the Greeks, give their praises to that exploit, and vow that vigilance must be used to render that triumph eternal.

" Never, Powers of Heaven, may any brow of the Immortals be bent in approval of that prayer! Rather, if it may be, breathe even into these men a better mind and heart; but if so it is that to these can come no healing, then grant that these, and these alone, may perish utterly and early on land and on the deep: and, to us, the remnant, send the swiftest deliverance from the terrors gathered above our heads, send us the salvation that stands fast perpetually." (Trans. by Jebb)

The remaining four orators of the Canon of the Ten are: Aeschines, an eloquent but insincere rival of Demosthenes; Lycurgus, statesman and financier; Hyperides; and Dinarchus.

IV. THE ALEXANDRIAN PERIOD

The Alexandrian Period (300–146 B.C.) was an age primarily of scholarship and criticism. After the fourth century B.C., Athens was no longer the supreme mistress of Greece in literature and the arts. Athenian political decline inevitably followed Macedon's military supremacy. Alexander's conquest of Asia and Africa spread Hellenic culture through lands formerly "barbarian" and gave the impulse to the founding and rapid growth of new Greek cities. Alexandria, in Egypt, founded by Alexander in 332 B.C. became a center of learning with a Museum and a large library which attracted numerous students, scholars, and teachers. Grammar and lexicography were much studied. Editions of selected classical writers of previous centuries, with commentaries, were industriously produced by such learned scholars as Zenodotus, Aristophanes of Byzantium, and Aristarchus, all of whom won fame, particularly in the study of the Homeric poems. In general, however, the creative age in literature had passed. Erudition, scholarship, and criticism flourished during the Alexandrian Period, but there were few works of great originality such as had been the rule during the Attic Period. A brilliant exception is Theocritus, of the third century B.C., who lived in Sicily, in Alexandria, and on the Island of Cos.

Theocritus was the founder of a new literary type, the pastoral idyll, and his charming Doric bucolic verses have enjoyed great popularity and have ever profoundly influenced poetry of this kind, as, for example, the Greek poets, Bion and Moschus, in their poems, the *Lament for Adonis* and the *Lament for Bion,* the Roman poet Vergil, in his *Bucolics* or *Eclogues* and, in English, the pastorals of Milton, Shelley, Tennyson, and many others.

Greek pastoral poetry is composed in the dactylic hexameter verse, but a lyric quality was secured by the use of a refrain, or recurring verses. Certain poetic conventions are peculiar to the pastoral. Rustics, in alternating competitive verse, sing to the accompaniment of the shepherd's pipe for a prize, such as a carven cup or young animal. Unrequited love is a frequent theme, a special favorite being the tale of the handsome young shepherd Daphnis, who pined away and died for love, deeply lamented by all nature.

The first idyll of Theocritus, the *Death of Daphnis,* is the most beautiful, perhaps, of his pastorals. The characters are Thyrsis and a goatherd:

THYRSIS. Sweet are the whispers of yon pine that makes
    Low music o'er the spring, and, Goatherd, sweet
    Thy piping; second thou to Pan alone.
    Is his the hornèd ram? Then thine the goat.
    Is his the goat? To thee shall fall the kid;
    And toothsome is the flesh of unmilked kids.

GOATHERD. Shepherd, thy lay is as the noise of streams
    Falling and falling aye from yon tall crag.
    If for their meed the Muses claim the ewe,
    Be thine the stall-fed lamb, or if they choose
    The lamb, take thou the scarce less-valued ewe.

TH. Pray, by the nymphs, pray, Goatherd, seat thee here
    Against this hill-slope in the tamarisk shade,
    And pipe me somewhat, while I guard thy goats.
GO. I durst not, Shepherd, O I durst not pipe
    At noontide, fearing Pan, who at that hour
    Rests from the toil of hunting. Harsh is he,
    Wrath at his nostrils aye sits sentinel.
    But, Thyrsis, thou canst sing of Daphnis' woes;
    High is thy name for woodland minstrelsy.

THE SONG OF THYRSIS

    Begin, sweet maids, begin the woodland song.
The voice of Thyrsis, Aetna's Thyrsis I.
Where were ye, Nymphs, oh where, while Daphnis pined?
In fair Peneus, or in Pindus' glens?
For great Anapus' stream was not your haunt,
Nor Aetna's cliff, nor Acis' sacred rill.
    Begin, sweet maids, begin the woodland song.
O'er him the wolves, the jackals howled o'er him;
The lion in the oak-copse mourned his death.
    Begin, sweet maids, begin the woodland song.

    Forget, sweet maids, forget your woodland song.
From thicket now and thorn let violets spring.
Now let white lilies drape the juniper,
And pines grow figs, and nature all go wrong;
For Daphnis dies. Let deer pursue the hounds,
And mountain owls out-sing the nightingale.
    Forget, sweet maids, forget your woodland song.
                   — *Trans. by Calverley.*

Some of the idylls of Theocritus are not purely pastoral. The fifteenth idyll is dramatic, a highly entertaining example of the *Mime* in which two gossipy Syracusan women resident in Alexandria attend the festival of Adonis.

Other poets of the Alexandrian Age are the erudite Callimachus, of Alexandria, composer of hymns, elegies, and epigrams, and Apollonius of Rhodes, author of the rather artificial epic, the *Argonautica*, a narrative of Jason's voyage in search of the golden fleece. In this period likewise we may place the *Mimes* of Herondas, and the astronomical verses of Aratus. The excellent history written by Polybius is a valuable source of information, particularly for the first Punic War.

V. THE GRAECO-ROMAN AGE (146 B.C.–526 A.D.)

There is no sharp line of delimitation separating the Alexandrian from the Graeco-Roman Age. Literary, or rather scholarly, activity continued to flourish without any break throughout the Greek world under Roman sway, or rather, let us say, throughout the politically supreme Roman Empire, dominated by Greek culture. The one great original literary genius of this age is Lucian, of the second century A.D., the pioneer and master in a new field, the Romance. Born in Syria, he traveled and studied in many lands, and resided for a time in Athens. Lucian is rhetorician, satirist, sceptic, and wit all in one. Very famous are his entertaining satiric dialogues, *Of the Dead*, *Of the Gods*, and *Of the Sea*. His *True History*, an extravaganza of adventurous travel, is the prototype of the tales of Baron Münchhausen and Swift's *Gulliver's Travels*.

Plutarch, first century A.D., is famous for his biographies (the *Parallel Lives*) and for his work called the *Morals*. Worthy of mention are the geography of Strabo (first century B.C.), the guide-book of Pausanias (second century A.D.), a work of great value for a knowledge of Greek monuments and topography, the general history of Diodorus Siculus, the excellent literary criticism of Dionysius of Halicarnassus (resident at Rome in the first century B.C.), the Pseudo-Longinus, the Roman Histories of Appian and Cassius Dio, the historical treatise on Alexander by Arrian, the History of the Jews by Josephus, that useful miscellany the *Deipnosophistae* of Athenaeus, the compilations of Stobaeus, the medical works of Galen, and the *Meditations* of the great Stoic Roman Emperor, Marcus Aurelius. The beginning of the novel should also be noted in the romances of Longus, Heliodorus, and Achilles Tatius.

Our brief survey of Greek literature will be concluded with a few words concerning the *Greek Anthology* (Garland of Flowers), or collections of epigrams, which began with Meleager (first century B.C.), and were augmented by Agathias (sixth century A.D.). This great body of verse was further increased in the Anthology of Cephalas (tenth century A.D.), now known as the *Palatine Anthology,* and the *Planudean Anthology* (fourteenth century). In these large collections we possess several thousand short poems or *epigrams* (in the Greek sense), largely in the elegiac meter, dating roughly from 700 B.C. to 1000 A.D. Many of their little poems treating of Love, Life, Death, Fate, etc., are charming; some have genuine inspiration. A few are given in translation to illustrate their nature:

PLATO

Thou wert the morning star among the living,
Ere thy fair light had fled;
Now, having died, thou art, as Hesperus, giving
New splendour to the dead.

— SHELLEY.

PLATO

Thou gazest on the stars, my star!
Ah! would that I might be
Myself those skies with myriad eyes,
That I might gaze on thee.

— LILLA C. PERRY.

CALLIMACHUS

To Heraclitus

They told me, Heraclitus, they told me you were dead;
They brought me bitter news to hear and bitter tears to shed.
I wept, as I remembered, how often you and I
Had tired the sun with talking and sent him down the sky.

And now that thou art lying, my dear old Carian guest,
A handful of gray ashes, long, long ago at rest,
Still are thy pleasant voices, thy nightingales, awake,
For Death he taketh all away, but them he cannot take.

— CORY.

Anonymous

Of our great love, Parthenophil,
This little stone abideth still
    Sole sign and token:
I seek thee yet, and yet shall seek,
Though faint mine eyes, my spirit weak
    With prayers unspoken.

Meanwhile, best friend of friends, do thou,
If this the cruel fates allow,
    By death's dark river,
Among those shadowy people, drink
No drop for me on Lethe's brink:
    Forget me never!

— Symonds.

Meleager

I'll twine sweet violets, and the myrtle green,
Narcissus will I twine, and lilies sheen;
I'll twine sweet crocus, and the hyacinth blue;
And last I twine the rose, love's token true:
That all may form a wreath of beauty, meet
To deck my Heliodora's tresses sweet.

— Goldwin Smith.

Simmias of Thebes

Wind, gentle evergreen, to form a shade
Around the tomb where Sophocles is laid;
Sweet ivy, wind thy boughs, and intertwine
With blushing roses and the clustering vine:
Thus will thy lasting leaves, with beauties hung,
Prove grateful emblems of the lays he sung;
Whose soul, exalted like a god of wit,
Among the Muses and the Graces writ.

— Anonymous.

Ion of Chios

Hail, dear Euripides, for whom a bed
In black-leaved vales Pierian is spread:
Dead though thou art, yet know thy fame shall be
Like Homer's, green through all eternity.

— Symonds.

Democritus (?)

All life's a scene, a jest: then learn to play,
Dismissing cares, or bear your pains alway.

PAULUS SILENTIARIUS

My name, my country — what are they to thee?
What, whether base or proud my pedigree?
Perhaps I far surpassed all other men;
Perhaps I fell below them all; what then?
Suffice it, stranger! that thou see'st a tomb;
Thou know'st its use; it hides — no matter whom.
— W. COWPER.

AGATHIAS

I love not wine, but shouldst thou wish
   That I its slave might be,
Thou needst but to taste the cup,
   Then hand it back to me.

For unto me that cup would bring
   From thy dear lips a kiss,
And while I drank would softly tell
   How it received such bliss.
— LILLA C. PERRY.

Here we must conclude our rapid survey of Greek literature. Only the skeleton has been given, which the reader will clothe for himself by more extensive reading. For, as Lord Bryce has said, " The ancient writings enter into and have done much to instill what is best in modern literature and are the common heritage of civilized peoples, the permanent foundation on which the republic of letters has been built. . . . Let no one be afraid of the name, ' dead languages.' No language is dead which perfectly conveys thoughts that are alive and are as full of energy now as they ever were. An idea or feeling grandly expressed lives forever, and gives immortality to the words that enshrine it."

CHAPTER XI

ATHENIAN EDUCATION

IT IS the actual educational practice rather than the theory with which we are most concerned in this chapter on education in Athens. Athenian and Spartan ideals and practice in education were very dissimilar. At Sparta, education was strictly controlled by the State, it was characterized by rigid discipline in all respects, and it was largely physical, as the aim was the production of brave and hardy soldiers. Girls, as well as boys, received a rigorous physical training. In short, at Sparta education was military, and was based on the theory that the citizen exists primarily for the State.

On the other hand, at Athens, a democratic community where it was believed that the State exists for the citizen, a wholly different ideal was dominant — that the training of the boy should be for citizenship and for living. Such an education involved the cultivation of mind even more than of body, and had as its goal the attainment of character, taste, and, above all, *sophrosyne,* or temperance, moderation, and good-behavior in word, thought, and deed.

This striking fact, of profound importance to the modern world, is to be observed in Athenian education. Although Athens was an important commercial center, and, although trade, industry, and arts were essential to the welfare of the city-state, yet no vocational or technical training as such was taught in the schools. Technical education in what we call the trades, industries, and professions was given by fathers to sons and by masters to apprentices in the actual work-shop or factory. Education, to the Athenian, was a training for living and not for a livelihood; the ideal was to attain health of mind and body, and not to gain proficiency in trade, arts and crafts, and money-making. Not that the claims and importance of these pursuits were actually ignored or despised by the Athenians, as is sometimes mistakenly asserted. But training in these specialized branches was regarded as something to be obtained after the youth had laid the foundation of a liberal training for living.

At Athens, education was largely a private matter. Some exceptions, however, are to be noted. Certain large gymnasia and *palaestrae* were built and maintained by the State, which were open to the public. The sons of Athenian citizens who had fallen in battle were supported and educated by the State. Free training in singing and dancing provided by the *choregi* was given to some 750 boys a year — the youths who composed the choruses in the contests at the festivals of the Dionysia and the Thargelia. Finally, there was the ephebic military training furnished by the government.

How general was education in Athens? Did all boys have regular schooling and for how long? We do not know with certainty. That some formal education was quite general is evident from the references in the literature and from the conspicuous intelligence of the average Athenian citizen. The sons of the rich naturally started to school earlier and remained longer than those of the less well-to-do. Advanced education, even the secondary education offered to boys over fourteen, could be afforded by the more prosperous only. But there were schools of all classes and tuition fees were very small in certain elementary schools. Athens herself was a great school of boundless opportunity and rich and poor alike constantly were being educated in the Assembly, the Senate, the theater, the court-room, and the agora. Nor should the fact be overlooked that in the fourth century B.C. Athenian youths of the age of eighteen were drafted for military training of two years' duration, an education in itself primarily physical and military, yet to this gradually was added mental discipline.

Little children were taught at home by their parents or by nurse and *paedagogus*, their attendant slave. At six or seven the boys were sent to primary school, usually to a school of the neighborhood. Girls were taught exclusively at home by their mothers and did not receive the formal training given their brothers. The elementary school-teachers were men; as a rule they were not persons of much education and their social standing was insignificant. They gained a meager livelihood from the tuition fees paid monthly by the parents. The amount of the fee and the course of study were determined by the teacher. The daily session began early in the morning and continued in the afternoon after the boys had returned from luncheon. Holidays were numerous and in some months, as, for example, *Anthesterion* (February–March), the school sessions were much broken. Theophrastus tells us of a stingy parent who regularly kept his children out of school during this month, thereby saving the tuition fee! In the school-room the boys sat on plain benches, while the master enjoyed an arm-chair, or *cathedra*. Vase-paintings show us writing-tablets, rulers, and baskets full of rolls of manuscripts hung on the walls and, in the music-school, lyres and flutes.

Athenian education comprised *music* and *gymnastic*. By music in the broad sense, the Greeks meant that training of the mind and character in any art presided over by a Muse. In the elementary school, music included reading, writing, the learning of poetry, counting, singing, and playing on the lyre, and, for a period after the Persian Wars, on the flute. In the better and larger schools reading, writing, and arithmetic would be taught by a special teacher, called the *grammatistes*, instruction in music and poetry was given by the harpist, the *kitharistes*, while physical training was directed by the trainer, the *paidotribes*. Formal primary education occupied the Athenian boy roughly from the age of six until fourteen; secondary, largely for the prosperous, from fourteen until eighteen; and the ephebic military training from eighteen to twenty. The elements of reading, writing, arithmetic and music naturally comprised the primary schooling; in the secondary period, literature, grammar, rhetoric, drawing, and geometry were added as advanced courses. Higher instruction, roughly comparable with a modern college course, was attainable by young men whose means, time, and interests permitted. This training might be in philosophy, under the direction of philosophers, or in rhetoric and oratory, under the tuition of popular teachers, the Sophists.

The Athenian school-boy may well be envied by the modern youth because of the comparative simplicity of his program of studies. He could concentrate upon the Greek language and literature because no other language was studied. Mathematical studies were simple and elementary. Little knowledge of the sciences existed in the fifth and fourth centuries B.C., at any rate of a popular kind. The basis for reading was furnished by Homer, Hesiod, Theognis and the lyric poets and probably, towards the end of the fifth century, the tragedians. Especially emphasized was the study of the Homeric poems, which were the very backbone of the school course. Fine passages were intimately studied and many books were even learned by heart. Books and materials were expensive, hence dictation by the master and copying and memorizing by the pupil were largely employed. This method encouraged wide knowledge of the poets and also explains the remarkable memories of the Greeks.

It is difficult, but vitally important, for the student of Greek education and literature ever to keep in mind that reading, to the Greeks, meant not silent perusal of a text, but always *reading aloud*. Enunciation and clearness of expression were essential, and voice training was constant. The method of instruction was largely oral, by dictation, as has been said, and in the class-room recitation of lessons, and not writing, was the rule. Books were not generally owned because of their expense, and the spoken, not the written, word characterized and profoundly influenced every form of intellectual activity. If this fact is constantly remembered, it is much easier to understand the prominence in the ancient world of oratory and speaking, of the drama, of recitation, of the public recitals and contests, and of the influence and popularity of the Sophists.

Writing was practiced on tablets of wax with a pointed instrument. Papyrus gradually came into use for more permanent records, the writing being done with a reed pen and ink. The poet was regarded by the Athenians as primarily a teacher rather than a literary artist. While pupils were taught to observe and to admire literary excellence and diction, and form and beauty in verse, yet the *moral* teaching in the poet was stressed by the instructor, and influence on character was regarded as the *summum bonum*. The poet is to be admired, says Aristophanes, insofar as he makes men better and makes them better citizens. In the comedy, the *Frogs,* Aeschylus is rebuking Euripides for the evil conduct of some of his heroes and heroines. Euripides retorts: "But is it not true, this evil which I have depicted? Is there not evil and are there not bad people in the world?" Aeschylus answers: "Certainly, but it is the duty of the poet to conceal this evil and not to parade it and teach it. Everyone who talks at all is a teacher to little children, but poets are the teachers to the young. It is therefore the duty of us poets to speak only the Good." This passage is of particular interest to us at present, when there is so much discussion relative to realism on the stage and in literature and of the need or the possibility of censorship. Just before these lines from the *Frogs* Aeschylus had claimed for his plays that they were essentially moral, and inspired in the reader or the auditor conduct of a like kind. For example, the *Seven against Thebes* had made the Athenians more martial and braver. This

was the effect, too, of the teaching of the *Persians*.
Aeschylus (i.e., Aristophanes) says that poets should
train men: " The great poets have been great teachers,
as Orpheus, who taught religious mysteries; Musaeus
taught healing of diseases and oracles and Hesiod agriculture, while the great Homer himself inculcated brav-
ery and gave instruction in the marshalling and arming
of men."

In the *Clouds,* also, Aristophanes has something to
say on education. In his usual rôle of the *laudator
temporis acti,* the comic poet compares the old system
of education with the new, much to the disadvantage
of the latter: " In the ancient system of education it
was incumbent that no one should hear the voice of a
boy uttering a syllable; and next, that those from the
same quarter of the town should march in good order
through the streets to the school of the Harpmaster,
lightly clad and in a body, even if it were to snow as
thick as meal. Then the master would teach them —
the boys not sitting cross-legged — to learn by heart a
song — either the *Pallas,* or *Loud Strain of the Lyre*
— raising high their voices in the strain our fathers
handed down to us. But if any one of them should
play the buffoon or start any of those flourishes, such
as musicians nowadays affect, those intricate flourishes
à la Phrynis, he got well-drubbed, being beaten with
many stripes for spoiling good music. Nor was it
formerly allowed, when a boy was dining, to take
even the head of a radish, or to snatch from his seniors
dill or parsley, or to eat fish, or to giggle, or to keep
the legs crossed."

The moral results of the good old instruction are
further humorously stressed as a discipline " which
produced the heroes of Marathon, and taught youths
to hate the market-place, to keep away from the hot
baths, to blush at things that are shameful, to give up
their seats to their elders, to be respectful to their
parents, to refrain from running after chorus-girls,
not to 'talk back' to a father, e.g., calling him an old

fogy. If a youth today choose the former good
schooling, he will pass the time in the wrestling-schools
healthy and blooming, not chattering in the market-
place; he will go down to the Academy to run with
well-behaved comrades 'neath the olive trees with a
garland of light reed upon his brow, and fragrant with
iris, and heartsease and silver poplar, rejoicing in the
season of springtime, what time the plane-tree whispers to the elm."

A passage of interest to the student of Athenian
education is found in the *Protagoras* (325 C) of Plato:

" Education and admonition commence in the first
years of childhood, and last to the very end of life.
Mother and nurse and father and tutor are vying with
one another about the improvement of the child as
soon as ever he is able to understand what is being
said to him: he cannot say or do anything without
their setting forth to him that this is just and that is
unjust; this is honourable, that is dishonourable; this
is holy, that is unholy; do this and abstain from that,
and if he obeys, well and good; if not, he is straightened by threats and blows, like a piece of bent or
warped wood. At a later stage they send him to
teachers, and enjoin them to see to his manners even
more than to his reading and music; and the teachers
do as they are desired. And when the boy has
learned his letters and is beginning to understand what
is written, as before he understood only what was
spoken, they put into his hands the works of great
poets, which he reads sitting on a bench at school; in
these are contained many admonitions and many tales,
and praises, and encomia of ancient famous men which
he is required to learn by heart, in order that he may
imitate or emulate them and desire to become like
them. Then, again, the teachers of the lyre take
similar care that their young disciple is temperate and
gets into no mischief, and when they have taught him
the use of the lyre, they introduce him to the poems

of other excellent poets, who are the lyric poets; and
these they set to music, and make their harmonies and
rhythms quite familiar to the children's souls, in order
that they may learn to be more gentle, and harmonious, and rhythmical, and so more fitted to speech and
action; for the life of man in every part has need of
harmony and rhythm. Then they send them to the
master of gymnastic, in order that their bodies may
better minister to the virtuous mind, and that they
may not be compelled through bodily weakness to
play the coward in war or on any other occasion "
(Trans. by Jowett).

Plato gives us in the above passage an admirable
account of the old Athenian early education. Virtue,
he believed, is teachable. Other passages in Plato of
interest and value might be quoted, particularly from
the *Republic,* as for example, in Book II (376ff), and
from the *Laws;* Aristotle's *Politics* should also be con-
sulted.

The two great branches of higher education at
Athens, which developed toward the end of the fifth
century B.C. and flourished exceedingly in the fourth
century and thereafter, were rhetoric and philosophy.
They were rival studies and each was claimed by its
teachers to be of greater value than the other as an
instrument of education to fit the young men of the
day for all duties and activities of life.

RHETORIC first claims our attention as taught by the
Sophists. The word *rhetoric* in the Greek sense is of
much wider connotation than in English. It meant,
first of all, the art of persuasion by speaking. More
than oratory, it had as its aim the moving of men in
public matters. The word *Sophistes* in Greek was applied at an early time to one who was regarded as
possessing wisdom. Originally it was a term of respect. Thus Homer, Hesiod, and the lyric poets are
called *sophistai.* The Seven Wise Men —Thales,
Solon, Pittacus, etc., — were also designated by this

term. In the latter part of the fifth century the changing political and social conditions at Athens profoundly stimulated intellectual activity and inquiry. Curiosity was rife concerning questions of every sort and great interest was evoked in such fields as ethics, government, history, grammar, religion, mathematics, and the sciences. Foremost, however, was the interest in public speaking and the art of persuasion. In the democracy every citizen had a chance to influence his fellows, to gain position and power, and to win reputation by public speaking in Assembly or in Senate. In fact, it was even obligatory that every participant in a law-suit plead his own case. There was inevitably a demand by youths of mature years for a more advanced education than was afforded by the comparatively elementary training of the schools. A veritable crop of teachers arose to satisfy this demand. These teachers, lecturers, and professors came from all over the Greek world — from Ionia, and from Thrace, from Sicily, and, of course, from Athens itself. The teachers from Sicily and Magna Graecia were especially interested in rhetoric proper, whereas those from Ionia embraced a much wider field, encyclopaedic in scope, stressing grammar and literary criticism with dialectic as a basis. Many of these men became immensely popular and their lectures were attended by throngs of youths who paid large tuition fees for the privilege. Some of the Sophists were itinerant lecturers, traveling about and teaching in various parts of the Greek world; others established flourishing schools in Athens. Certain of these teachers were persons of superior attainments, excellent and sincere men, who had at heart the welfare of their students. Ethical training formed the basis of their instruction. Their fees were honestly earned in an effort to ground their pupils in the thorough knowledge and effective use of the Greek language and literature. They tried not merely to give information in various fields of knowledge, but sought also to train their disciples in

thinking, and in the exercise of judgment and the use
of imagination.   Readiness of thought, wide information on many topics, and ability to speak, especially
extemporaneously, were cardinal features of their
pedagogical system.   But it is not surprising that amid
the restless conditions which then obtained, when the
old standards of conduct and thought were being swept
away and a new world was being ushered in, that
charlatans appeared who sought and found a rich field
for harvest.   The road to popularity and to affluence
lay open to many men who were able to attract attention by skilful advertising, personal magnetism and
extravagant claims.   These dishonest and insincere
professors of the new education, with their much ad-
vertised short cuts to knowledge, filled their lecture
rooms with hearers and their purses with money.
At the same time, however, they brought disrepute
upon themselves from the discriminating, and by the
fourth century B.C. had fastened upon the term
sophistes an invidious meaning which survives to the
present day in its English derivatives, *sophist, sophistry,* and *sophism.*

Who were some of the famous men who played at
Athens prominent rôles as influential teachers in this
great educational movement?   Socrates himself is
really an example of the Sophist in the best sense.
He was at variance with the professional Sophists,
however, in that his teaching was ever informal, he
charged no fees, and he made no claims to superior
knowledge — in fact, with characteristic irony he
always asserted his ignorance — but the spirit of the
age inspired him to devote his life to instructing his
fellow-citizens in the field of ethics, and aroused him
to combat popular misconceptions and hence to discredit the vain assumptions of the Sophists of the
baser type.   The Socratic ideal of education was this,
that it should prepare the individual for living, and
that it should train and fit him for leadership in the
State.   In spite of Socrates' sterling integrity and

absolute honesty it was his misfortune to be confused with the charlatans and actually to suffer martyrdom, being convicted through popular prejudice and calumny on the charge of corrupting the youth!

Especially prominent representatives of the New Education as Professors of Practical Culture were Protagoras, Prodicus, Hippias, Gorgias, Isocrates, and Alcidamas. Protagoras of Abdera, who gives his name to Plato's well-known dialogue, enjoyed great repute and apparently deservedly so. He was the first of the Sophists proper, and for forty years traveled and taught throughout Greece receiving, we are told, for a course of lectures some $2000. He was famous for his dialectic, and his teaching of *commonplaces* for use in speaking by means of which his students were able " to make the weaker argument appear the stronger." His best known utterance is that " Man is the measure of all things." He was interested, too, in logic and grammar. Protagoras claimed to make his pupils better and wiser men by " teaching them prudence in affairs private and public; in short, the science or knowledge of human life."

Prodicus of Ceos, somewhat younger than Protagoras, was especially concerned with synonyms and the exact meaning of words. He taught morals and rhetorical style and achieved reputation and considerable wealth.

Hippias of Elis boasted an encyclopaedic culture and professed to teach economics, ethics, and politics; " the faculty of managing public affairs along with one's own."

We come now to Gorgias of Leontini in Sicily, who is a striking and extremely important figure in the history of rhetoric and education, a teacher and orator who made a profound and lasting impression on the theory and the practice of rhetoric. His chief concern was with style and poetic rhetorical embellishment. Not the message, but the manner, not the thought, but the expression — this sums up his belief

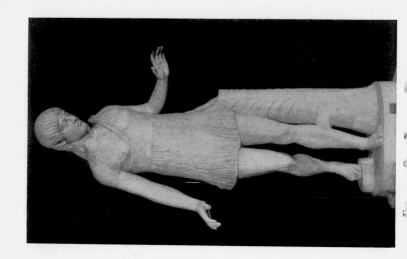

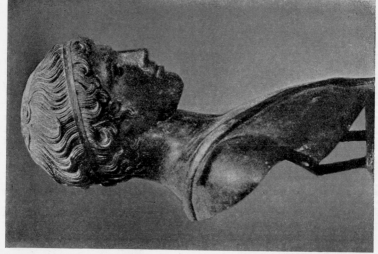

FIG. 12. BRONZE HEAD OF AN EPHEBE (Madi...

and practice. Greek prose as Gorgias found it was
stiff, hard, austere, and inartistic. It was a rather
unwieldy instrument, as for centuries verse had been
the only means of literary expression. For this reason
even the early philosophers wrote in verse rather than
in prose. Gorgias conceived the idea of marrying to
prose the polish, the finish, and the embellishments of
poetry. Accordingly he sowed figures and rhetorical
devices as with a sack, and achieved a style which was
characterized by a plethora of words and a paucity
of ideas. These figures and poetic devices are antith-
esis, paronomasia, alliteration, repetition of words,
likeness of sound in final syllables of successive words
and clauses, and arrangement of words in nearly equal
periods. Added to these are alternating amplifica-
tion and brevity, bold metaphors, unusual epithets,
and poetic rhythm. In 427 B.C. Gorgias came to
Athens as the head of a Sicilian embassy and addressed
the Assembly. The effect of his speech was electri-
fying, as the younger men were swept away by the
brilliancy, eloquence, and the unwonted style of his
oration.

These stylistic characteristics — seen later in the
Asiatic school of Greek oratory and in Euphuism in
English literature — which impress us as inartistic and
frigid in the extreme, met with high praise and imitation, or with strong censure and avoidance, in his
own and subsequent generations. The Gorgian influence was beneficial insofar as it gave greater polish,
smoothness, and flexibility to the Attic prose of Antiphon, Thucydides, Isocrates, and their successors.
His influence was pernicious, when he was followed
slavishly to excess. But Gorgias' great contribution
to Greece was this: he was the founder of artistic
prose, and with him begins *epideictic* literature, or the
rhetoric of display. Of the writings of Gorgias we
possess a fragment of a *Funeral Oration,* and a discourse *The Encomium on Helen* which most scholars

believe genuine. The latter composition deserves our further consideration.

In the centuries succeeding Homer we find in Greek literature numerous disparaging animadversions on Helen of Sparta and Troy. The praise of Helen, however, became a favorite theme with the rhetoricians, since the difficulty of a vindication was a constant challenge to their rhetorical skill and ingenuity. *The Encomium on Helen* of Gorgias is a short but astounding composition, in which the master of poetic and figurative prose fairly outdid himself. In justice to the author it must be remembered that he characterizes his effort as a sportive piece, a *jeu d'esprit*. A translation of the most interesting portions of the discourse is given below, in which I have made an effort to reproduce in the English as faithfully as possible the florid and frigid Greek.

" Embellishment to a city is the valor of its citizens; to a person, comeliness; to a soul, wisdom; to a deed, virtue; to discourse, truth. But the opposite to these is lack of embellishment. Now a man, woman, discourse, work, city, deed, if deserving of praise, must be honored with praise, but if undeserving must be censured. For it is alike aberration and stultification to censure the commendable and commend the censurable.

" It is the duty of the same individual both to proclaim justice wholly, and to declaim against injustice holily, to confute the detractors of Helen, a woman concerning whom there has been uniform and universal praise of poets and the celebration of her name has been the commemoration of her fame. But I desire by rational calculation to free the lady's reputation, by disclosing her detractors as prevaricators, and, by revealing the truth, to put an end to error.

" That in nature and nurture the lady was the fairest flower of men and women is not unknown, not even to the few, for her maternity was of Leda, her pater-

nity immortal by generation, but mortal by reputation,
Tyndareus and Zeus, of whom the one was reputed in
the being, the other was asserted in the affirming; the
former, the greatest of humanity, the latter, the lord-
liest of divinity. Of such origin she was endowed with
godlike beauty, expressed not suppressed, which
inspired in many men many mad moods of love, and
she, one lovely person, assembled many personalities
of proud ambition, of whom some possessed opulent
riches, others the fair fame of ancient ancestry; others
the vigor of native strength, others the power of
acquired wisdom; and all came because of amorous
contention and ambitious pretention.

"Who he was, however, who won Helen and attained
his heart's desire, and why, and how, I will not say,
since to give information to the informed conduces
to confirmation, but conveys no delectation. Passing
over in my present discourse the time now past, I will
proceed to the beginning of my intended discussion
and will predicate the causes by reason of which it
was natural that Helen went to Troy. For either by
the disposition of fortune and the ratification of the
gods and the determination of necessity she did what
she did, or by violence confounded, or by persuasion
dumbfounded, or to Love surrendered. If, however,
it was against her will, the culpable should not be
exculpated. For it is impossible to forestall divine
disposals by human proposals. It is a law of nature
that the stronger is not subordinated to the weaker,
but the weaker is subjugated and dominated by the
stronger; the stronger is the leader, while the weaker
is the entreater. Divinity surpasses humanity in
might, in sight, and in all else. Therefore, if on fortune and the deity we must visit condemnation, the
infamy of Helen should find no confirmation.

" But if by violence she was defeated and unlawfully
she was treated and to her injustice was meted, clearly
her violator as a terrifier was importunate, while she,
translated and violated, was unfortunate. Therefore,

the barbarian who verbally, legally, actually attempted the barbarous attempt, should meet with verbal accusation, legal reprobation, and actual condemnation. For Helen, who was violated, and from her fatherland separated, and from her friends segregated, should justly meet with commiseration rather than with defamation. For he was the victor and she was the victim. It is just, therefore, to sympathize with the latter and anathematize the former.

"But if it was through persuasion's reception and the soul's deception it is not difficult to defend the situation and forefend the accusation, thus. Persuasion is a powerful potentate, who with frailest, feeblest frame works wonders. For it can put an end to fear and make vexation vanish; it can inspire exultation and increase compassion. I will show how this is so. For I must indicate this to my hearers for them to predicate. All poetry I ordain and proclaim to be composition in meter, the listeners of which are affected by passionate trepidation and compassionate perturbation and likewise tearful lamentation, since through discourse the soul suffers, as if its own, the felicity and infelicity of property and person of others.

"Come, let us turn to another consideration. Inspired incantations are provocative of charm and revocative of harm. For the power of song in association with the belief of the soul captures and enraptures and translates the soul with witchery. For there have been discovered arts twain of witchery and sorcery, which are consternation to the heart and perturbation to art.

"Now, it has been shown that, if Helen was won over by persuasion, she is deserving of commiseration, and not condemnation. The fourth accusation I shall now proceed to answer with a fourth refutation. For if love was the doer of all these deeds, with no difficulty will she be acquitted of the crime attributed to her. The nature of that which we see is not that which we wish it to be, but as it chances to be. For through the vision the soul is also in various ways smitten.

" If, then, the eye of Helen charmed by Alexander's beauty, gave to her soul excitement and amorous incitement, what wonder? How could one who was weaker, repel and expel him who, being divine, had power divine? If it was physical diversion and psychical perversion, we should not execrate it as reprehensible, but deprecate it as indefensible. For it came to whom it came by fortuitous insinuations, not by judicious resolutions; by erotic compulsions, not by despotic machinations. How, then, is it fair to blame Helen who, whether by love captivated, or by word persuaded, or by violence dominated, or by divine necessity subjugated, did what she did, and is completely absolved from blame?

" By this discourse I have freed a woman from evil reputation; I have kept the promise which I made in the beginning; I have essayed to dispose of the injustice of defamation and the folly of allegation; I have prayed to compose a lucubration for Helen's adulation and my own delectation."

The greatest of the permanent teachers of rhetoric in Athens was Isocrates, who was born in Attica in 436 B.C. and lived to the great age of 98 years. He was a pupil of the greatest teachers of his time, namely, Protagoras, Prodicus, and Gorgias, and was influenced by Socrates.

Early in life he was by profession a *logographos* or writer of speeches for participants in law-suits, until, about 390 B.C., he opened a school of rhetoric. For fifty years his school was an influential educational center and was attended by ambitious young men from all parts of the Greek world, even from Pontus, Sicily, and Cyprus, and many of these subsequently distinguished themselves. Among these pupils were the orators Isaeus, Lycurgus, and Hyperides, the historians Ephorus and Theopompus, and the statesman Timo-

theus. The course of study occupied three to four
years and the tuition fee charged for the whole course
was a thousand drachmas, about $180. Isocrates pro-
fessed to train young men for public life through the
study of rhetoric and eloquence, that is, oratory in the
broadest sense. Now this study he taught as a
" philosophy," because his rhetorical instruction
formed, he claimed, no mere orator or advocate, but
trained the taste, judgment, and character. In short, he
professed to conduct a school of morals. His definition
of an educated man, as given in his *Panathenaic* discourse (30ff), is interesting, and is even more pertinent and worthy of reflection than when it was formulated. Particularly challenging is the first sentence:

" Whom, then, do I call educated, since I refuse this
name to those who have learned only certain trades,
or certain sciences, or have had only certain faculties
developed? First, those who manage well the daily
affairs of life as they arise, and whose judgment is
accurate and rarely errs when aiming at the expedient.
Then, those who associate in dignified and honorable
fashion with all with whom they come in contact, bearing easily and good-naturedly what is unpleasant or of-
fensive in others, and softening, as much as possible,
their own asperities of manner. Further, those who
never become the slaves of pleasure, and who by mis-
fortunes are not unduly cast down — bearing themselves in their presence manfully and in a manner
worthy of our common nature. Fourthly, and most important of all, those who are uncorrupted by good fortune and do not lose their heads and become arrogant,
but, retaining control of themselves as intelligent beings,
rejoice not less in the good they have acquired at birth
by their own nature and intelligence than in the benefits that have been cast in their way by chance. Those
whose souls are in permanent and harmonious accord,
not with one of these things, but with all of them,
these, I say, are wise and perfect men, possessed of
all the virtues. This is my opinion with regard to

educated men." (Translation from Walden's *Universities of Ancient Greece*.)

Isocrates' school ended at his death, but the influence of the man, his teaching, and his writings, has been permanent. In his own day, the success of his school, and the views he held relative to education, expounded chiefly in the discourses *Against the Sophists* and *On the Antidosis,* which he expressed with the utmost vigor and indeed with condescending and patronizing frankness, involved him in keen rivalries and disputes. The greatest of his rivals was the Sophist Alcidamas, the successor to Gorgias.

Alcidamas devoted his talents to practical oratory. Isocrates held that if a student had natural ability, then discipline and practice would bring success. Training in written composition on worthy themes was emphasized. Alcidamas, on the contrary, contemned and belittled the written word and lauded extemporaneous speech and vigorously argued his case in an extant composition, *On the Sophists* or *On the Writers of Written Discourses.*

The second great branch of Athenian higher education was the study of philosophy. After the death of Socrates there arose four great schools in Athens, somewhat comparable with our colleges: the *Academic,* founded by Plato; the *Peripatetic,* originated by Aristotle; the *Stoic,* founded by Zeno; and the *Epicurean,* the school of Epicurus. The doctrines of these schools are discussed in the chapter devoted to Greek Philosophy. At the death of Plato, in 347 B.C., his house, which was located near 'the grove of the Academy, was inherited, together with its contents, by his nephew Speusippus and his successors, and became a permanent school with an appointed or elected Head, called the *Scholarch.* The Peripatetic School was held in trust as a college by Aristotle's successor, Theophrastus, and his followers. The Stoics possessed no private property. In fact, their very name comes from their original public place of meeting, the Painted Stoa (portico). The Epicurean school for a long period occupied the house and garden in Athens of its founder, Epicurus.

It remains to consider briefly a form of education to which all Athenian youths were liable — the military *ephebic* training. Our information relative to the ephebes, though by no means complete, is considerable and is gained from the inscriptions. The Greek word *ephebe* (Fig. 42) means youth, but the term was officially applied to young men of Athens of citizen status who served as apprentices in arms to the State for two years, during their eighteenth and nineteenth years. The date of the founding of the College of the Ephebes is uncertain. Such military service had been compulsory to a certain degree in the fifth century B.C. Certainly by the fourth century the institution had been officially established, with its supervision placed in charge of the generals and the Court of the Areopagus, and with numerous instructors who were employed by the State. During the first year of service the cadet was trained in gymnastics, the use of weapons, riding the horse, and tactics. In the second year, he had patrol and guard duties and service in the Attic forts. The Ephebes, as a cavalry contingent, found place, too, in festal processions.

The oath, sworn to by all the Athenian ephebes on entering service, is a model of its kind. It is inscribed in the hall of the Y. M. C. A. building in Chicago:

" I will never disgrace these sacred arms, nor desert my companion in the ranks. I will fight for gods and home, both alone and with many. I will transmit my fatherland, not only not less, but greater and better, than it was transmitted to me. I will obey the magistrates who may at any time be in power. I will observe both the existing laws and those which the people may unanimously hereafter make, and, if any person

seek to annul the laws or to disobey them, I will do
my best to prevent him, and will defend them both
alone and with many. I will honor the religion of
my fathers. And I call to witness Agraulos [daughter
of Cecrops], Enyalios, Ares, Zeus, Thallo [daughter
of Zeus and Themis], Auxo and Hegemone [Graces]."

Various important changes in the ephebic training
and service took place during the fourth and third
centuries. Military disciplines were relaxed and intellectual studies became increasingly important. The
ephebes in a body, led by their Director, attended
lectures in philosophy or in rhetoric in the gymnasia.
The term of service was reduced from a period of two
years to one year. Attendance, originally compulsory,
became, after the Macedonian conquest, voluntary.
Toward the end of the second century B.C. foreigners
were freely admitted to the college.

CHAPTER XII

THE GREEK THEATER AND THE PRODUCTION OF PLAYS

"In a romantic wooded dell on the northeast slope of Mt. Pentelicus, a short half-day's journey from Athens, lie the scanty remains of a little village — Icaria — which should be the Mecca of all lovers of the drama, for it is the legendary birthplace of both tragedy and comedy." — EDWARD CAPPS.

DRAMATIC performances in ancient Greece were given always out-doors in places of assembly open to the sky. Originally the country folk sat on the ground on a sloping hill-side and watched the dancing and the action which were enacted below them about an altar on a level floor of earth. The developed theater was an amphitheater of considerable size, and was composed of three parts; the *auditorium* (*theatron* or *cavea*), where the spectators sat, the *orchestra,* or level circular dancing floor, and the *scene-buildings,* which furnished a background for the action and provided dressing rooms, etc., for the actors. The slope of a hill was generally chosen for the auditorium, to save labor of construction. The seats were at first of wood, as was the case in the theater at Athens during the fifth century B.C. Later, permanent seats of stone were employed. As the auditorium was shaped somewhat like a horseshoe, artificial elevation of the sides for the seats on either side of the orchestra was necessary. To facilitate the entrance and exit of the audience, stairs ran from the orchestra to the top, thus dividing the auditorium into a number of wedge-shaped sections of tiers of seats. In the larger theaters it was also found desirable to have a wide passage (*diazoma*), one-half to two-thirds of the distance from the orchestra to the top, dividing the structure into a lower and an upper section.

The *orchestra* (the word in Greek means *dancing-place*) was a complete circle and was originally of leveled hard earth, although later, in Roman times, it was paved with stone or marble. Entering the orchestra on both sides were passage-ways (called

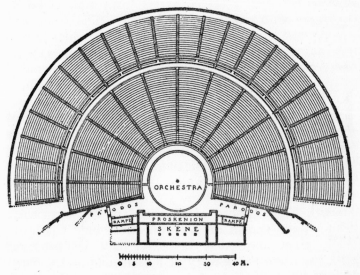

FIG. 44. GROUND-PLAN OF THEATER (EPIDAURUS)

parodi) by means of which the entrance of the chorus was effected. Actors also might enter and depart through the *parodi* and before and after the performance these passages were naturally used by the spectators.

Behind the orchestra were the *scene-buildings*. In early times there stood at this place a simple dressing-room for the convenience of the actors and the chorus. This tent, or booth (Greek, *skēnē;* Latin, *scaena;* Eng. *scene*), originally of skins, then of wood, finally was erected as a permanent structure of stone and naturally came to be used, not merely as a dressing-room and place of storage for properties, but also as a back-scene or background for the action of the drama. Hence the derivation of the English word *scenery*. Fronting the scene-building proper was a decorated wall or *proscenium*, a covered place ten to thirteen feet in height, of shallow depth, with a flat or sloping roof. In Greek tragedy the action generally takes place before a temple or a palace and accordingly the front of the proscenium represented such a scene, as its front wall could be decorated with columns and statues. The front wall was pierced by three, later by five, doors, which served as entrance and exit for the actors. The proscenium also served to join the *parascenia*, the two symmetrically projecting wings of the developed scene-buildings.

Of scenery and decorations in the Greek theater of the fifth and fourth centuries B.C. our information is scanty. No curtain was employed and the mounting must have been extremely simple, leaving much to the imagination of the spectators. But this does not mean that the ancient plays were given in primitive fashion. Modern presentations of classical and Shakespearean drama have shown us how effective and impressive really great plays may be when they are produced with the utmost simplicity of background and scenery. Few changes of scene are required in the extant Greek tragedies; Aristophanic comedy demands more. In the *Suppliants* of Aeschylus an altar alone is needed. In only two of the extant tragedies is the scene changed. In the *Eumenides* of Aeschylus the action shifts from Apollo's temple at Delphi to the temple of Athena at Athens, and in the *Ajax* of Sophocles there is a change from the tent of the hero to a place by the sea-shore. Tradition assigns to Sophocles the "invention" of scene-painting; painted canvas or boards (*pinaces*) could be placed between the pillars of the proscenium. Statues might be put before palace or temple. We hear of other scenic accessories and machinery: e.g., the *machine* (*mechane*), or crane, often employed by

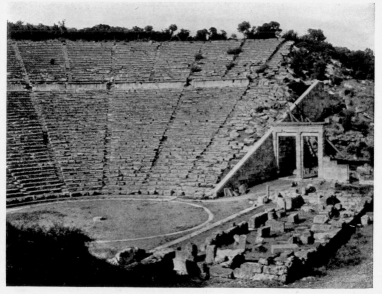

FIG. 45. THE THEATER AT EPIDAURUS

FIG. 46. THE THEATER OF DIONYSUS AT ATHENS

Euripides, by means of which a god, or a hero could be raised or lowered (this device is the famous *deus ex machina,* or " god from the machine "); and the *eccyclema,* or moving platform on wheels. This last conventional contrivance, of construction and appearance unknown to us, served to disclose to the spectators the interior of the scene-building. For example, when an act of violence resulting in death had taken place within — it was a convention of the Greek theater that such deeds should not occur before the eyes of the spectators — it was possible by the use of the *eccyclema,* to roll out of doors the group of persons involved. The later Greek theater seems to have been provided with numerous other scenic accessories, such as the *periacti,* or large revolving triangular prisms, which were decorated on their three faces with different scenes thus allowing for a change of scene; the *bronteion,* or thunder-making apparatus, consisting of a sheet of metal upon which stones were thrown; and *Charon's Steps,* or trap-door, by means of which, for example, the ghost of Darius in the *Persians* of Aeschylus could suddenly appear. An example of this device is found in the theater at Eretria in Euboea, where an underground passage-way runs from behind the scene-buildings to the middle of the orchestra and steps lead to the surface.

Our discussion of the physical aspect of the Greek theater must now return to the scene-buildings, or, more accurately, to the proscenium and to a most interesting and much-vexed question. Did the Greek theater of the fifth and fourth centuries B.C. have and employ a raised stage? Until recent years the existence of a stage was not doubted. Vitruvius, the celebrated Roman writer on architecture, who lived in the time of Augustus, describes, in his extant work, *De Architectura,* the Greek theater as having a lofty stage. Remains of a stage have been found in some Greek theaters. The Roman theater had a stage. The modern theater is always thus provided. Yet a majority of Greek scholars today believe that no elevated stage was in use in the Greek theater of the fifth and fourth centuries B.C., and that, in consequence, both actors and chorus performed on the level dancing-floor, the orchestra. This view is held for the following reasons. In the extant plays there are numerous passages necessitating intimate action between actors and chorus, action which would be difficult, if not impossible, if they were separated by a lofty platform. Professor Capps has shown that in the forty-four extant dramas the action requires that the chorus pass over the boundary — conceived to be the edge of a ten-foot stage which separated actors and chorus — at least sixty-eight times, the actors thirty-nine times, and chorus and actors together nine times. For example, in the *Iphigenia among the Taurians* of Euripides the heroine touches and embraces each member of the chorus when she is entreating them to preserve her secret. In the comedies actual physical contact between actors and chorus is extremely frequent. The Greek proscenium, furthermore, was much too narrow to accommodate the action of a play. Of course the roof of the proscenium could be used, and was used occasionally, by an actor in the rôle of a god, or a watchman, as in the scene at the beginning of the *Agamemnon*. No theater of the fifth century is in existence. In the fourth century theater, as at Athens, no traces of a stage are to be found. The remains of a stage in some existing Greek theaters may be accounted for by the fact that these structures were remodeled and changed in the Roman period. The Roman theater did have an elevated stage and it is perhaps the Graeco-Roman theater which is described by Vitruvius in the first century B.C. No confusion resulted by having both actors and chorus perform on the same level because they were differentiated in costume and appearance; the members of the chorus would withdraw to either side or to the rear of the roomy orchestra when the dialogue proper was

taking place. Nor was there any difficulty with regard to seeing, since the spectators were seated on a
steep incline and could look down into the orchestra
with unobstructed view; no elevated platform was
needed, then, and would have been an interference to
the action.

Every city and town throughout the Greek world
had its theater. The best preserved of all Greek theaters is that at Epidaurus (Fig. 45) in the Peloponnesus, in the auditorium of which some of the end seats
on the sides only are missing. It was much larger than
the theater at Athens. The orchestra, a perfect circle
surrounded by a ring of limestone, is sixty-five feet in
diameter. The proscenium is about seventy-five feet
long and eleven and one-half feet high. As is usually
the case in Greek theaters, the acoustics in the theater
at Epidaurus are excellent; a person in the orchestra
speaking in a clear voice can be distinctly heard in the
farthest removed seats.

The largest theater in Greece was that of Megalo-
polis, seating twice as many spectators as the Athenian
theater, with an orchestra no less than ninety-nine feet
in diameter. Little of this theater is preserved. Remains of theaters have been found in many places
throughout Greek lands, as for example at Delphi,
Eretria, Sicyon, Thoricus, Oropus, Delos, and Pergamum.

No Greek theater possesses such interest for us and
arouses such veneration as the Athenian Theater of
Dionysus (Fig. 46), located on the steep slope of the hill
at the southeastern corner of the Acropolis. On this site
were presented the dramatic masterpieces of Aeschylus, Sophocles, Euripides, and Aristophanes. The seats
of the auditorium originally were of wood, later of
stone. The stone seats which partly cover the site today belong to the time of Lycurgus, Athenian minister
of the treasury, 338–326 B.C., who rebuilt the theater

with limestone, with an orchestra of a diameter of sixty-four feet four inches (sixty Greek feet), and a stone scene-building, one hundred and fifty-two feet in breadth by twenty-one feet in depth.   The theater was rebuilt several times in Hellenistic and in Roman times, and orchestra and scene-buildings have been repeatedly remodeled.   But the Athenian theater unfortunately, unlike that at Epidaurus, has suffered sadly in the passing of the centuries; all the upper tiers of seats have been carried away.

The stone benches which remain are without backs, but are cut so as to allow plenty of room from front to back and for the feet of the spectators.   At a later date, a circular tier composed of extremely comfortable chairs of marble with backs was added as a front row. These chairs, which remain today, were for ecclesiastic and civic dignitaries.   In the exact center is a commodious throne with arms, which is elaborately decorated with designs in low relief.   There are borings in the arms showing that metal supports upheld a canopy to shield from the sun the august head of the occupant. The inscription on the throne informs us that this best seat in the theater was for the use of the High Priest of Dionysus.   In the time of the Roman emperor Nero (first century A.D.) a stage, with a new proscenium, was built infringing upon the full circle of the orchestra. A marble pavement was laid as a flooring for the orchestra, which previously had been hard earth, and a balustrade of marble was constructed to protect the spectators from injury during gladiatorial exhibitions. The inept sculptured frieze of the front wall of the stage, which is today conspicuous, was put in place in the third or the fourth century A.D., when a certain Phaedrus was governor of Attica.

The seating capacity of the Athenian theater was about seventeen thousand, according to the calculations of archaeologists.   Possibly somewhat more could be crowded in.   Certainly Plato's reference to the presence of thirty thousand spectators is a rough estimate, or rather guess.

THE PRODUCTION OF PLAYS

The modern theater, which is largely a commercial venture and which primarily exists for the purpose of providing amusement and entertainment for its patrons, presents theatrical performances throughout the year. Altogether different was the situation in ancient Greece. The Greek drama was founded on religious observances, and plays were given only twice a year and then for very limited periods. These occasions, when tragedies, comedies, and dithyrambs were presented, were the two great special festivals in honor of Dionysus, the patron god of wine, fertility, and the drama, namely, the festival of the *Lenaea* (the winepress), at the end of January, and the *City Dionysia*, at the end of March. A lesser festival, the *Rural Dionysia*, was celebrated in country districts of Attica at the end of December, when the successful plays which had been given at Athens were repeated. The most important of the festivals was the City Dionysia, which lasted at least five days and was devoted primarily to tragedy, although some comedies also were enacted. The Lenaea was the festival of comedy, although the production of tragedies was a late addition (about 433 B.C.). The dramatic performances followed each other continuously from early morning until evening; at the Dionysia tragedies were given in the morning and comedies in the afternoon. These dramas were all *new* plays during the fifth century, as original playwrights and new dramas were extremely numerous at this time. In the fourth century, however, when Attic dramatic and literary genius was on the wane, the practice of reviving the masterpieces of the past became popular and indeed necessary.

The presentation of plays in Athens was controlled by the government, and poets, actors, and *choregi* were selected by State officials. The festival of the City Dionysia was in charge of the *Archon Eponymus;* the Lenaea was supervised by the *Archon Basileus.* A tragic poet who wished to compete in the dramatic competition submitted his plays to the appropriate Archon.   In the first part of the fifth century a tetralogy (i.e., three tragedies and a satyric play) in which a single theme was developed, was presented and from the numerous dramas offered the Archon selected the three tetralogies judged best.   To these he " gave a chorus," or rather, assigned a *choregus*.   The choregus (literally chorus-leader) was a wealthy citizen whose duty it was to choose and to pay the expenses of a dramatic chorus. It was obligatory also for him to engage a trainer or " coach " for the presentation, to pay for the musical accompaniment furnished by the flute-players, and also to defray the expense of the costumes.   This duty was called the *choregia* and was one of the *liturgies*, or public services, exacted by the State as taxes on wealthy Athenians.

The minimum expense of the *choregia* was considerable and might be great if the choregus were wealthy, generous, and eager to win.   In an oration of Lysias a speaker affirms that he spent, within seven years, about $540 for a tragic choregia, $288 for a comic choregia, and no less than $900 for a dithyrambic chorus of men, and $270 for a boys' chorus.

The poet himself in the early part of the fifth century might act in his own plays, or select his actors.   Later, however, the State took charge of this also and distributed by lot the protagonists, or chief actors, among the poets.   A professional class of trainers, actors, and singers arose who were available for the dramatic festivals.   The trainer was called a *didascalus*, or teacher of a chorus.   To " teach " a play became synonymous with producing it.

The huge audience of many thousands assembled in the theater at Athens early in the morning for the performances which were to continue through the day.   If the spectators were wise, they brought cushions for comfort, and likewise refreshments.   The weather was pretty certain to be pleasant as the festivals were held

at a time when in Greece open-air performances are delightful, and the sun is warm but not oppressively hot.
The admission was originally free, but because of the
crowds competing for seats the practice was introduced
of selling tickets (usually small stamped leaden disks)
in advance for one day's session at the small price of
two obols (six cents) for all seats without distinction
of location, with the exception of the comparatively
small number of front seats reserved for priests,
officials, and honored guests. At the end of the fifth
century we find the State instituting a fund (the Theoric
Fund) which provided admittance fees to any citizens
who were too poor to pay for their entrance. This
theater fund for the needy was not established on the
principle of the Roman *panem et circenses* for the proletariat. The Greek theater was a religious and educational institution. All citizens, therefore, should for
their own welfare and that of the State be encouraged
and assisted to attend and this was made possible by
the Theoric Fund. All classes of the population, including women, children, resident aliens, and slaves
could attend, athough adult male citizens must have
formed the large majority of the spectators. Many
strangers, too, were present for the celebration of the
City Dionysia, which enjoyed wide fame. Navigation
at the end of March was safe and, furthermore, this
was the time of the year when the tribute was sent to
Athens by the allies. At the end of each competition
of three tetralogies, the judges, apparently five in number, who had been chosen by lot to avoid any possibility of partiality, rendered their decision. The victorious
poet and his choregus were crowned with ivy. In the
dithyrambic contests the successful choregus received
a tripod. To each of the competing dramatists was
given a sum of money and the records of the awards
were inscribed upon public tablets.

The subject of costume, particularly in tragedy,
bristles with difficulties, and much foolishness has been
written about it. Vase-paintings, and the literature

give us some light, although all of this information is by no means contemporaneous or complete. The Greek tragic actor of tradition is truly a portentous figure. He is represented as greatly increasing his height by the use of the *cothurnus* (buskin), a boot with prodigiously thick soles; he is supposed to have padded his body to grandiose proportions and to have increased his height by wearing a towering head-dress; upon his face he is represented as wearing a grotesque mask. We are now inclined to believe, however, that this impressive, but rather absurd, personage must be "scaled down" to proportions of common-sense and to accord with the Greek sense of propriety. The evidence for the use of all this apparatus is late. While the cothurnus or buskin seems to have been commonly worn by the tragic actor, at least in later times, the conception of the extreme thickness of its sole is based partly on very late literary evidence and partly on the misinterpretation of works of art. The "invention" of tragic costume is traditionally credited to Aeschylus. In general it may be reasonably asserted that actors and chorus were clad in costumes befitting their rôles. The nature and needs of comedy gave rise to variety and picturesqueness of costume, especially as to the members of the chorus, who impersonated, in the Old Comedy, animals, birds, etc. Women did not appear as actors in Greek plays; men or youths assumed all feminine parts.

The origin of the use of the mask is uncertain. Some have naïvely thought that the mouthpiece of the mask served to magnify the actor's voice. But the physical construction and contour of the Greek theater with the concave auditorium of the steep hillside provided remarkable acoustics, as may be proved by actual demonstration today in the theater at Epidaurus, where the words, clearly enunciated merely, of a person in the orchestra are easily heard in the most remote part of the auditorium. It is possible that the mask is of religious origin and that it was introduced to enable the actor to assume a rôle appropriate to the performance of religious rites in honor of the god Dionysus. Its use indubitably had many advantages; for example, it permitted one actor to play several parts — an economical device — and men to assume feminine rôles. While facial expression was lost through its employment, yet in any case the large size of the open-air Greek theater would have largely nullified that asset of the modern actor's art. In our large indoor theaters and operahouses the play of features of the actors is largely lost to spectators in remote seats, often even when they are provided with opera-glasses.

Three actors, the protagonist, who assumed the leading rôle, the deuteragonist, and the tritagonist, were sufficient by the change of mask and costumes to assume all the rôles in a majority of the plays. It is a mistake, however, to assume that a fourth actor could not be employed. Certain tragedies (e.g., the *Oedipus at Colonus*) could have been given only with great difficulty, and some comedies (e.g., the *Frogs* of Aristophanes) could not have been presented at all with fewer than four actors. Mutes were frequently used, as well as extra performers for crowds, attendants, slaves, and others. At Athens, unlike Rome, the profession of the actor was in good social repute, and in the fourth century and thereafter there flourished Actors' Guilds or Unions.

Of the music in the Greek drama we know little. A flute-player, occasionally also a harpist, in the orchestra, furnished the simple musical accompaniment for the lyrics and the dance evolutions of the chorus. The dialogue portion of the play, written in iambic trimeters (i.e., six iambic feet), was spoken or declaimed; trochaics and anapaests were delivered in recitative; other meters might be accompanied; the lyrical passages were always sung to music. The singing of the chorus was in unison and unlike modern opera could be clearly understood, as the musical element was subordinated to the recitation. In the latter part of the fifth century there was a tendency to emphasize and elaborate the musical element to a degree formerly not customary. Euripides especially was reprehended by the conservative Aristophanes for this practice. The chorus generally sang alone, as in the *stasima* (choral lyrics proper), though choristers and actor might join in a lyric passage, as in the *commus* (a lamentation). A monody was a solo by an actor. A fine sonorous voice, clear enunciation, and exact rendering of the verse were absolutely essential to an actor's success in the Greek theater. The original dithyrambic chorus had consisted of fifty members. In the earliest extant play, the *Suppliants* of Aeschylus, the chorus is actually composed of the fifty daughters of Danaus. Aeschylus reduced this unwieldy number to twelve, which was subsequently raised by Sophocles to fifteen. This increase probably allowed superior marching and dancing evolutions. The leader of the chorus was called the coryphaeus. Twenty-four constituted the number of the chorus in comedy.

CHAPTER XIII

GREEK TRAGEDY

GREEK tragedy, according to Aristotle, in his *Poetics*, originated among the Dorians in the worship of Dionysus, the god of vegetation, fertility, and in particular, the vine.[1] It was the custom in the spring, when the wine of the previous autumn was broached, for the country-folk to hold festival and to sing and dance in honor of the god of wine. This song, known as the *dithyramb* — a choral lyric relating the adventures of Dionysus — was performed in a circular dancing-place (*orchestra*) to the accompaniment of the flute, by a chorus of fifty men and boys, dressed as satyrs, the sportive attendants of the god. The dithyramb, according to tradition, had been developed by Arion — originally of Lesbos, but resident at Corinth — who had the leader of the chorus address his fellows. However this may be, tragedy arose when Thespis (about 535 B.C.), of Icaria in Attica, impersonated a character alluded to in the song and conversed with the chorus, or its leader. Aeschylus added a second actor and Sophocles a third. Dialogue naturally and gradually developed at the expense of the original lyric element, plots became more complex, and stately and dignified language was used. The early satyric element, playful but distinct from comedy, was

[1] The traditional view here given has recently been attacked by two scholars, who are, however, not in agreement. Professor William Ridgeway maintains that the origin of Greek tragedy is to be found in the ritual performed by the chorus worshipping dead heroes at the tomb. Professor Gilbert Murray, on the contrary, thinks the origin is in the ritual which celebrated the annual death and rebirth of vegetation, a rite which was a feature of the cult of Dionysus. A composite origin, however, for the gradually developing tragic art may reasonably be assumed, since various elements may be seen in the fully perfected drama.

developed independently of tragedy, but was conservatively retained, being incorporated in the short concluding play of the fifth century tetralogy. It may be remarked here that only two examples of the satyric drama are extant — the *Cyclops* of Euripides, and the recently discovered *Trackers* of Sophocles.

The Greek word *tragōdos* means " goat-singer," but why the tragic singer was so called is not clear. Perhaps it was because of the singers' original satyr costume or, more probably, because a goat may have been given as a prize.

Epic and lyric poetry had preceded tragedy as popular and perfected art-forms. The new tragic art, therefore, had abundant materials for its use. Subject-matter was obtained from that treasure-house of ancient story, the great epics, both Homer and the *Cyclic Poems*. Lyric poetry, particularly the dithyramb, with its religious origin and feeling, poetic idiom, and varied meters, lent its resources to the tragic choral odes. In the dialogue element of the drama there was substituted for the epic dactylic hexameter, as better suited to conversation, the iambic verse of six feet (iambic trimeter) which had been perfected by Archilochus of Paros (seventh century B.C.).

THE EXTANT TRAGEDIES

Of the hundreds of tragedies written during the great period of the Attic drama only thirty-three are extant. We possess seven plays of Aeschylus, seven of Sophocles, and nineteen of Euripides. Scanty fragments only remain of plays written by Aeschylus' predecessors, Choerilus, Pratinas, and the great Phrynichus. Two plays of Phrynichus are of special interest, the *Phoenissae* (476 B.C.), of which the theme was the Greek victory at Salamis, and the *Capture of Miletus*, which dramatized the loss of that Greek Ionian city to Darius. These two plays, written on contemporary historical events, show that Aeschylus in writing his historical play, the *Persians*, had been anticipated in this novel choice of story, although the practice did not become popular.

AESCHYLUS, born in 525 B.C. at Eleusis, fought at Marathon and was present at Salamis. The period of his dramatic activity falls between 499 and 458 during which time he won thirteen victories. To him are traditionally ascribed the introduction of a second actor, the lessening of the importance of the chorus, and the invention of tragic costume. He died in Sicily in 456 B.C. His seven plays, given below in chronological order, will be very briefly summarized.

The *Suppliant Women* shows its early origin by the overshadowing importance of the chorus, the scant attention paid to characterization, and the comparative absence of action. The scene lies near Argos and the story is concerned with the escape of the chorus, the fifty daughters of Danaus, from Egypt to avoid marriage with their cousins, the sons of Aegyptus. The maidens find asylum with the King of Argos.

The scene of the *Persians* (472 B.C.) lies before the palace of Xerxes, at Susa, the Persian capital. The chorus is composed of aged Persian councillors. The theme was calculated to be pleasing to an Athenian audience, as it relates the rout of the barbarian fleet at Salamis and the despair of Xerxes, who, with his royal mother, Atossa, are characters in the drama. The play contains a poetic and extremely vivid narration of the great sea-fight.

The *Seven against Thebes* (467 B.C.), aptly characterized by Aristophanes as a "drama full of Ares," belongs to the Theban cycle of legend and deals with the fortunes of the sons of Oedipus. Eteocles, the elder, having assumed the throne, is besieged by an Argive army gathered by his brother Polynices, who had been expelled from Thebes. In the assault upon the city its seven gates are defended by Eteocles and

six fellow champions and attacked by Polynices with
an equal number of combatants. The brothers fall
by each other's hand. The Theban councillors decree
honorable burial for the patriot Eteocles, while the
edict declares that Polynices' body must be thrown to
the dogs and the vultures. The play ends with the
announcement of Antigone that she will defy this decree.

The *Prometheus Bound,* of uncertain date, is a
magnificent poetic drama and is one of the most impressive of all the Greek tragedies. It has been
translated by Mrs. Browning, and inspired Shelley's
poetic drama, *Prometheus Unbound.* The Titan hero,
Prometheus, has disobeyed and flouted Zeus, who had
wished to destroy utterly the impotent and imperfect
human race, by stealing from Heaven the forbidden
fire. With this flame, conveyed in the fennel-stalk,
he has succored man and likewise has taught him the
arts of civilization and cheers his heart with hope.
For this grave disobedience the hero is ruthlessly
nailed and bound to a rock in a solitary gorge in
Scythia. The chorus is composed of maidens, the
daughters of Oceanus, who come to give him sympathy. In his torment and humiliation the hero is
visited by the patronizing Oceanus, the wandering Io,
and Hermes, messenger of Zeus. Prometheus, rely-
ing on his knowledge of a secret, namely, that Zeus,
if he make a certain marriage, is destined to be de-
throned by his son, is obdurate. Amid thunder and
the whirlwind the chasm yawns and he, together with
his chorus, sink into the earth. It is probable that
the *Prometheus* is only one play of a trilogy and that,
in a drama which followed, his release by Heracles
and reconciliation with Zeus were represented.

The *Oresteia* (the story of Orestes) is the name
given to the only extant trilogy, composed of the
Agamemnon, Libation-Bearers, and the *Eumenides.*
The *Agamemnon,* the greatest of the Greek plays in the
sheer poetic merit of the lyric element, relates the

homecoming of the victorious general Agamemnon
from Troy, and his foul murder at the hands of his
faithless wife Clytaemnestra, and her paramour Aegisthus. The *Libation-Bearers* tells of the return of
Orestes, son of Agamemnon, from exile to punish
the guilty pair. He slays them both, but is mad-
dened by his crime and flees from the pursuing
Furies to supplicate Apollo, at whose instigation he
had accomplished the deed of vengeance. In the
Eumenides, Orestes, who has been purified by Apollo,
must be reconciled with the *Erinyes* (Furies). Arriving at Athens, he is tried before the Court (known
later as the Areopagus). The vote of the jury of
Athenian elders is a tie, and Athena, as presiding
magistrate, casts her vote for Orestes and thereby he
secures acquittal. The Furies are pacified by the
goddess and are given residence beneath the hill, the
Areopagus. Henceforth, they are designated Eumenides (Kindly Spirits), guardians of the land.

SOPHOCLES (495–406 B.C.), second of the Athenian
tragedians, is known to us by seven extant tragedies,
all of the greatest interest and merit. These are, in
approximately their chronological order, *Ajax*, *Antigone*, *Electra*, *Oedipus Tyrannus*, *Trachiniae* (the
Women of Trachis), *Philoctetes*, and the *Oedipus at
Colonus*.

In the *Ajax*, the hero, who has been defeated by
Odysseus in the contest for the arms of Achilles, seeks
vengeance upon Agamemnon and Menelaus. Made
mad by Athena, he has slain a herd of cattle, mis-
taking them for his enemies. On regaining his sanity,
in his humiliation he commits suicide. Honorable
burial, at first denied him by the chiefs, is grudgingly
granted him at last through the intercession of Odysseus.

The *Antigone* is a play of great appeal and has ever
been deservedly admired. It is a sequel, so far as
action is concerned, to the *Seven against Thebes* of

Aeschylus.   Antigone, despite the edict of Creon, king
of Thebes, gives honorable burial to her slain brother,
Polynices, who is pronounced a traitor by the king.   In
consequence of her act the heroine suffers a martyr's
death.   Creon's punishment is terrible, for the death
of Antigone is followed by the suicide of Haemon,
his son and Antigone's lover, and of his wife, Eurydice.

The *Electra* develops the same theme as the *Libation-Bearers* of Aeschylus, a story which was likewise
used by Euripides in his play of the same name.   It tells
of the return of Orestes and of the vengeance inflicted
by him upon his guilty mother Clytaemnestra and Aegisthus, the slayers of his father.   His intrepid sister
Electra aids and abets him in the dread deed.

The *Oedipus Tyrannus* (*Oedipus the King*) is the
greatest of all the Greek plays in excellence of plot
and in the element of suspense.   It is quoted by Aristotle more frequently than any other Greek drama
in his discussion of tragedy in the *Poetics*.

The hero had come to Thebes years before and had
found the city oppressed by the Sphinx.   Oedipus
had solved the riddle of the monster and had been rewarded with the throne.   He had married Queen
Jocasta, the widow of the former king Laius.   At the
beginning of the play Thebes is suffering from a devas-
tating pestilence.   Creon, the brother of the Queen,
brings word that the oracle of Apollo at Delphi proclaims that the source of the pollution, the unknown
murderer of Laius, must be discovered and expelled
from the land.   Oedipus pledges himself to succor his
people, and vows that he will find the guilty person
upon whose head he pronounces dread curses.   Tiresias, the blind soothsayer, summoned before the king,
refuses to tell all he knows, as this would involve the
king himself in guilt.   At length, the aged seer, stung
by the king's hot words, denounces Oedipus himself as
the murderer.   Oedipus, in sore wrath at this accusation, so unjust as he believes, accuses Tiresias as the
tool of Creon, who, he thinks, is conspiring for the

throne. The queen Jocasta, to quiet the fears of Oedipus, tells him that oracles are not to be trusted, since Apollo had prophesied Laius' death at the hand of his own son, whereas the babe had been exposed on the mountain and Laius had been slain by robbers, *at the meeting of three roads*. Jocasta's recital alarms Oedipus, as he had once met and slain an old man in Phocis at a place where three roads meet. Could this have been Laius? A messenger comes from Corinth — Oedipus' previous home — to report the death of King Polybus, and that Oedipus has been chosen as his successor. Oedipus, who thinks himself the son of Polybus, is now partly relieved from his fear that he may fulfil the oracle, which said that he was destined to slay his father and wed his mother. The messenger, to dispel all dread from Oedipus' mind, assures him that he is not the son of Polybus and Merope, but a foundling, a babe exposed on Mt. Cithaeron, whom he himself had received from a shepherd of Laius. This shepherd is summoned and unwillingly tells the whole truth. All now is known. Jocasta, in horror of the situation, hangs herself, and Oedipus puts out his eyes that they may be dark forever " when naught to be seen is good." He begs Creon that he may be sent forth from the land. The play ends with the solemn utterance of the Chorus:

Ye citizens of Thebes, behold, 'tis Oedipus that passeth here,
Who read the riddle-word of Death, and mightiest stood of mortal men,
And Fortune loved him, and the folk that saw him turned and looked again.
Lo, he is fallen, and around great storms and the out-reaching sea!
Therefore, O Man, beware, and look toward the end of things that be,
The last of sights, the last of days; and no man's life account as gain
Ere the full tale be finished and the darkness find him without pain. — G. Murray.

The *Trachiniae* is a play wherein love is a powerful motivating element in the action. Deianira, wife of

Heracles, to regain the affections of her absent husband, who is enamoured of a captive maiden, Iole, innocently sends him a love gift, a robe. This garment is deadly, however, as it had been anointed with the poisonous blood of the Centaur Nessus, who had been slain by Heracles. Heracles, having put on the garment, dies in agony, while Deianira, in despair, slays herself.

In the *Philoctetes* the poet relates how Odysseus and Neoptolemus, the young son of Achilles, come to the desolate island of Lemnos to bring the hero and his bow and arrows, formerly the weapon of Heracles, to Troy. Ten years before, the Greeks had abandoned Philoctetes, as he had been bitten on the foot by a venomous snake, and the wound would not heal. Subsequently, when the Greeks learned that Troy could not be taken without Philoctetes and his weapon, the mission to Lemnos is sent. By a trick of the wily Odysseus, Neoptolemus gains possession of the bow, but later, moved by the despair of the hero, restores it. This development in the character of young Neoptolemus is of particular interest. The play is concluded by a device favored by Euripides — the intervention of the *deus ex machina*. The deified Heracles appears and commands Philoctetes to go to Troy.

The *Oedipus at Colonus* is the last play of Sophocles' long and happy life written when the tragedian was nearly ninety years of age. But the drama shows no sign of failing powers and is characterized by religious feeling and great poetic beauty. Particularly fine is the ode in praise of Colonus, which was the birthplace of the dramatist himself. Hither to Colonus, near Athens, the aged and blind Oedipus, an exile from Thebes, comes for refuge, led by his daughter Antigone. He is welcomed by Theseus, king of Athens, and protected from Creon of Thebes, who appears to take him back. Here, the sorely-tried hero at last finds eternal rest. Seen only by Theseus, he is miraculously translated to the world below.

To EURIPIDES (480–406 B.C.) fate has been kind, as the dramatist's works are known to us through nineteen extant plays. These are: *Alcestis, Medea, Hippolytus, Hecuba, Cyclops, Children of Heracles, Mad Heracles, Andromache, Suppliants, Trojan Women, Iphigenia among the Taurians, Ion, Electra, Helen, Phoenician Women, Orestes, Iphigenia at Aulis, Bacchantes,* and *Rhesus.* The story of only a few of the most noteworthy of these plays may be indicated here.

The *Alcestis* (438 B.C.) is a tale of a wife's devotion. The Fates have decreed that Admetus of Pherae in Thessaly may evade approaching death only on condition that he find a substitute. All refuse to assume the sacrifice until his wife consents. As her strength fails at the approach of Death, Heracles arrives. His host allows the hero to remain in ignorance of the situation. While jovially drinking, the demi-god learns the truth, and going to the tomb, wrestles with Death and restores Alcestis to her husband.

The *Medea* (431 B.C.) is perhaps the best known of the plays of Euripides. Medea, a barbarian princess from Colchis, has accompanied Jason to Greece when he returns with his Argonauts from the successful quest for the Golden Fleece. This success has been achieved only through Medea's assistance. At Corinth, Medea is cast aside by Jason, who contemplates the taking of a Greek wife, the daughter of the king of Corinth. Medea and her two boys are to be banished. The play relates the terrible revenge of the deserted and passionate Medea, who slays the intended bride and her father through the medium of a poisoned robe, and, to punish her recreant and selfish husband, kills her own children.

The *Iphigenia among the Taurians* has always been extremely popular. Iphigenia, daughter of Agamemnon, supposedly sacrificed at Aulis, so that the Greek fleet might have fair winds to sail to Troy, has been saved by Artemis and transported to the Crimea, the barbarian Tauric land. Here she is priestess of the temple, and her dread duty is to sacrifice strangers.

Hither, at Apollo's instigation and in quest of an ancient image of Artemis, come her brother, Orestes, pursued by the avenging Furies because of his matricide, and his faithful companion, Pylades. Orestes is about to be sacrificed, when sister and brother recognize each other and plan a successful escape.

The *Trojan Women* is a pathetic and moving presentation of tragic scenes following the fall of Troy. The recent revival of this war-time drama made a powerful impression upon minds and hearts poignantly aroused by the tragic realities of the Great War.

THE TRAGIC POETS

The three great Athenian tragedians cannnot be carelessly considered as a unit as if they typified a single school. Although they are all of Athens and of the fifth century B.C., and wrote for an Athenian audience and theater, they differ widely in thought, methods, aims, and achievement. AESCHYLUS, first in time, is first in creative genius, and loftiness of poetic powers. Of the tragedians he is the exemplar of the " grand style " or, as Longinus, the Greek literary critic designates it, " the sublime." His plays abound in sonorous Miltonic lines, in bold and original epithets and compound words, in striking figures of speech, and in solemn and inspired lyrics. His style is ever lofty and his verse dignified. To Homer he is greatly indebted. The characters in his drama are gods, demigods, or great heroes, and the world in which they move and act is not ours. In his thought he is conservative, and in his religious views orthodox. It is customarily asserted that Hellenism and Hebraism in their religious conceptions are poles apart. In general, this is true. Yet there is something of the old Hebraic element in the religious teachings of the Aeschylean dramas in their stern insistence on moral doctrines, such as " the sinner must pay the penalty," " he who transgresses against Heaven in word, in thought, or in

deed, will be brought low by divine will," " the sins of
the fathers shall be visited upon their children," and
" we learn through suffering." Of great influence and
power, and playing great rôles in the Aeschylean tragedies, are Moira, Necessity, Atê, and Nemesis. *Moira*
is Fate personified, an agency which in the beginning
was more powerful than the gods themselves. Even
Zeus, in the *Prometheus,* is thought of as being sub-
servient to Moira, although in the *Agamemnon* the conception has somewhat changed and Fate is an instrument in the hands of the Father of gods and men, or
rather, Fate and Zeus are identified. But Fate does
not work blindly nor is man its mere plaything; Fate
overwhelms the sinner. *Atê* is the personification of
sin, a blind obsession which pursues the sinner, takes
possession of his mind, and accomplishes his ruin. Over-
much prosperity may fill a man with overweening pride
and wanton insolence (*hybris*); *Nemesis,* the personification of divine retribution, then overtakes him and
humbles him. As a dramatist Aeschylus is a pioneer
and his plays are naturally simple in technique, and
plot and action are not highly developed. One thinks
of Aeschylus, first, perhaps, as a moral and religious
teacher, next as a great dramatic poet, and lastly, as
a playwright.

Than SOPHOCLES there is no more attractive figure in
ancient Athens. In the circumstances of his life he was
happy, in his relations with his fellow-men he was popular, and in his chosen life-work he was successful.
Sophocles is the embodiment of the Greek genius; he
is the personification of Greek good-taste and *sophrosyne,* or the golden mean in all things. His predecessor,
Aeschylus, had cleared the way. Sophocles, of gentler
mold, although of lesser originality, refined and im-
proved the dramatic art. As Cicero boasted he had
done with philosophy, so Sophocles brought tragedy
" down from the clouds," and made it of strong human
appeal. His characters, unlike those of Aeschylus, are
essentially human and arouse human sympathies, yet

idealism dominates them.   In delineation of character he marks a distinct advance upon Aeschylus.   Particularly in plot-construction is he a master; in this respect his *Oedipus Tyrannus* is the greatest of all Greek plays. His style is restrained, yet ever polished.   His iambic verse is perfect.   Poetic inspiration in his dramas, while not compelling as in Aeschylus, is never bombastic in its expression, is ever sustained, and is consistently maintained at a high level of excellence.   In the dialogues and the speeches of his plays he is rhetorical in the good sense and is never swept away into *bathos,* as is Euripides occasionally.   Prominent and of tremendous effect in his plays is the use of *tragic irony*.   This is in evidence when a hero, unaware of his real tragic situation, which is clear to the audience, utters words which he thinks refer to others but which, in reality, apply to himself.   A moving example of this effective dramatic device, this irony often called " Sophoclean," is found in the *Ajax*, when the hero thanks Athena for her favors, although it is she who has betrayed him. The most striking cases are in the *Oedipus Tyrannus*, especially where Oedipus imprecates curses upon the head of the murderer of Laius, and thereby unwittingly pronounces his own doom.

With religion Sophocles is not so much concerned as is Aeschylus.   A calm religious spirit, however, breathes through his plays and the unwritten laws of Heaven are supreme.   He who does them violence suffers divine chastisement.   In general, in his survey of the universe, to use the true and oft-quoted criticism of Matthew Arnold, " he saw life steadily and saw it whole."

The virtues of the Athenian genius are to be found in the tragedies of Sophocles: side by side we find simplicity and finish, directness and urbanity, frankness and reserve.   Over all and in all is beauty, Grecian beauty, difficult truly to define but conspicuous in Athenian art and literature at its best.   Sophocles is indeed a lovable figure to those who are privileged to know him and thereby enter into the spirit of ancient Athens.

If Aeschylus is to be regarded as a religious and moral teacher of great poetic and dramatic gifts, and Sophocles as a consummate dramatic artist of deeply religious convictions, EURIPIDES is to be characterized as a master of the theater. In his religious views he is often sceptical, as a poet he is uneven in performance, but as a writer of plays for a real audience he is seldom ineffective. In consequence, although during his lifetime he was far from winning the dramatic popularity of Aeschylus — of the nearly one hundred plays of Euripides only four received first prize — or the personal esteem given to Sophocles, after his death for some centuries his plays, and not those of his great predecessors, were constantly revived, annotated, and imitated. Aeschylus, with his old-time religious orthodoxy and grandeur of concept and language " needs interpreters for the many," as Pindar says of his own odes; Sophocles is the embodiment of the Attic genius of the Age of Pericles; Euripides, however, is an apostle of unrest and of a world in ferment and change. Passion, conflict, and strong emotion blaze up in his plays.

Roman tragedy as it has come down to us in the plays of Seneca is largely Euripides. The Euripidean influence on French drama through the medium of Seneca has been enormous. Today, for popular reading and presentation the dramas of Euripides are the Greek plays chosen. Why is this? Many reasons are apparent. In comparison with Aeschylus, the creative artist, and Sophocles, the idealist, Euripides is ever " modern," for he is theatrical in his technique as a playwright, and a realist in his thinking, handling, and presentation of dramatic material. There is much truth in the familiar saying of Sophocles, quoted by Aristotle: " I paint men as they should be, Euripides as they are."

Many of the plays of Euripides show his great ability to delineate character, as, for example, the

Medea; they reveal originality in construction of plot
and ingenuity of innovation in handling the old themes,
as in the *Iphigenia among the Taurians*. In poetic
merit his work is singularly uneven; lyric passages of
haunting beauty may alternate with banal speeches and
dialogue which is frigidly rhetorical. The influence of
his teachers, the physicist-philosopher Anaxagoras, and
the popular Sophists of the day, is seen in his writings.
For Euripides the myths, the stories of the gods, the
dogmas of old-time, even the gods themselves are no
longer credible and sacred and must be weighed in the
balance and even rejected. By him, conventions were
to be disregarded. As had been said, it was his choice
" to put new wine into old bottles," and this made him
anathema to conservatives, such as the comic poet
Aristophanes, but it endeared him to the younger generation, the disciples of the " new thought."

It is strange that Euripides should have been regarded through the centuries as a woman-hater — a
dramatist who so strongly championed woman's rights,
as in the *Medea,* and revealed so nobly a woman's self-
sacrifice, as in the *Alcestis*. This erroneous conception
of the tragedian is probably based on his own supposedly unhappy domestic life and on the fact that evil
women as well as noble are presented in his plays.

The virtues of Euripides are numerous, evident, and
have ever been admired. It is because of them that he
is the most popular of the Athenian tragedians. But
from his own day to the present time he has been
severely criticized for grievous faults and blemishes.
Some of these have been indicated and briefly discussed above. Aristophanes, in the *Clouds,* abuses the
dramatist for his ideas, supposedly heterodox, on religion, morality, and education; but in these views
Euripides is but representative of the changing ideas of
the times, the " new school " of thinking. Nor are we
perturbed by the charges of the comic poet that
Euripides is culpable in introducing mean characters
and trivial incidents into his plays, and that his inno-

vations in music and in meter are reprehensible. Aristophanes further alleges that Euripides' prologues are monotonous and mechanical, and Aristotle reprehends him for inconsistency, for faultiness in management of his subjects, and for his misuse of the *deus ex machina*.

To answer these numerous charges briefly we may say that Euripides was a master of the theater and knew his audience. The special prologues to his plays doubtless met with popular favor, as did the prologue common to the Elizabethan drama. The Euripidean prologues do not, as it has been frequently asserted, kill interest in the stories to follow. As Professor D. C. Stuart has shown, they do not tell the plot in detail, but serve to create suspense by foreshadowing possible dread happenings. In regard to Euripides' use of the *deus ex machina,* it may be said that this device of introducing a deity at a critical moment must have been extremely effective to an Athenian audience. Religiously, the epiphany, or envisagement of the god, was awe-inspiring in highest measure; theatrically, the effect must have been thrilling. Not through poverty of invention, it is certain, did Euripides employ this artifice; it was rather through his sure theatric instinct. In a late play, the *Philoctetes,* we see Sophocles paying Euripides the great compliment of imitation in this matter.

CHAPTER XIV

THE CHARACTERISTICS OF ATTIC TRAGEDY

NOWHERE is the genius of the Athenians more strikingly manifest than in the tragedies they wrote and produced. These dramas are permanent contributions to culture and of eternal interest because they are appealing as plays, they are great as literature, and they are true as an interpretation and criticism of life. In this chapter we shall consider some of the chief characteristics of Attic tragedy.

Extremely striking is the literary quality of all the extant dramas of the three great tragedians. The thought was ever clothed in suitable language, exemplifying Aristotle's definition when he says in the *Poetics* that "Tragedy is an imitation of an action that is serious, complete, and of a certain magnitude, in language embellished with each kind of artistic ornament." The Athenian drama was exclusively poetic drama. The verse form was employed throughout, the iambic trimeter for the dialogue and speeches of the actors, and free meters for the lyrics of the chorus. As is the case with the plays of Shakespeare, therefore, Greek tragedies may be read with enjoyment as literature, for they are noble as poetry.

It is not enough, however, that a play be expressed in beautiful language; it must be dramatic. The first essential of a drama is, that it shall interest, impress, and satisfy an audience in the theater and not that it shall please a reader in his study. Shelley's *Prometheus Unbound*, Swinburne's *Atalanta in Calydon*, and Matthew Arnold's *Merope* are fine poems, but poor plays. Granting that the tragedies of Athens are excellent poetry and that they possess literary artistry of style and symmetry of form, do they meet the inexorable test of the theater? This question may be truthfully and emphatically answered in the affirmative, but at the same time the answer demands elucidation.

One who tries to understand and interpret a play and to judge of its dramatic qualities and effectiveness must take into consideration several fundamental factors — the time and place of the production of the drama, why it was written by the playwright, the nature of his theater, and the character and sophistication of the audience before whom it was produced. A facetious reviewer of a recent book on the Greek theater remarked that the author had discussed at length various topics, but had remained silent on the most important subject of all, whether ancient Greek audiences were not really bored by ancient Greek plays. Now every student of ancient Greek life knows the eagerness, curiosity, and interest of the Greek audience, and understands what meaning, value, and influence Greek drama had for the people themselves. To the Athenians the plays as given during the festivals were at once entertainment, literature, moral and ethical instruction, and religious worship. Every community had its theater and the plays presented in these theaters were written for hearers and spectators and were not intended for readers, since a reading public in those days scarcely existed. Few of the contemporaries of the dramatists would read their dramas, but nearly all would hear and see them. And the plays produced were the best only, chosen in keen competition during the glorious days of the fifth century or revived in later times because of their proved excellence.

But do these plays interest a modern audience when they are presented today? Again it must be said by way of proviso that the conditions underlying the writing and the production of a Greek tragedy are very different from those obtaining today. The Greek drama was essentially religious in origin and always remained as the culmination of the celebration of a religious festival, whereas modern drama, originally religious, has become thoroughly secular. The Greek dramatist was regarded primarily as a teacher; the modern is first and foremost an entertainer. To the cultivated Athenians the plays were literature; in the strictly modern drama literary quality is more likely to be a handicap than a help and an esteemed virtue. But it may be emphatically said that Athenian trage- dies do greatly interest modern audiences when the play is judiciously chosen, sympathetically presented, intelligently acted, and the audience itself is cultivated. To be sure it cannot be expected that all the Greek plays, differing widely one from another as they do, and originating among a people living over twenty- three hundred years ago, amid conditions so different from the world of today should make equal appeal to modern taste and feeling. For example, the *Ajax* of Sophocles was a thrilling play to the Greek audience and held their interest to the very end because the question at issue, all important to Greek religious feel- ing, is this—Shall the dead hero receive religious burial or not? To us, however, it may seem that the high point of interest is reached in the middle of the play when Ajax slays himself. Again, a modern audience might not relish particularly the long prophetic recital in the *Prometheus* of Aeschylus where the tortured Titan describes to the wandering and persecuted Io her future peregrinations. It is possible that this detailed passage would seem to many in an audience today an impertinent interpolation, but to the Athenian auditors of the fifth century B.C. the geographical, ethnological, and mythological allusions in the recital were unques- tionably of engrossing interest. But the numerous and intelligent presentations in recent years of certain Greek plays have evoked genuine interest and admira- tion. The pathos of the *Trojan Women* of Euripides, unhappy victims of war, is profoundly moving; the scene in the *Iphigenia among the Taurians*, where a dramatic recognition at a critical moment saves Orestes from sacrifice by his sister's hand, still has power to arouse keen suspense; the *Iphigenia at Aulis* in many scenes is thoroughly modern; the *Electra* of Sophocles holds spell-bound an audience today; and the *Oedipus Tyrannus* of Sophocles, in its marvelous technical handling of a difficult plot, splendid delineation of character, and successful working out of all the essential dramatic values is, in the opinion of many competent and unprejudiced critics, the greatest play ever written.

The absence of the love element in most Greek plays tends to render them somewhat alien to modern taste. In perhaps nine-tenths of modern plays the motive of romantic love between the sexes is the very essence of their structure and being. While the motive of love is often found in one form or another in Greek New Comedy, it is rare in Athenian tragedy. It is true that in the *Antigone* of Sophocles the love of the affianced pair, Antigone and Haemon, intensifies the pathos of the tragic dénouement, yet the love element is not stressed as it would be in a modern play. The Greek dramatist allows nothing to distract the attention from the great issue of the play, the conflict between the eternal and wise laws of Heaven, venerated and obeyed by the heroine, and the foolish edicts of the State as promulgated by the stubborn and short-sighted Creon. The *Trachinian Women* of Sophocles is remarkable for the revelation in many ways of the tender affection of Deianira for her absent husband, Heracles, whose doom she innocently brings to pass by the gift of the fatal love-token. Yet it is the fortunes of the great hero that are all important in the play. Love, too, plays a part in the life and fate of characters in the *Hippolytus, Medea,* and *Alcestis* of Euripides, but in general Greek tragedy is based on other themes.

Greek and modern tragedies differ, too, in this respect that the Athenian dramatists were limited by tradition and by conservative religious feeling to the portrayal of old stories. Homer and the Cyclic poets,

Hesiod, and the " epic-lyric " poet Stesichorus furnish most of the plots. Phrynichus had attempted to break away from this custom by a tragedy based on the capture of the Ionian city Miletus by the Persians in 494 B.C. But the Athenian people, distressed by witnessing this presentation of the sorrows of an allied and related people, and reminded, doubtless, of their own derelictions, fined the dramatist one thousand drachmas and forbade further performances of that play. Aeschylus wrote of a contemporary event in his *Persians*, but this gave no offense to his fellow-citizens as the play relates the downfall of the hated enemy and the Athenian victory at Salamis. These examples, however, were not generally followed and the cycles of mythical tales gathered about Troy, Thebes, and Argos were the inexhaustible quarry from which all three of the great tragedians obtained their material. The same story might be used by all three playwrights. For example, all three dramatists base tragedies on the unhappy plight of Electra. Yet this use of old and familiar material was not a handicap to them and their art. Variations in details and masterly handling of character and situation enabled them to avoid monotony and sustain dramatic interest. The audience could not hear too often the familiar, but ever new, stories. As we know so well from Shakespeare, familiarity does not detract from our enjoyment of his plays. On the contrary familiarity may enhance our pleasure, provided that the play is genuinely great in the true dramatic qualities, such as construction of plot, delineation of character, inevitability of consequence, and the arousing of suspense.

To some modern readers of the Greek drama the presence and participation of the Chorus is a stumbling-block to full appreciation. The introduction of choral lyrics at frequent intervals seems to impede the swift action of the play and to cause cooling of interest in the unfolding of the story. It must, however, be remembered that Greek tragedy was merely a development of the dithyramb, the Doric choral lyric sung and danced by a chorus of fifty in honor of Dionysus. The song and dance, of religious origin and meaning, was the very essence of the play. To a Greek, tragedy would have been unthinkable without the singing, dancing, and interpretation of the Chorus. While it is true that the history of Greek tragedy shows a gradual decline in the participation and the importance of the Chorus as an active and indispensable factor, from our earliest extant play, the *Suppliants* of Aeschylus — a drama mostly lyric with the Chorus the chief actor — to the later plays of Euripides — where the choral element is comparatively insignificant so far as dramatic action is concerned — yet religious feeling and conservatism forbade its total omission even though plot, action, and characters became gradually paramount. To the Athenian audience the Chorus was felt to be both actor and audience. In the early plays, as in those of Aeschylus, the songs of the chorus actually served to further the plot; excise the lyrics and the action would be scarcely intelligible, as in the *Agamemnon*. Through the *coryphaeus,* or leader, the Chorus might, and did, participate in the dialogue. Always an interested spectator, the Chorus served not merely as a sympathetic background for the action, but expressed, or actually *created,* the mood at any given moment of the audience. The choral lyrics eased the emotional shock at the moment of the *peripety* (the reversal of fortune) or gave voice to the general exultation at the announcement of glad news. Suspense might be heightened by the expression of the Chorus' fears and forebodings. Lyric prayers for help and songs of thanksgiving are frequent. Especially important is the Chorus in Aeschylus which he used as the instrument of profound religious expression. As has been said, the Greek tragedian was primarily a moral teacher; the Chorus was a powerful medium for religious instruction.

In general, when the chief character is a woman, the

Chorus is composed of women, as, for example, in the *Iphigenia among the Taurians,* whereas a Chorus of men usually serves as support for a male protagonist. Yet there are noteworthy exceptions whereby the effect of the play is greatly enhanced, e.g., the rugged Prometheus, surrounded by the gentle maidens, the daughters of Oceanus, and Antigone, in striking isolation, with a background of stern Theban elders.

Modern critics of the Chorus in the Greek drama, and apologists also, fail lamentably to do justice to their theme insofar as they forget that it was a highly important function of the Chorus to enhance the dramatic picture. One of the great elements in dramatic art is *spectacle,* and this was provided richly by the Chorus. Recall, for instance, the opening scene of the *Eumenides,* where the Chorus of grim Furies, who surround their exhausted quarry, the unhappy Orestes, lie sleeping. Greek tragedy is replete with these stage-pictures which must have been always theatrically effective and frequently beautiful. In the Greek open-air theater the lighting naturally could not be changed, and a change of scene in tragedy was rare. But by way of compensation for the lack of lighting and of elaborate scenery — theatrical accessories so dear to the modern theater-goer — the costumed chorus gave pleasure to the eye. The modern *reader* of the plays fails to realize the dramatic beauty and impressive dignity of Greek tragedy. The esthetic value and the emotional effect of a Greek play as a picture is largely lost to us, unless we can, in imagination, conjure forth the accompanying elements of the dramatic representation — the occasion itself of the production as part of the sacred annual festival, the religious atmosphere, the music of the flute, the voices of the singers, and the evolutions and grouping of the dancers. The spectators, seated on the slope of a hillside in the warmth of a spring sun, surrounded by a beautiful landscape, watched with profound and changing emotions the unfolding of the drama.

Attempts have been made to compare the Greek tragedies with modern opera, as, for example, the music-dramas of Richard Wagner. It is true that there are resemblances, and the results of these studies are valuable. Yet in modern opera the musical element is paramount, whereas this was not the case in the Greek drama. The Wagnerian orchestra is a rich and powerful instrument frequently dominating lyric recitation and dramatic action. In the Greek plays only the slender notes of a single flute accentuated the rhythm of the dancers' steps and evolutions and provided lyric accompaniment for the clear enunciation of the odes sung in unison, songs which, unlike modern operatic and choral singing, could be completely understood by all in the audience.

It is interesting to observe that the Greeks drew a sharp distinction in dramatic composition between tragedy and comedy. No Athenian writer of tragedies wrote comedies and no comedian essayed tragedy although the versatile Ion of Chios is said to have been an exception. How different this is from modern drama! Shakespeare, for example, was a master in both provinces, and united the types, as, for example, in *Measure for Measure*, technically a comedy, yet generally serious in tone. There is to be seen, however, a growing tendency in Greek tragedy to erase the sharp dividing line between tragedy and comedy. Even in Aeschylus and Sophocles there are occasional flashes of humor and comic touches in the scenes in which rustic shepherds or messengers appear, while Euripides, in such plays as the *Iphigenia among the Taurians* and the *Alcestis*, which are not tragedies in the Shakespearian sense, as they have scenes almost comic, and happy endings, paved the way for Greek New Comedy. These Euripidean tragi-comedies, however, are real tragedies in the Aristotelian sense, and illustrate his definition that " a tragedy is an artistic imitation of an action that is serious, complete in itself, and of an adequate magnitude." These plays, morever, have throughout the potentialities of tragedy according to the modern definition of the term.

It seems appropriate at this point to consider certain pronouncements of modern criticism that have as their aim a sharp and convenient differentiation of Greek and modern tragedy. First, the dictum that the Greek drama is one of inaction, the modern of action. There is enough of truth in this categorical statement to make its enunciation intelligible. The *Prometheus Bound* of Aeschylus, for example, taken as a single play — although it should not be forgotten that the *Prometheus* is doubtless only one of three plays, or acts, in a trilogy — has little plot and action: it consists largely of a masterly and poetic portrayal of the character of the Titan rebel as he rages against what he considers to be his cruel, humiliating, and undeserved punishment at the hands of an ungrateful Zeus. Now the *Prometheus* would probably not interest greatly a modern audience accustomed and eager for action, more action, and still more action. Yet is there not splendid plot and an abundance of action with consequent " pity and fear " in such plays as *Oedipus Tyrannus* and *Antigone* of Sophocles, and in the *Medea* and *Iphigenia among the Taurians* of Euripides? A consideration of Greek tragedy as a whole will show that too much emphasis has been placed on the supposed absence of action therein. The generalization, superficially attractive and true, needs strong qualification.

In an excellent lecture on Greek tragedy Professor J. R. Wheeler says: " Greek drama is a drama of ideas; the modern of character. Call to mind the characters of Antigone, Orestes, and Oedipus and we think of their tragic situations in which they found themselves and their woeful circumstances; call Hamlet to mind, and his tragedy lies within his own nature." Is this wholly true? By no means, as it seems to me, although the whole tendency of Greek literature is towards simplicity and objective handling and direct description of subjects, whereas the modern taste is inclined to subjective analysis and detailed and psychological introspection. But Antigone as portrayed by Sophocles stands forth as a vivid and vigorous personality; she is no mere victim, helpless and colorless, caught in the meshes of an inexorable net, but a forceful character, fighting for the right as she sees it, making her own decision as to action and willing to abide by the consequences. Orestes, as depicted in Sophocles' *Electra,* abetted by his sister, in contrast to Hamlet, carries through his plan to avenge his father and slays the murderers. If one familiar with the Sophoclean play calls to mind Oedipus, he thinks not merely of the tragic situation of the hero, but of his kindly although impetuous nature and his noble mind but over-hasty conclusions and utterance. One thinks of him at the beginning of the play as the wise and paternal ruler; then, in the scenes with Tiresias and Creon, as haughty, suspicious, and wrathful; finally, one recalls his horror, grief, and resignation at the end.

It is true that Hamlet furnishes a character study such as no personage of Greek — or any other — tragedy presents, yet, as one recalls Medea, Jason, Prometheus, and Deianira, circumstances do not stand forth more prominently than the motivation of their acts and the inner meaning and outward expression of their personal characters.

The element of Fate, called by many names, is important alike in ancient and modern drama. It is popularly thought that Fate is the be-all and end-all of Attic tragedy. One might assert, doubtless with little fear of contradiction, that the characters in the Greek drama are but helpless puppets, themselves and their acts and circumstances completely predestined. This current misconception of the nature of the Greek drama accounts in a measure for the dogmatic and unqualified assertion that Greek tragedy is a drama of ideas, of situations, and of woeful circumstances, and that it is quite lacking in character portrayal.

In this general conception of Fate as a powerful factor in the Greek drama there is, to be sure, much truth. Particularly is this the case in Aeschylus, in whose plays *Moira* (Fate) is at times all powerful; indeed, in the *Prometheus*, Fate is conceived as being superior to Zeus himself. But especially in Sophocles and Euripides, what men do themselves, and of themselves, is of the greatest influence upon the outcome. The element of human volition, of character swayed by emotion, and the part they play in the Greek drama must not be ignored, although it is not always easy to separate the twisted strands of apparently foreordained happenings from those calamities which are the result of human weakness, frailty, or error. Here we have Fate and character largely the same thing, although called by different names.

What is the connection, or relation, between modern and ancient tragedy? Some rashly say there is none. Is there a close tie, whether of descent or of kindred aims and characteristics? While direct and pure descent from the Greek drama is not easily proved in all respects for modern tragedy with its religious origins, yet the Elizabethan drama was strongly influenced through the study of Greek tragedy by the playwrights of that period. Profound, indeed, has been the influence of the plays of the Roman tragedian Seneca upon the modern drama, and Seneca, without Euripides, is unthinkable. Ibsen, for example, has been justly called the modern Euripides. Truly, to conceive of the modern drama without the works of the Greek theater is impossible.

But comparisons, often odious, are generally difficult and inaccurate. All Greek tragedies are by no means of one pattern. It is impossible to make a safe and unqualified generalization with respect to a dramatic literature which includes the *Suppliants* of Aeschylus and the *Medea* of Euripides. And modern plays, whether

Shakespearian or of more recent date, by no means follow one set form. But common to all great tragedies are certain powerful, omnipresent, and eternal elements. These are the clash of wills, the unfolding of an inevitable sequence of cause and effect, the delineation and development of character, the portrayal of a sympathetic personality, the arousing and holding of suspense, the appeal to the emotions, and the revelation of good and evil — not misery, for, as Aristotle says, " Tragedy is a drama or representation of goodness and nobility, not of misery." And this revelation and interpretation of human life with its strivings, victories, and defeats must, in a play which may properly be called *classic,*—i.e., a play which will be of universal and eternal appeal, as the drama of a Shakespeare or of a Sophocles, be presented with dignity and with power, in suitable form and in beautiful language and with a logical sequence of events. Above all such a play, to be successful, must be genuinely dramatic, with a potent appeal to the minds and hearts of the audience.

CHAPTER XV

ATHENIAN COMEDY

COMEDY flourished by the side of tragedy, although it reached its full development somewhat later than the tragic art. The City Dionysia as an official festival had been instituted by Pisistratus with contests in tragedy, whereas comedy was not officially supervised in Athens until 486 B.C. at the City Dionysia, and about 442 B.C. at the Lenaea.

As was the case with tragedy, comedy originated among the Dorians and in connection with the worship of the god Dionysus. The germ of comedy seems to be found in the revels of rustic festivals when the god of wine and fertility was worshipped by a joyous band of dancers in fantastic costume, singing impromptu wanton songs to the accompaniment of the flute, and often wearing the *phallus* or sign of fertility. Such a revel was called a *comus;* the Greek word *cōmōdos* means revel-singer. Old Attic comedy seems to have developed from this primitive comus when actors were added to the chorus, and when, according to literary tradition, Epicharmus of Sicily clothed the primitive ceremony in literary dress and gave it plot.

The structure of Old Comedy is similar to that of tragedy, but with certain additional features. As in tragedy, there is the introductory part of the play, the prologue which preceded the entrance song (*parodus*) of the chorus, and there are episodes alternating with choral lyrics. Peculiar to comedy, however, are the *agon,* and the *parabasis.* The agon is a " dramatized debate " — a scene in which two actors, each aided by a semi-chorus (comedy had a chorus of twenty-four),

212

engaged in a heated verbal contest sometimes accompanied by blows. The parabasis, or coming forward by the chorus, was a lyric of complicated structure, following a set metrical form, in which the chorus as the mouthpiece of the poet, directly addressed the audience.

The course of Greek comedy can be divided into three periods: Old Comedy to *ca.* 390 B.C.; Middle Comedy, *ca.* 390–330 B.C., and New Comedy, after 330 B.C. The Old Comedy, represented by Aristophanes, and New Comedy, exemplified by Menander, are sharply differentiated in their nature and purpose; the Middle is a period of transition and no plays of this class are extant.

Athenian OLD COMEDY is characterized by personal and political satire and abuse. It enjoyed the greatest license of speech and boldly and mercilessly attacked prominent individuals and social and political tendencies of the day. Its chief aim, however, was to amuse and in this it admirably succeeded. But always with the comical or farcical element went a serious purpose, as the comic poet wished to correct abuses, improve society, or discredit individuals. Present in Old Comedy are ribaldry of speech and frank indecency, and at times the obscenity which had characterized the original Dionysiac revel.

Comedy, unlike tragedy, was not limited as to subjects. The latter was largely restricted to stories taken from mythology, whereas comedy drew freely from contemporary life and society, politics, religion, and education. Animal life might enter into its nature and the chorus was sometimes dressed to represent birds, wasps, fishes, goats, etc.

Our sole representative of the Old Comedy is Aristophanes (445–385 B.C.), a comic poet of great and imaginative powers, of keen wit, and remarkable lyric gifts. His eleven extant comedies are *Acharnians, Knights, Clouds, Wasps, Peace, Birds, Lysistrata, Thesmophoriazusae, Frogs, Ecclesiazusae* and *Plutus.*

The activity of Aristophanes was largely contemporaneous with the course of the long Peloponnesian War
(431–403 B.C.) and condemnation of this war and long-
ing for peace motivated the *Acharnians, Knights, Peace*
and *Lysistrata*. The *Wasps* satirizes the Athenian
mania for litigation. In the *Birds,* an exceedingly witty
and lyrical play, expression is given to disgust of certain undesirable features of Athenian law and government and there is a description of the founding of an
ideal city-state, a Utopia of the Birds, *Cloud-Cuckoo-
Town*. Best known of the Aristophanic comedies are
the *Clouds* and the *Frogs*. In the *Clouds* the dramatist
discredits the teaching, influence and character of
Socrates, who is unjustly but cleverly identified with
the dishonest sophists or charlatan teachers of the day.
This extremely entertaining play, in which the victim
Socrates has the leading rôle, undoubtedly did much to
arouse local prejudice against the noble philosopher,
who later suffered martyrdom.

The *Frogs* is a very diverting play, containing a
wealth of wit and humor. In it there is much to inspire serious thought. Aristophanes had a three-fold
purpose in writing it: First, he wished to lampoon
Euripides, whom he often attacked in his comedies
as a bad poet, a dangerous playwright, and an evil
influence; secondly, he was eager to restore and re-
habilitate the Eleusinian Mysteries which had been
somewhat neglected during the latter and critical years
of the Peloponnesian War; thirdly, he urged that there
must be political harmony and general amnesty if
Athens was to be saved.

The plays of Aristophanes are not, and cannot be,
popular at the present day with readers or an audience
who do not possess a fairly intimate knowledge of
Athenian civilization, because of the local and personal
allusions in which they abound. Satisfactorily to trans-
late them for readers ignorant of Greek is well-nigh
impossible, as the dramas bristle with coined expres-
sions, plays on words, and references which are mean-

ingless without explanation. But these comedies are
the works of a genius of a high order; they are clever
in conception and striking and successful in dramatic
execution. As documents throwing light on Athenian
society they are of great value when interpreted with
caution and judgment.

The NEW COMEDY was a drama of very different
type. The abuse, the personalities, the moral teaching,
and the obscenity of the school of Aristophanes have
disappeared and a comedy of manners has taken its
place. To this transition the plays of Euripides with
their emphasis on human relations doubtless contributed much. Changed social and political conditions
in Athens are likewise responsible. Human nature, its
follies and weaknesses, are reflected in this mirror of
life (*speculum vitae*). Certain types of characters are
generally present: the credulous old father, the extravagant and somewhat undisciplined son, the fawn-
ing parasite, and the shrewd slave. Love is an important theme in the New Comedy. It is sometimes
portrayed in its lower aspects, often in its nobler manifestations, but love-scenes are seldom presented before
the audience. The importance of the chorus dwindled
and it was retained merely to entertain the audience between the scenes with song and dance. The great representative of the New Comedy is Menander (342–
291 B.C.), a playwright of great fame. Despite his
popularity and dramatic fecundity no complete comedy
of his has come down to us. Until recent years we
knew his drama only through the Latin adaptations of
his works, namely the *Eunuch, Adelphi, Self-Tor-
mentor*, and *Andria* of Terence and the *Poenulus,
Bacchides*, and *Stichus* of Plautus. In 1905, papyrus
manuscripts were found in Egypt which contained
large portions of four comedies, the *Girl with the Shorn
Locks, Hero, Samian Girl*, and *Arbitrants.* While these
plays, as we have them, by no means justify the extravagant praise of Menander by some ancient critics,

as, for example, Dio Chrysostom and Plutarch, who actually preferred Menander to Aristophanes, yet they reveal a skilful dramatist, who is particularly successful in his portrayal of character. And, as Professor Capps well says, " the literatures of Rome and modern Europe bear witness to the qualities of universality and permanence in the New Comedy of Athens and of its greatest representative, Menander."

CHAPTER XVI

PHILOSOPHY

"The history of Greek Philosophy is, in fact, the history of
our own spiritual past, and it is impossible to understand the
present without taking it into account." — J. BURNET.

"There may be greater philosophical conceptions than these
the Greeks have left us, but I know not where they are unless
they are in the future." — F. J. E. WOODBRIDGE.

AMONG the many signal achievements of the
genius of the Greeks, their contribution to
human thought in the realm of philosophy is
one of the greatest. Unlike the peoples by whom they
were surrounded the Greeks had intense intellectual
curiosity, a thirst for knowledge, and a desire for truth
for truth's sake. Tradition and dogma, it is true, were
their inheritance from primitive times, as is the case
with all peoples, but the Greeks were saved from the
blight of superstition and from intellectual servitude
by the originality and the fearlessness of their minds
and by the nature of their religion. Unlike the code of
the Hebrews, the Greeks had no sacrosanct laws to dis-
courage, or to prohibit altogether, independent thought
and judgment. There was no tribal God, conceived as
omnipotent, whose word was absolute law. No hier-
archical or ecclesiastical dictation permanently banned
original inquiry. On the contrary, the gods were
of human origin, although of greater than human power
and influence. Goodness, justice, and virtue were
to be sought as things of excellence in themselves
and not as mere accompanying attributes of a personal
deity to be attained through unquestioning obedience.

In the first place it must be understood that the term
philosophia did not at first have for the Greeks its

modern metaphysical connotation. It meant simply " the occupation of the *philosophos* " and a *philosophos* was " he to whom wisdom is dear "; so Pythagoras, who first used the word, called himself. A little later the term meant " a learned man " or " one of liberal education." Not until Plato did the word come to have its peculiar significance of " one who speculates on the nature of things." Aristotle was subsequently called " the philosopher " in this more technical sense.

In the course of Greek philosophic thought the first speculation of the earliest thinkers dealt largely with the origin and nature of the physical universe. This school of inquirers is called the *Pre-Socratics* (the predecessors of Socrates). Somewhat later, questions relating to knowledge and conduct, ethics or human relations, and ideas and ideals, engaged the attention of Socrates and Plato and, to a certain extent, of Aristotle. In the schools of thought following Aristotle the Post-Aristotelians, like Socrates, were concerned with ethical problems, but more from the viewpoint of the person and the emotions. Thus we have Greek philosophy successively engaged in the study of physical science, practical life and ethics, and religion.

For convenience of study the field of Greek philosophy may be divided into the three great divisions indicated above: I. The Pre-Socratics; II. Socrates, Plato, and Aristotle; III. The Post-Aristotelians.

I. THE PRE-SOCRATICS

It must be confessed at the outset that it is extremely difficult, if not impossible, to gain a thoroughly intelligent comprehension of early Greek philosophy (the Pre-Socratics) because of the very fragmentary nature of the extant ancient Greek writings bearing on the subject. The written records are extremely scanty and consist largely of meager excerpts handed down in the form of quotations. It is, therefore, and always will be, a matter of dispute as to the exact meaning of the doctrines and hypotheses which were formulated and maintained by these early thinkers.

It is sometimes said that Greek philosophy begins in the cosmogonies and theogonies of Homer and Hesiod. This is true only if we understand the term philosophy in its broadest significance so that it includes cosmogony, mythology, and scientific speculation. The germs of more speculative thinking are seen in the sayings attributed to the Seven Wise Men who were legislators and rulers throughout the Greek world — Thales, Solon, Periander, Cleobulus, Chilon, Bias, and Pittacus. With the exception of Thales, these were men of practical wisdom merely: they were *sophoi,* not *philosophoi.* Two famous sayings are " Know Thyself " and " Nothing to Excess," the former attributed to Solon, the Athenian statesman, and the latter to Chilon, a Spartan ephor of the sixth century B.C.

It was in Ionia, in Asia Minor, that Greek philosophy had its real beginnings.

A. The Ionic School. The subject which concerned the Ionian thinkers was the nature of the world, or, rather, that " something out of which everything in Nature grows and is made." Three thinkers of Miletus, who belong to the sixth century B.C., attempted to answer this question: Thales, who said it was *Water;* Anaximander, who declared it was the *Indefinite*—i.e., an original substance, " a limitless something," out of which by separation all things have their origin — and Anaximenes, who made it *Air.* It is difficult indeed to comprehend just what these thinkers meant by these explanations. Thales apparently wrote nothing. Anaximander, it is true, wrote a book, perhaps the first Greek book in prose, but it has perished, as has Anaximenes' prose work. The *Indefinite* of Anaximander we should call perhaps the ether. It is that illimitable substance, that original something which occupies all space; out of this Anaximander believed that all things originate. The *Air,* or rather vital *breath* of Anaximenes produced, as he thought, all things by rarefaction and condensation. As regards the world itself, we are told that Thales believed the earth to float on the water; Anaximenes thought it was flat and that it floated upon the air, as did also the heavenly bodies; Anaximander, however, was of opinion that " the earth does not rest on anything, but swings free in space, being, in shape, a short cylinder." Modern evolutionists should note the striking conjecture of Anaximander that man has developed from an aquatic animal protected by a covering.

In the latter part of the sixth century B.C. there arose in the western world two schools of thought founded by Greeks who came from Asia Minor — Pythagoras of Samos, and Xenophanes of Colophon.

B. The Pythagoreans. The school of Pythagoras, originally from Samos, was located at Croton in Southern Italy, and was a society or sect the members of which concerned themselves with religious and political as well as philosophical questions. Pythagoras left no writings, but the fame and influence of his school endured for centuries and references in literature to the beliefs and practices of the brotherhood are numerous. From these statements we learn that Pythagoras, who was revered by his followers and whose word was law (*ipse dixit*), held that *number* is immanent in all things and is not a mere abstraction, and that the square is the symbol of perfection. The doctrine of transmigration of souls or rebirth (metempsychosis), a belief of the Orphics, was taught by Pythagoras and, in addition, his disciples followed certain Rules of Life and Conduct. These rules prescribed a strict regimen as to diet, beans, for example, being eschewed, because, as was said by some, they contain the souls of the dead! Thus Horace (*Satires* II. 6.63) humorously speaks of beans as the kinsmen of Pythagoras (*faba Pythagorae cognata*). The philosophy of Pythagoras was concerned with religion, practical life and conduct, and with science. In fact, certain discoveries in arithmetic, geometry, and acoustics are attributed to the master. Aristotle, too, credits the Pythagoreans with a table of opposites, or antitheses, such as the Odd and the Even; the One and the Many; the Good and the Bad, etc. Antitheses, adapted and taught as a stylistic device by the Sicilian rhetoricians through Gorgias, became fashionable in Greek literary composition and are familiar and effective features of the style of the orator Antiphon and the historian Thucydides.

C. The Eleatics. Xenophanes of Colophon is a picturesque figure and occupies a place among both the thinkers and the elegiac poets of Greece. For sixty-seven years, as he tells us in an extant fragment of a poem which he wrote at the age of ninety-two, he wandered about Greece as a minstrel. Finally, he is reputed to have founded a school at Elea, a city in southern Italy, where he taught and wrote.

The independence of the views of Xenophanes is remarkable, and it is as a reformer and a protestant of an early day that he arrests our attention. The excessive adulation and material rewards given to professional athletes he sternly reprehended, since brain and intellectual virtue, he asserted, should be more highly esteemed than brawn. Moderation, temperance, and good behavior in human society and relations he preached. Current religious views he strove to combat. Pantheism he denied, since " there is but one God, the greatest among gods and men, not like mortals in body or in mind and He, with His whole being, sees and thinks and hears." Xenophanes anticipated Plato in censuring the poets who represent the gods as sinful, saying, " Homer and Hesiod have ascribed to the gods all things that are a shame and a disgrace among mortals, e.g., theft, adultery, and deceit." Anthropomorphism, or the common belief that the gods are human in form and appearance, especially aroused his ire. Men merely make gods with their own image: " If oxen and lions had hands wherewith to portray their gods in art, they would give to them the bodies of oxen and lions." The fearless independence of these views maintained in the sixth century B.C. is remarkable.

Parmenides of Elea was a hearer of Xenophanes and of far greater originality as a thinker. He wrote a work on Nature, in hexameter verse, of which some lines are preserved. In this treatise he denied the possibility of change as expounded by his predecessors and maintained that Being alone exists. Whatever is, is, and can not have arisen from nothing. Being is immovable, indivisible, continuous, and finite. Other prominent Eleatics were Zeno and Melissus.

D. Physicists of the Fifth Century B.C. Heraclitus of Ephesus (early fifth century B.C.) was picturesquely designated by ancient writers as " the weeping philosopher " because of the supposed sadness of his thought, and " the Dark " because of the obscurity of his utterances. The two chief doctrines associated with his name are that " All things are in a State of Flux," nothing being fixed, the elements freely changing from one to another, and that " Fire is the primal Element." Some of his striking sayings as revealed by the scanty fragments are: " Much learning does not teach men to think "; " You cannot step twice into the same river "; " War is the father of all things." Of interest in Heraclitus' thought is his idea of the soul, which to him was real, not a wraith, although " You cannot discover the boundaries of the soul; so deep it is." As fire is the purest element, so the soul when most perfect has most fire.

Of the Pre-Socratics it remains for us to consider briefly Empedocles, Anaxagoras, and the Atomists, Leucippus and Democritus, all of the fifth century B.C.

The fame of Empedocles, of Akragas (Agrigentum) in Sicily, has been greatly enhanced by the praise awarded him by the great Roman philosophical poet

Lucretius (I. 716ff) and through the poem, *Emped-ocles on Aetna,* of Matthew Arnold. Empedocles, a person of versatile genius, was distinguished for his achievements not only in philosophy, but in politics, medicine, science, mysticism, and poetry. Numerous fragments of his bold verses *On Nature* survive, "verses of his godlike genius." Empedocles won great favor as a statesman with his fellow-citizens by his democratic measures, while his cures in medicine gave him the reputation of a worker of miracles. In philosophical speculation he postulated four immutable elements or roots, fire, water, earth and air, and explained change as due to a combination or mixture of these four. It is to be observed that Empedocles thus added earth to the water of Thales, the fire of Heraclitus, and the air of Anaximenes. A further important contribution to physical speculation was made by Empedocles when he essayed to assign a moving or motivating cause to account for the relation of the elements to one another, since he conceived of the four elements as originally gathered together in a sphere which he asserted was maintained by love (attraction) and separable by hate (repulsion).

In his religious views Empedocles held the beliefs of Pythagoras and the Orphics, for he believed in reincarnation and asserted that he could recall the various forms of his previous existences. A story popular in antiquity, but unworthy of credence, related that Empedocles committed suicide by throwing himself down the crater of Aetna.

Anaxagoras of Clazomenae, a city of Ionia, early went to Athens where he lived and taught for many years. As a popular teacher his influence upon the younger generation was great, in particular, upon Euripides. He was compelled finally to leave Athens ostensibly on the charge of atheism, although it is probable that his intimate friendship with Pericles had exposed him to attack from the statesman's enemies.

Anaxagoras was greatly interested in astronomy and

physics.   Matter, the sum of which can neither be increased nor diminished, he believed to be composed of
an infinite number of particles or seeds; he held, too,
that these extremely minute particles, each having its
own qualities, can be divided.   A thing has individual
character according as certain corresponding seeds pre-
dominate.   Order or arrangement is produced in the
relation of these particles to one another, originally
indiscriminately mixed, by *Mind* or *Reason* (*Nous*),
which is the source of motion and of knowledge, and
Mind alone is pure, infinite, and not mixed with anything.   An object into which Mind has entered is animate.   Anaxagoras was highly praised by Plato and
Aristotle in that he introduced Reason as an intelligent
moving cause, but they censure him for regarding it
as too much in the light of a mechanical and material
agent.

   To the modern world and to modern science the
doctrines of the Atomists are of surpassing interest.
The author of the Atomic Theory was Leucippus of
Abdera, of whose life we know little.   The views of
Leucippus were expanded and taught by Democritus,
also of Abdera, who conceived the doctrine that there
exist the *Full* and the *Empty,* or *Atoms* and the *Void.*
The Void is the infinite space or vacuum in which the
atoms are constantly moving and striking upon one
another.   Thus a vortex or rotary whirl is caused, and,
as like atoms come together and hold together, bodies
and even worlds are formed.   The atoms, very fine
and infinite in number, are thought of as hard, permanent, and indivisible and as differing in size and shape.
If the atoms are close together the body is hard, otherwise it is soft.   It will be seen that the atomic theory
reconciles the opposing views of Parmenides and
Heraclitus, since it combines the idea of the eternity
of reality with the belief in perpetual change.   To
Greek religious feeling, however, it did violence in that
the doctrine of atomism is essentially materialistic
and mechanical.   Empedocles had thought of Love

and Hate, Anaxagoras of Reason, as directing agents, but Democritus considered the universe to be accidental and not produced by design, as it was the result of the descent of atoms through space and of their fortuitous association.

The Atomic Theory of Leucippus and Democritus ranks with the greatest discoveries of antiquity in our estimation, but it met with slight favor in the fifth and fourth centuries B.C. It remained for Epicurus to adopt it to support his views antagonistic to current theology, and in the great didactic Roman poem, the *De Rerum Natura* of Lucretius, we have its lengthy exposition.

Our study thus far of early Greek philosophical thought shows us that the chief concern was with the origin and nature of the universe. The majority of the Pre-Socratic thinkers, in fact, were keenly interested in the physical sciences and in mathematics; their fame, in part, rests on their attainments in these fields. Thales, for example, was a mathematician and astronomer and predicted, we are told, an eclipse of the sun. Anaximander created geographical science and drew the first map of the world. To Pythagoras tradition attributes various important discoveries in arithmetic, geometry, and acoustics. Empedocles was physician as well as philosopher and Anaxagoras was deeply concerned with physics and astronomy. Furthermore, all these men were largely cosmologists, although Xenophanes and Pythagoras were thinkers and teachers more in the field of religion and conduct and the maxims " Know thyself " and " Nothing to excess " of the wise men were familiar precepts.

II. Socrates, Plato, and Aristotle

In our sketch of Greek philosophic thought thus far we are struck by the fact that no Athenian appears in the list of these early inquirers. To be sure, the flower of the Athenian genius did not come to full bloom until after the Persian Wars. But the fact remains that Athens produced only two great native philosophers, Socrates and Plato — Aristotle was born at Stagira of a Thracian mother. Further, these thinkers were not interested in cosmology or in physical science, but in humanism. The subjects which concerned Socrates and Plato are human conduct and relations, society, education, and politics. And these same subjects dominated even the thought of Aristotle, catholic scientist as he was.

It was the Sophists who were chiefly responsible for giving this direction to Athenian thought. Although these thinkers and teachers are more fully discussed in connection with education, yet a few words should be devoted to them here.

The discordant views of the early thinkers relative to cosmogony and to the nature of things in general inevitably invited scepticism and encouraged disbelief in the possibility of the attainment of truth. The pronouncement of Protagoras that " Man is the measure of all things," therefore, met with eager welcome and Socrates and Sophists alike turned to the study of humanism.

The term Sophist was originally a title of respect, applied, for example, to the Seven Sages, but it gradually acquired an invidious sense because of the vain pretensions, the moral insincerity, and the greed of gain of certain teachers of the fifth and fourth centuries to whom the name was given. These men, some of whom we might call Professors of Practical Wisdom, assumed certainty of knowledge and claimed infallible success in teaching matters relating to virtue and conduct, education and government. They were, in any case, genuinely interested in moral science, practical statesmanship, and rhetoric and grammar, and deprecated, as futile, speculation regarding the nature of the universe. Best known of these teachers were Protagoras, Gorgias, Prodicus, Hippias, Polus, and Thrasymachus. The ability of these men is unquestionable and their services were of value to the education of the time and were a stimulation to thought and independent thinking. But, as Plato and Aristotle clearly show, there were charlatans among the Sophists as a whole, particularly those who are called the *Eristics,* i.e., those who for gain practiced and taught unfair disputation or the use of fallacious arguments in representing the false as true, in the winning of a lawsuit, or in swaying the Assembly. The *Clouds* of Aristophanes shows us, although in exaggerated fashion, the methods and the results of sophistry as an art. The word sophist in English has inherited the opprobrious sense only. Yet Socrates himself and Isocrates the rhetorician were Sophists in the best sense of the term.

The way is now clear for a discussion of the great Athenian teachers of philosophy.

A. Socrates. Socrates, one of the greatest and most influential thinkers in the history of human thought, was born at Athens in 469 B.C. and was put to death by the State in 399 B.C. He was the son of a sculptor, and seems to have received the usual education to which he constantly added by a lifetime of thought and study. As a youth he entered upon the career of a sculptor, but early gave up this profession to devote himself to the mission of educating his fellow-citizens in ethical standards. Accordingly, he did not concern himself much with politics and public office, although he actively and courageously did his duty as a citizen and a soldier. As a soldier he fought bravely as a hoplite at Potidaea, where he saved the life of Alcibiades, at Delium, and at Amphipolis. As a citizen he showed great moral courage on two occasions particularly, as we learn from passages in the *Apology* of Plato.

In appearance, Socrates fell far short of the Greek average of personal attractiveness. In several passages in Plato there are humorous references to his homeliness, his flat nose, rather thick lips, and prominent eyes. In stature he was rather short and corpulent; in physique rugged, powerful, and of the greatest endurance. In dress he was extremely simple, as he went barefoot throughout the year and even wore the same weight of garments in winter and summer alike. In food and drink he was abstemious. These eccentricities of person and conduct made him rather conspicuous, but he won hosts of friends among the discriminating by his generally attractive personality, cheerful disposition, modest demeanor, democratic manners, and sterling virtues. His wife, whom he married rather late in life, was named Xanthippe, whose misfortune it is to be accounted by ancient and modern tradition a scold and a shrew. If the lady really was of this disposition, it may be that the philosopher gave her some grounds for complaint by reason of his daily pursuits, which were calculated to improve the morality of his fellow-citizens, but not the material welfare of his own family!

In his youth, Socrates had naturally studied the teachings of the early philosophers and scientists. But he soon decided that in these subjects sure conclusions and permanent and valuable results could not be achieved. In consequence, he turned to the study of conduct, to ethics, and to practical morality devoting to these subjects a powerful mind and moral virtues. He conceived it his duty, furthermore, to educate his fellow-men, to " rouse, persuade, and rebuke " them, and to disabuse their minds of ignorance, prejudice, and pretence. As an educator he did not establish a school, as Plato, Aristotle, Isocrates, and others did, nor did he accept money from his pupils, as was the case with the Sophists, but he spent his days talking informally with all who cared to converse with him in the public places of Athens, the streets, the gymnasia, the workshops and the market-place.

Socrates' method was *dialectic,* or question and answer, used in an endeavor to arrive at an accurate definition and truthful conclusion. In this method and in its results is to be found the basis of all subsequent metaphysical and abstract thinking. Socrates would ask of his respondent, What is Justice? What is Piety? What is Courage? Love? Temperance? A superficial, thoughtless answer would generally be forthcoming. His manner of conducting the discussion then would be to start with some thesis or principle, which was readily admitted, and to proceed to its logical consequences. These conclusions, unforeseen by the respondent, would be incompatible with the original definition and obviously false and prejudiced. In the Socratic dialogues the dialogue at times ends at this point, because of the irritation and pique of the respondent; sometimes the questioning and answering continue step by step until a satisfactory conclusion is reached. To Socrates the assumption of accurate knowledge and smug intellectual complacency were unpardonable. It was his aim to substitute for this a realization of ignorance and a striving for the truth. The hypocrisy, insincerity, pretence, and false premises of certain of the Sophists especially aroused his indignation.

Knowledge, to Socrates, was the chief desideratum. By this he meant practical wisdom, since absolute knowledge he regarded as unattainable. He went so far as to declare that " We err through ignorance. No one knowingly does wrong. Virtue is knowledge. Knowledge is attainable through education, training, and careful definition. Through knowledge we arrive at the good, which is the useful and the advantageous." If men err seeming to have knowledge, we must believe that their knowledge is really ignorance. Knowledge thus lies at the basis of all virtues; or rather, there is but one virtue. As Mr. Henry Jackson states: " Piety, justice, courage and temperance are the names which ' wisdom ' bears in different spheres of action: to be pious is to know what is due to the gods; to be just is to know what is due to men; to be courageous is to know what is to be feared and what is not; to be temperate is to know how to use what is good and avoid what is evil." Socrates himself constantly assumed ignorance. This is his so-called *irony,* which was very vexatious to those who at first were sure that they knew, only to discover that they did not.

Many of the great moral teachers of the world, as, for example, Christ, themselves wrote nothing; and this is true of Socrates, but his philosophy survives for us in the dialogues of Plato. The personality of the philosopher is revealed to us not only by Plato, but by Xenophon in his *Memorabilia.* The influence of the teachings of Socrates, who himself established no school, was profound on all the post-Socratic schools. Thus, the Academy of Plato adopted it entire; the Peripatetics took over much of it; the Cyrenaics accepted the Socratic ethics, but made pleasure the basis thereof; the Epicureans, with a saner conception of pleasure, sprang from the Cyrenaics; the Stoics adopted the simplicity and sincerity of the Socratic beliefs and conduct; the Cynics exaggerated this simplicity and made it asceticism.

We have next to consider the question of the manner of death of Socrates. How is it possible that the Athenians, of all people, actually put to death a man like Socrates, a personality so attractive, a character so noble, a teacher so sincere, a patriot and a lover of his fellow-citizens?

The facts are briefly these. In the year 399 B.C., three men, Meletus (the spokesman), a poet little known, Lycon, an orator, likewise insignificant, and Anytus, a wealthy banker and prominent democratic leader, brought an indictment against Socrates charging him " (1) with disbelief in the gods which the city believes in and of introducing other and new divinities, and (2) of violating the laws by corrupting the youth." The trial was held before a jury of 501 Athenian citizens. Plato has preserved for us the simple but noble and impressive speech, *Apologia,* which gives essentially, no doubt, Socrates' own words on that

momentous occasion. It is largely a statement of his
life-work and teachings and a justification thereof,
but there is no effort to conciliate; rather the speech is
a defiance. In it there is no appeal for clemency, there
is no acknowledgment of error, there is no promise of
different behavior. The result was a condemnation
by a small majority, 281 against 220 in his favor. Socrates was then asked to suggest a penalty other than
that of death, which Meletus had proposed. Xenophon
declares that Socrates might have been acquitted " if
in any moderate degree he would have conciliated the
favor of the jurymen." Instead of proposing a fine
or exile as an alternative to the death penalty, Socrates
asserted that not punishment as a malefactor, but reward as a benefactor, was his real desert and declared
that he should be awarded free maintenance by the
State in the Prytaneum. At the close of his speech, he
grudgingly offered to accept a fine of one *mina* ($18)
raised finally to 30 *minas;* the latter sum was pledged
by his friends, Plato, Crito and others. The judges,
alienated still further by these statements and by an
attitude which seemed to them inexcusable and un-
intelligible, condemned him by a much greater majority,
80 larger than the former vote, according to Diogenes
Laertius. The execution was delayed for thirty days,
since, according to the Athenian law, the return from
Delos of the sacred ship must be awaited. During
these days spent in prison, Socrates' calm demeanor was
absolutely unchanged. He was visited repeatedly by
his friends and his discussions of life, death and the
immortality of the soul are preserved in the Platonic
dialogues, *Crito* and *Phaedo.* He might have escaped
from prison had he cared to accept a plan arranged by
his friend Crito, but he refused to do so on the ground
that he could not disobey the laws and that the truly
wise man will regard approaching death with equanim-
ity as being in fact a boon. He drank the poison-cup,
the hemlock juice, with utmost calm and thus died in
his seventieth year.

What is to be said briefly of the truth of these charges? (1) Socrates did not disbelieve in the gods — on the contrary, he was sincerely pious. Xenophon says that no one ever knew of his doing or saying anything profane or unholy. He did not, of course, accept literally the current mythology in all its traditional forms. He did not believe, for example, in the disgraceful acts attributed from prehistoric times to the gods. While he conceived of a creator, of a god who was supreme above all, yet he did not deny, nor could he have escaped from, the polytheism of his time. He scrupulously observed therefore the current religious worship and observance. (2) What is meant by the charge "introducing other and new divinities"? This doubtless refers, as Xenophon says, to his "Daimonion," that inner voice or conscience which, as he said, dissuaded him from certain actions. But in any case, it was not illegal in Athens to introduce new divinities. (3) The final charge, namely, that he "corrupted the youth," is the most important. It was asserted that Socrates had contempt for Athenian political institutions, and especially for election by lot. It is true that he was not entirely in sympathy with the democracy as then constituted, but he was not alone in holding those views. He was, however, always patriotic and law-abiding. Socrates was further blamed for his pupils, Critias and Alcibiades, but these men turned out badly in spite of, rather than because of, Socratic teachings. Finally, it was said that Socrates taught the young to disobey parents and guardians and that he quoted passages from Homer and Hesiod in a manner subversive to public morality; these charges are, of course, absurd.

It is evident that these charges are not the only reasons for the condemnation of a man whom we regard — if Plato's portrait of him is genuine — as Athens' greatest citizen. They are the cloak which conceals the real animosity originating in political and personal prejudice. In his political views Socrates was not in sympathy with the oligarchical faction on the one hand, or with the extreme democrats on the other. He had clearly shown, by word and deed, his hatred for the former, as in his resistance to the Thirty Tyrants in 404 B.C. And because of his disbelief in the practice of the election by lot of important officers of state, and by reason of his adverse criticism of other features of an unrestricted democracy, he was regarded with hostility by the extreme democrats. His accusers, Meletus and the others, were members of the extreme democratic party of Thrasybulus. The actual condemnation of Socrates, however, was the result not so much of political animus as of personal prejudice and popular misunderstanding. Although Socrates was surrounded by a fairly large number of eager listeners, understanding pupils, and even devoted disciples, who fairly worshipped him, he seems to have been popularly regarded by the multitude as at best an eccentric bore and at worst as a pernicious menace to state and society. His personal appearance, his dress and manner of life, his opinions, which often were unconventional and heterodox in popular estimation, his dialectic, which had discomfited and humiliated so many prominent and conceited persons, the conduct of some of his pupils who were Socratic in method only — all these were powerful influences in rendering him unpopular. His openly expressed dissatisfaction with traditional views offended the conservatives, who sincerely believed that his teachings and influence were certainly unsettling and probably harmful to the younger generation. Thus, both the thinking and the unthinking elements in the population came to look upon him with ever greater disfavor. A powerful single factor which aroused and fanned popular feeling against Socrates was the comedy of Aristophanes, the *Clouds*. This interesting and powerful play, originally produced in 423 B.C., taking advantage of the license of the Old Comedy and following the broad path of caricature, ruthlessly ridiculed the philosopher as a man, and grossly misrepresented his views and his teachings. The playwright ignorantly, or wilfully, confused Socrates with the most pernicious of the Sophists, and represented him as accepting money for tuition in charlatanism and knavery. The play was amusing, but grossly unfair, as Socrates himself says to the jury in his *Apology:* [1] " Well, what do the slanderers say? They shall be my prosecutors, and I will sum up their words in an affidavit. ' Socrates is an evil-doer, and a curious person, who searches into things under the earth and in heaven, and he makes the worse appear the better cause; and he teaches the aforesaid doctrines to others.' Such is the nature of the accusation: it is just what you yourselves have seen in the comedy of Aristophanes, who has introduced a man whom he calls Socrates, going about and saying that he walks in air and talking a deal of nonsense concerning matters of which I do not pretend to know either much or little."

Socrates was a thinker ahead of his time and paid the penalty. Unhappily, through a combination of untoward circumstances, his life had a tragic, although triumphant, end. The life and thought of the man have been and always will be a source of inspiration. As Socrates himself wrote nothing, the world is fortunate in having such a life and teaching brilliantly handed down to us in the writings of Plato, although it is quite probable that the Platonic Socrates is an idealized person.

B. Plato. Plato, one of the most profound philosophers that ever lived, is also one of the greatest writers and masters of prose style. He was born, perhaps, in 427 B.C., in Athens, and of an aristocratic family, and was certainly well educated. About 407, he joined the group of followers of Socrates, and became one of the most devoted of the disciples of that master for some years, until the death of Socrates in 399 B.C. The next few years Plato spent in travel, visiting

[1] The translations of the Platonic passages are by Jowett.

Egypt, Sicily, and Magna Graecia. About 387, Plato established a school of philosophy in the Academy, one of the three great gymnasia of Athens. With the exception of two brief visits to Syracuse, he wrote and taught at Athens until his death there, in 347 B.C., at the age of eighty.

The writings of Plato are voluminous and seem to have been preserved to us in their entirety. Forty-two dialogues and thirteen letters are extant under Plato's name. Most scholars regard the letters as spurious; of the other writings — all dialogues with the exception of the *Apology* of Socrates — these compositions are generally accepted as genuine: *Apology, Euthyphro, Crito, Charmides, Laches, Lysis, Hippias Minor, Ion, Menexenus, Protagoras, Meno, Euthydemus, Gorgias, Cratylus, Symposium, Phaedo, Republic, Phaedrus, Parmenides, Theaetetus, Sophist, Statesman, Philebus, Timaeus, Critias* and *Laws*. It is difficult to estimate the indebtedness of Plato to Socrates,[1] who is the chief speaker in most of these dialogues, and a subordinate speaker in four of them. In the *Laws* alone he does not appear. Much of the philosophical thought is certainly of Socratic origin, but the whole elucidation and interpretation have been elaborated and refined and transmuted by Plato's alchemy. The dialectic method of the master, the favorite cross-examination by question and answer, is followed by the pupil who likewise is chiefly concerned with questions of conduct and with the formulation of the laws that govern moral behavior. Plato subscribes to the Socratic thesis that virtue is knowledge and sin is ignorance. No one willingly chooses evil. The virtuous life is the happy life.

In this necessarily brief sketch it is impossible to characterize in detail all the dialogues. The nature of a few of the most important may be indicated.

---

[1] The traditional view that the real source of the Dialogues of Plato is Socrates and his teachings is attacked by Eugène Dupréel, *La Légende Socratique et les Sources de Platon* (Oxford, 1922), who substitutes, without convincing proof, the Sophists.

Four compositions tell us of the trial, last days in prison, and death of Socrates, namely, the *Euthyphro* (an attempt at a definition of piety), the *Apology* (Socrates' speech at his trial), the *Crito* (so named from Socrates' wealthy friend who vainly tries to save him and effect his release from prison), and the *Phaedo* (named after a follower who, in this dialogue, relates the events of Socrates' last days and reports the argument whereby the master shows that the wise and virtuous man will meet death cheerfully, because the soul is immortal). The *Lysis* discusses friendship; the *Charmides*, temperance; the *Laches*, courage. Four, *Protagoras, Gorgias, Euthydemus*, and *Cratylus*, named after the famous Sophists, explain the attitude and teaching of those teachers. The theme of the *Meno* is, "Virtue is Knowledge," while the *Phaedrus* discusses philosophic love. The *Symposium* delightfully describes a banquet at the house of the tragic poet Agathon and the discussion of Love by the guests; the *Republic* deals with the nature of justice and the founding of an ideal city-state based on justice; the *Timaeus* is a cosmogony; the *Laws*, a modification or revision of the *Republic*, is a discussion of legislation for the best state practicable.

These numerous dialogues are extremely dramatic in setting and execution. In fact, many can be analyzed on the analogy of a Greek tragedy and have easily discerned parts, which may be designated prologue, episodes, and epilogue. Dramatic, too, is the dialogue with the clash of wills and the rhetorical contention. The language is of singular beauty and appropriateness. As Professor Shorey says: "Plato's prose is of wonderful variety and power, varying from the colloquial, to dialectic precision; it is imaginative, mystical, everything but oratorical. It combines quotation, parody, literary and historic allusion, idiom, proverb, dialect, allegory, technical vocabularies of all arts, sciences, and professions. Composite, suggestive, polychromatic, literary prose was created by Plato."

The *Republic* is Plato's greatest work. It is a
lengthy dialogue in ten books, the scene being the
house of Cephalus, father of Lysias the orator, in the
Piraeus. Socrates is the leading speaker in the discussion, which begins with a conversation on old age,
continues with attempted definitions of justice, and is
developed and concluded with the practical application
of justice in the establishment of an ideal state. This
perfect, speculative Greek city is to be no faulty
Athenian democracy, but an ideal aristocracy. There
are three classes in the ideal state: (1) the artisans and
husbandmen, or the producers, who have nothing to do
with the government; (2) the auxiliaries or guardians,
the warriors who, chosen in infancy, have been trained
in philosophy for their duties as commanders in war
and subordinate magistrates; (3) the philosopher-
statesmen, a small and highly select class who have
been rigorously and successfully disciplined and have
accurate comprehension of the greatest of the Platonic
Ideas, the Idea of the Good. In describing this Utopia,
Plato allows his vivid fancy and fertile imagination to
have full play, and the progress of the discussion un-
folds before us a bewildering succession of suggestions,
recommendations, and hypotheses. Many fundamental
problems of government, education, and society in general are acutely stated and discussed with striking conclusions. Professor Shorey has summarized these questions in this pregnant sentence:

" The division of labor, specialization, the formation
of a trained standing army, the limitation of the right
of private property, the industrial and political equality
of women, the improvement of the human breed by
artificial selection, the omnipotence of public opinion,
the reform of the letter of the creeds to save their spirit,
the proscription of unwholesome art and literature, the
reorganization of education, the kindergarten method,
the distinction between higher and secondary education, the endowment of research, the application of
higher mathematics to astronomy and physics — such

are some of the divinations and modernisms of that
wonderful work."

In consequence of the wealth and striking nature of
suggestions for an ideal society, the *Republic* must be
studied by all students of politics, education, and society. It has inspired such ancient works as Cicero's
De Republica and St. Augustine's *City of God,* and
such modern treatises as More's *Utopia,* Bacon's *Atlan-
tis,* and Bellamy's *Looking Backward.* The *Republic*
certainly shows that Plato was not an admirer of Athenian institutions, but more inclined to the education,
laws, and government of Sparta.

The reader of the *Republic* must not entertain the
belief, however, that every suggestion found in that
work is the final, sober dictum of the philosopher which
he thought could be, and should be, immediately
realized in Athens of the fifth century B.C. This conception is often erroneously held. The *Republic* is an
imaginary, speculative commonwealth, which is gradually evolved in the course of a long discussion and is
hypothetical and purely tentative. In this work Plato
is more poet than prose-writer, and the mythical, the
mystical, the imaginative, and the poetical elements
alternate with sober and reasoned practicality. It is
unreasonable, therefore, for the literal-minded to query
every speculation in the *Republic* and ask if Plato
thought every proposal capable of realization then, or
at any time, and desirable of attainment if realizable.

This is the question, by the way, of Glaucon in Book
V who asks: " Is such a state possible? " and Socrates
replies, " We were led to form our ideal polity in the
search after justice, and the just man answered to the
just state. Is this ideal at all the worse for being im-
practicable? Would the picture of a perfectly beautiful man be any the worse because no such man ever
lived? Can any reality come up to the idea? Nature
will not allow words to be fully realized. *Until kings
are philosophers, or philosophers are kings, cities will*

never cease from ill; no, nor the human race; nor will our ideal polity ever come into being."

So, too, in the *Laws*, Plato speaks of his ideal state, based on philosophy and communism, as impossible of realization in his age, although it is to be regarded as a model.

Some of the suggestions for the ideal state are familiar, indeed, to us. Some have been put into effect in our own state; others would be adopted, if certain thinkers had their way.

A small community is postulated both by Plato and Aristotle, as the Greek political thinker thought in terms of a small, compact, homogeneous population; with this only was he familiar. The ideal state in the *Republic* has a population of about 1000 warrior-citizens; in the *Laws* it has about 5000. Plato would be surprised, indeed, to see the democracy of the United States, a commonwealth comprising dozens of great states, and a population of over a hundred millions. A real and permanently successful democracy was to him unthinkable, because perfect liberty for the individual would inevitably degenerate into license and into discord, prejudicial and fatal to the general welfare. Genuine democracy, which is our ideal, doubtless seemed to Plato utterly unattainable, as indeed it was in his day, and for that matter still is yet to be realized in our grievously imperfect modern world, in spite of the long, slow, painful steps forward which the human race has made in order to arrive at its present condition. Thus it is, that Plato's *polis* is a military state, trained for war, and aristocratic in nature. The citizens form an upper class; the toilers and slaves are below them as a permanent lower caste. Harmony, and universal social and political brotherhood, Plato can not conceive.

Plato's silence with regard to international relations is a glaring and regrettable omission to many modern readers of the *Republic*, who forget the time and the place of the composition, or ignore the racial origin of the writer. To the Greeks of the fifth century B.C., the world was divided into two classes — Hellenes and Barbarians. The former were supreme in language, literature, art, government, and civilization; the latter, non-Greeks, were immeasurably inferior in all these respects. The Greeks thought of the Persians to the east, and the races to the north, as wild hordes, against whom they must always be on the military defensive. It was not a question of international concord and amity with these races; it was the possibility of national and racial salvation, although surrounded by hostile and invading peoples. Furthermore, it must be remembered that the Greeks themselves were passionately fond of independence, and that this love of complete autonomy and craving for " self-sufficiency," discouraged amicable relations among themselves. A permanent and successful league of Greek states was therefore impossible. Even great crises affecting the Hellenes of the mainland as a whole, e.g., the Persian and Macedonian invasions, resulted only in imperfect, temporary, and by no means unanimous inter-state combinations. The student of Greek civilization in the time of Plato is not surprised, therefore, that the question of foreign relations is not discussed in the works of the Athenian philosopher.

Plato's preference for Spartan institutions may be seen in a number of regulations suggested for his ideal state. The more important of these are the common meals for men, the provision that youths should undergo compulsory military training, gymnastic exercises for women, the declaration that citizens should be soldiers and not tradesmen, the inculcation in the young of great reverence for parents and elders, the putting out of the way of deformed children, the equality of the sexes, and the communistic division of property.

With regard to Plato's advocacy of communism a word of warning must be spoken. The Platonic conception of community of property and life is not the modern. It is not socialistic. as we understand socialism. The communism of Plato is *class* legislation, affecting the highest classes, i.e., the guardians and auxiliaries in the commonwealth, and was not inspired by social ills, such as poverty and the exploitation of the poor by the rich or of labor by capital. Plato is not interested in collective property *per se*. His recommendation is, that guardians shall be forbidden the possession of private property to the end that selfishness, or the thought of personal and material gain, may be removed from their minds. We may quote from the fifth book of the *Republic:* " The guardians are not to have houses or lands or any other property; their pay is to be their food, which they are to receive from the other citizens, and they are to have no private expenses; for we intend them to preserve their true character of guardians."

So it is, that abolishment of property for the guardians is recommended with the purpose of removing temptation, that the guardians may be utterly disinterested and wholly altruistic for performing their duties in the public welfare.

The same idea underlay the proposal of a community of wives and children. Just as the possession of private property militates against thought for the common good, so the institution of the family makes a wholehearted devotion to the State impossible. " Both the community of property and the community of families, as I am saying, tend to make them more truly guardians; they will not tear the city in pieces by differing about " mine " and " not mine "; each man dragging any acquisition which he has made into a separate house of his own, where he has a separate wife and children and private pleasure and pains; but all will be affected as far as may be by the same pleasures and pains because they are all of one opinion about what is near and dear to them, and therefore they all tend towards a common end " (*Republic*, V).

The suggestion of a community of wives and children was as alien and repugnant to Greek ideals as to our own. For the sake of the argument of what impersonally is the ideal good of the ideal state the human relationships of husband and wife, parents and children, are swept away by Plato. In the interest of eugenics and racial improvement the breeding of children is to be supervised, parents are not to know and rear their own children, and offspring will be cared for by nurses and caretakers of the State. Plato's readers would admit that family life is responsible for serious distractions, but they would urge that there are compensations and advantages of a personal and social nature which heavily outweigh them. It is not surprising, therefore, that in his later work, the *Laws*, Plato gives up this recommendation.

Another perplexing and much discussed question in connection with Plato and, in particular, the *Republic*, is the philosopher's attitude towards poets and poetry. Plato himself wrote poetry in youth; his own prose style is poetic in the extreme, being rhythmical, imaginative, and figurative. In his compositions are numerous poetical quotations which show his fondness for the poets and his admiration for that inspired art. Why, then, in the *Republic* does he disapprove of the poets and even go so far as to banish Homer altogether from his ideal state?

An exact answer to this question is difficult and would require longer discussion than may here be devoted to it. Suffice it to say that Plato, in his analysis of education and of those influences which tend to inculcate an appreciation of truth in the young, is led to point out unfortunate passages in the poets who serve as the very foundation of the education of the young. Epic poetry, for example, is full of unbecoming stories of the gods which are unfit for the ears of the immature. And these stories are not only impure; worse still, they are false. Poetry, in general, is full of falsehoods, whereas the truth is the chief end of education. Furthermore, poetry is imitative and not real; it is emotional and not rational; it is productive of unwholesome excitement and illusion. Drama through its poignant appeal to the emotions is a harmful indulgence and a bad instrument of education. The exigencies of the argument gradually but inexorably compel Plato to exclude most poetry because only that which is pure, noble, beautiful, and elevating can be tolerated in a perfect state. Poetry and art are important, but above all it is the soul which must be fostered by the truth. Therefore, " we are ready to acknowledge that Homer is the greatest of poets and first of tragedy writers; but we must remain firm in our conviction that hymns to the gods and praises of famous men are the only poetry which ought to be admitted into our state. For if you go beyond this and allow the honeyed muse to enter, either in epic or lyric verse, not law and the reason of mankind, which by common consent have ever been deemed best, but pleasure and pain will be the rulers in our state " (Book X).

In the *Laws* a modified view of the poets is taken. Their art is not to be condemned outright, but a censorship of poetry must be exercised by the responsible magistrates to the end that poets of good repute shall sing of noble thoughts and noble deeds.

Finally in our consideration of Plato let us speak briefly of his Theory of Ideas, the very cornerstone of his philosophical edifice. The Greek word *idea* really means " form," i.e., (originally) *visible* form; the English word *idea* is simply a transfer, not a translation from the Greek. Plato believed that the things of this world about us are only imperfect and ephemeral copies of the eternal Ideas. The latter are the realities of the world of Ideas; the former are mere pictures of the perfect originals. In extremely poetic language Plato maintains the reality, the perfection, the precedence, and the eternal nature of the Ideas as compared and contrasted with the things of this world. To his mind the Ideas are personified and become as living shapes and beings. Of them we have knowledge, because our souls have beheld them in pre-natal vision.

The greatest of these ideas is the Idea of Good, which is the source of everything; this Idea only the thoroughly disciplined may apprehend. Such a one will be the real philosopher, the philosopher-king, who alone will be qualified to rule the ideal state.

C. Aristotle. Aristotle (384–322 B.C.) was born in Thrace, at Stagira, where his father was physician to Amyntas II of Macedon, but he obtained his philosophical education in Athens and for some twenty years was the pupil and companion of Plato. Aristotle's indebtedness to his teacher is very great but his independence, originality, and scientific type of mind caused him to pursue more exact and less imaginative studies. In 342 B.C., Aristotle accepted the tutorship of young Alexander of Macedon, then thirteen years of age. We are not in a position to know the extent of his influence upon the young prince. Milton, it is true, says that Aristotle bred Alexander to subdue the world, but this is unlikely in the extreme, since the keynote of Aristotle's philosophy was the golden mean. In 335 B.C., Aristotle established in Athens his school in the gymnasium called the Lyceum. His pupils gained the appellation *Peripatetics,* from the fact that the master frequently lectured while walking with his disciples along the garden path (*peripatos*). Here he taught for twelve years, until his retirement to Euboea where, too, he died.

Dante calls Aristotle the " Master of those who know." Certainly his intellectual curiosity was prodigious and the range of his studies and writings almost incredible. His works may be grouped in the following divisions: I Logic II Natural Sciences III Psychology and Metaphysics IV Ethics V Politics VI Rhetoric.

His *Organon,* to use the Peripatetic name for what was subsequently designated Logic, is, perhaps, Aristotle's most notable work. At any rate, with its study of the syllogism and its exposition of the ten categories or forms of thought, namely, substance, quantity, quality, place, time, relation, action, passion, posture or relative position of parts, and habit or state, it is the foundation of modern logic.

His investigations in the Natural Sciences, such as the *History of Animals, De Caelo,* and *Physics,* are to us the least important of his researches, because of the great achievements of modern science.

In his Psychology (*de Anima*) Aristotle maintained that soul is present in all living things. It is merely nutritive in plants; in animals it is nutritive and sensitive and may also be appetitive and motive; in man, soul, besides possessing the foregoing characteristics, is intellectual. The *Metaphysics* derives its name from its position in his works, coming as it did *after the Physics.* It deals with the four causes: formal (form), material (matter), efficient (moving), and final (the good). Plato's Theory of Ideas was not accepted by Aristotle.

The *Ethics* is called *Nicomachean* after Aristotle's son Nicomachus, who is thought to have edited them, to distinguish the work from the *Eudemian* Ethics, written by Eudemus on the basis of Aristotle's teaching. The basis of the ethics of Aristotle is practical. His object was not to distinguish the right and the wrong nor to lay down rules of morality, but to determine the best and most desirable scheme of life. The aim of life is happiness or well-being. He will attain happiness who, possessing external goods, lives and dies in virtue. Virtue lies in the " golden mean," in " nothing to excess " and is a habit of the soul, not, as Plato taught, the result of knowledge. Of virtue there are two kinds — moral and intellectual. Of the Moral Virtues the chief are temperance, justice, courage, gentleness, liberality, munificence, self-respect, and magnanimity. The Intellectual Virtues are practical judgment, speculative wisdom, and reason. Man's highest good is philosophy, or the life of contemplation, although the philosopher will be a good citizen.

In the *Politics,* Aristotle discusses the happiness or

well-being of the community, as in the *Ethics* he dealt with the individual well-being. From the family as a social unit comes the clan-village; from the village, the complex *polis*. For the government of the *polis* there are a number of polities or constitutions possible, of which some are good (e.g., aristocracy, monarchy, and *polity* proper) where the government rules for the good of the community, while others are bad — e.g., democracy, oligarchy, and tyranny — as being perversions, the reverse of the good. Aristotle believes that the best government would result from the exercise of absolute power by one superior person, or more than one, in the interests of all, although this government is not to be achieved. His ideal state is, therefore, aristocratic, small, and autonomous. Plato's ideal commonwealth as outlined in the *Republic* is rejected, and cogent arguments and objections are directed against his teacher's proposed institutions.

The *Constitution of Athens*, the papyrus manuscript of which was first published in 1891, is a description of the Athenian polity, and is of great interest and importance to students of Greek history and constitutional law.

The rhetorical works of Aristotle are well-known and long have exerted profound influence. In the *Rhetoric* we have the first real treatment of the subject as an Art, namely, the Art of Persuasion. Book I discusses the kinds of proof and the three types of rhetoric, — deliberative, judicial, and epideictic. Book II deals with the psychology of the audience, and Book III with style and arrangement.

In the *Poetics*, the first formal treatment of poetry, Aristotle essayed to define, analyse, and discuss the chief kinds of poetry. The work, as we have it, is incomplete. To Aristotle, the greatest of the arts is poetry, and the highest form of poetry is tragedy. A tragedy he defines as " imitation of an action that is serious, complete, and of a certain magnitude; in language embellished . . . in the form of action, not narrative; through pity and fear effecting the proper purgation of the emotions." The parts of tragedy are six: plot, character, diction, thought, scenery, and song. The *Oedipus Tyrannus* of Sophocles is Aristotle's favorite play for illustrative purposes. With regard to the so-called three unities, which are now generally believed to have rigidly bound and constrained the Greek dramatist, we may note that Aristotle does not even mention the unity of place, nor does he lay down any hard and fast rule relative to the unity of time, except to state that the limit of a tragedy should be a single revolution of the sun or only a little longer. Unity of action alone he insists upon, in that every part of the plot of a play must be necessary to the whole.

These are the extant works of Aristotle, but we know that he wrote, or inspired, many more. The writings we possess are in form incomplete and the style is generally devoid of charm. It is evident that they are unrevised and had not been prepared for publication. In fact, it is probable that some of the treatises are but the lecture notes of the philosopher or the notes taken by his pupils. Aristotle's knowledge was immense, likewise his ability to classify and to interpret. He stands forth as a giant among the world's great thinkers and his influence upon all subsequent thought is incalculable.

III. The Post-Aristotelians

As we have observed, Socrates himself founded no college, no permanent school of formal philosophy. But numerous schools sprang from his teaching and influence. We have already discussed the Academy of Plato and the Lyceum of Aristotle. It remains to consider several prominent schools of thought, which were destined to sway the thinking of the world for centuries. The founders of these schools largely discarded the method of dialectic dear to Socrates and Plato; nor were they in sympathy with the idealistic speculation and the theories of their predecessors. They emphasized, however, the ethical doctrines of Socrates and busied themselves with the elaboration and the enunciation of practical ethical creeds, practical philosophies, by which men might live to best advantage.

The earliest of the Socratic schools were those of the *Cyrenaics* and the *Cynics*. The *Cyrenaics* were founded by Aristippus, a pupil of Socrates, of the city of Cyrene, a rich and populous Greek colony on the coast of Africa. Aristippus rejected the Socratic dictum that virtue is knowledge and the greatest good. Happiness, he asserted, was the chief end of man. Pleasure, he held, must be sought. Knowledge results from sensation. The teachings of Aristippus had great influence upon the doctrines of the Epicureans and the Hedonists, but it should be noted that the Epicureans, unlike the Cyrenaics, believed in the Socratic pleasures of the mind, while the Hedonists went far beyond the Cyrenaics in the emphasis placed upon the pleasures of the senses.

The *Cynics* probably received their name originally from the fact that the founder of the school, Antisthenes, a pupil of Socrates, taught in the gymnasium of Cynosarges, just outside Athens. The name Cynosarges means " of the White Hound." Popular feeling, however, early derived the name " Cynic " directly from the Greek word for " dog," because of the snarling, contemptuous, and disagreeable nature of certain of the members of the school, in particular, Diogenes. Thus the English word " cynic " has come to mean a sneering fault-finder. The Cynics denied that wealth and pleasure are to be desired. Virtue is the supreme end and is won through self-denial, poverty, and self-sufficiency, which lead to independence of intellect. Here we have the germs of Stoicism. These doctrines, to be sure, point the way to asceticism, which was practiced by the notorious Cynic, Diogenes of Sinope (412–323 B.C.). Many

stories are told of this eccentric person — how he lived
in a tub (really, *jar*) and destroyed his only wooden
bowl when he saw a peasant youth drinking from his
hands. Famous, too, is the story of his supposed inter-
view with Alexander at the festival of the Isthmian
games, when Diogenes craved of the great Macedonian
a single boon — that Alexander would not stand between him and the sun. To which Alexander is said to
have replied: " If I were not Alexander, I would be
Diogenes."

The *Stoic* school of philosophy was founded by Zeno,
who was born in 336 B.C. The name of the school
comes from its place of meeting, the Painted Stoa, a
colonnade on the north side of the Athenian market-
place, which was adorned with mural paintings of Trojan scenes by the great painter Polygnotus. Although
Stoicism was first taught in Athens, its founder was of
Cyprus and of Phoenician descent; its devotees were
Hellenistic Greeks rather than Hellenes proper and its
stronghold came to be Rome, not Athens. The tenets
of the practical Stoic belief were such as to appeal to
the grave Roman character and temperament. Prominent among the Greek teachers and interpreters of
Stoicism were Cleanthes, Chrysippus, and Panaetius.
At Rome, the Stoic philosophy, which was the religion,
in theory at least, of all noble and educated Romans
for several centuries, was expounded by such great
thinkers and writers as Seneca, Cornutus, Persius,
Lucan, Epictetus, and Marcus Aurelius.

The chief doctrines of the moral philosophy of
Stoicism very briefly stated are these: Virtue, to the
wise man, is the highest good. Fixed laws govern the
Universe and these laws express the world-soul, of
which the human soul is a part. Goodness is to be
found in the true knowledge of nature, and this knowledge is to be won by reason. Wisdom consists in living
in accord with nature. The wise man is self-sufficient.
Self-control, therefore, is of paramount importance.
Serenity of mind is essential, whether in pleasure or

pain. Unlike the Cyrenaics and the Epicureans, the Stoics denied that pleasure should be sought; if it comes it is merely a concomitant of virtuous conduct.

The *Epicurean* school was founded by Epicurus (342–270 B.C.), of Athenian parentage, who bought a garden in Athens, where he established a philosophic school and taught a philosophic system which won a great following and was destined to have wide-reaching influence. Only scanty fragments of his numerous works have come down to us and we are largely dependent for our knowledge of his life and philosophy upon his biographer, Diogenes Laertius, and upon the great philosophical poem, *De Rerum Natura* of his Roman admirer Lucretius.

Epicureanism, like Stoicism, was more practical than speculative and was concerned with ethics more than with physics and logic. In physics, Epicurus followed Democritus in the atomic theory, as he believed that the universe consists of atoms and void; the atoms are without limit as to number, indestructible and indivisible, and are in perpetual motion in the void, " the illimitable inane." There are numerous worlds in the universe. The gods exist, it is true, in a realm of their own, but they do not concern themselves with humanity, nor do they rule the world. Consequently man should free his soul of all religious fear and superstition, and likewise of the terror of death. The soul, itself corporeal, perishes with the body, for death ends all. Sensation is alone to be trusted, for it is only through the senses that reality and the truth may be ascertained. Happiness is the chief end of life, and pleasure consists of pleasant sensations. But by this Epicurus did not mean sensuality — this is Hedonism. We must be on our guard lest we mistakenly accept the modern meaning of the word *epicurean,* i.e., " given to luxury or indulgence in sensual pleasures, especially in eating and drinking," as correctly characterizing the teachings and the practice of Epicurus and his school. Happiness, said Epicurus, was to be achieved through freedom from disturbance, by the living of a simple life, and by choosing only those pleasures which bring real and permanent contentment to mind and body. Wisdom enables us to make the proper choice.

Epicurus was a man of simple and temperate life and of attractive personality, and inspired love and veneration in his numerous disciples. His philosophy unchanged lived after him, and, about 150 B.C., was established at Rome where it won wide repute. As has been said, Lucretius was his Roman disciple and interpreter in a poem of great power and remarkable poetic excellence. Horace, in his thinking, was largely Epicurean. In fact, in the first century A.D., the prevailing philosophy at Rome was Epicurean in practice, although Stoic in theory. In the second century A.D., a chair of Epicureanism (along with Stoic, Platonist, and Peripatetic Chairs) was established by Marcus Aurelius.

Amid the discordant doctrines of these many schools as above outlined it is not surprising that the spirit of scepticism, the germs of which are to be found in the teachings of the Sophists, grew until it materialized into a definite school, that of the *Sceptics*, founded by Pyrrho of Elis (born about 365 B.C.), who held that truth is unattainable and dogmatism must be rejected. Happiness alone is the chief good, and this happiness, consisting of tranquillity or mental imperturbability, is attainable through an attitude of indifference to all things.

The scope of this volume forbids us to carry further the sketch of the late Greek philosophic schools, their subsequent influence, and their relation to Christianity.

CHAPTER XVII

RELIGION

"What has the religion of the Greeks to teach us that we are most in danger of forgetting? In a word, it is the faith that Truth is our friend, and that the knowledge of Truth is not beyond our reach." — W. R. INGE.

WHAT was the religious belief and what were the religious practices of the Athenians of the fifth and fourth centuries B.C.? To answer these questions completely is impossible; even to answer them satisfactorily is difficult. In truth, the same difficulty confronts any inquirer into the nature of the religion of any people of any period or land, because an inherited religious tradition, the result of the mingling of diverse elements which are of manifold and obscure origins, is inevitably complex. It is not easy, furthermore, to separate religion as such from mythology, and especially is this true in the case of the religion of the Greeks, a people without dogmatic religion, but the possessors of a rich and imaginative mythology. To us, religion is based primarily upon intimate relationship between man and God, but to the Greek this relationship was not felt as something constantly present which at every moment profoundly affected his happiness in this world and in the life hereafter. Then, too, the degrees and kinds of religious faith and belief may be as numerous as individuals, depending upon the intellect, the imagination, the education, and the environment of the individual. Again, even in a given person, religious belief is often subject to change. Nor were the religious beliefs and ideas of Plato, Socrates, or Euripides in all particulars identical with those of the average Athenian. Our task, too, is made more difficult by the fact that the Greeks, unlike so many other peoples, had no Bible, no sacred writings, and no formulated religious dogma. In consequence of these factors perhaps the best approach to this subject will be to give a brief historical sketch of Greek religious thought and teaching. A fuller treatment will be found in Professor C. H. Moore's *The Religious Thought of the Greeks.*

It was natural, and indeed inevitable, that the writings of early poets and thinkers, especially Homer and Hesiod, should powerfully affect and largely determine Athenian religious thought. These great poets were regarded by the Athenians not primarily as literary artists, whose chief value was their contribution to aesthetic pleasure, but they were venerated rather as inspired teachers and preceptors, whose utterances were of profound moral value.

Since the study and memorizing of Homer and Hesiod formed the very backbone of all instruction, it was from this source that the Athenians gained their prevalent conceptions with respect to cosmogony, the genealogy and the relationships of the gods, anthropomorphism, forms of worship, and views of the future world. It is true that Xenophanes, Plato, and Euripides repudiated certain teachings of Homer and the early poets, but it is probable that popular belief was little influenced by their protests.

In the poetry of Homer we find that the gods are made in man's image, although they are superhuman and immortal. They possess great power and may in varied ways profoundly affect human destinies, yet they are themselves subject to Fate, are not omnipotent or omniscient, and can suffer pain and humiliation. Ambrosia and nectar, not human sustenance, supply their nourishment, and *ichor*, not blood, courses in their veins. The gods, according to Homer, are all too human, however, in that they are subject to passion and show frailty, as evidenced by their quarrels, jealousy, and misconduct. The functions and prerogatives of the chief deities are thus defined by Homer.

Zeus is father of gods and men, and is lord of the Olympians: Hera is his wife. Apollo, the archer god, is lord of the lyre, a giver of inspiration to prophets, and a patron of war. Artemis, the huntress, is his sister. Athena is patroness of handicraft, and is also interested in war. Ares, however, is the chief god of warfare, Aphrodite of love, Hephaestus of fire, and Poseidon of the sea. Hermes is messenger god. The chief virtues, according to Homer, are those which were universally esteemed among the Greeks — the keeping of an oath, reverence for parents, and observance of hospitality. Soul and body are not clearly differentiated. At death the soul departs to Hades where, in gloom and sadness, it exists as the mere wraith and image of the living man, although retaining, in exceptional cases, consciousness.

Hesiod, in his *Theogony*, a genealogical epic, revealed the dynasties of the gods, showing that Uranus and Cronos had preceded Zeus. In his *Works and Days*, many myths are related, such as the story of the creation of Pandora and her fateful jar, whence escaped the diseases and evils of this world, and the tale of the Islands of the Blest, where the happy heroes dwell forever. To Hesiod, too, we are indebted for the myth of the Five Ages of Man. First came the Golden Age, under Cronos, when men lived like gods, knowing neither toil nor misery, with hearts free from care. Wretched age weighed not on them and when they died it was as though they were overcome by sleep and having become spirits they served thenceforth as guardians of mortal men. Next, under Zeus, was the Silver Age. The men of this Age, less noble, were destroyed for their sins and impiety. Third came the Age of Bronze, a generation of lovers of war and violence, with armor, weapons, and houses of bronze. These men were destroyed by their own hands and nameless went to the dank house of chill Hades. Fourth in the sequence

was the Age of Heroes, a god-like race of hero-men who
are called the demi-gods. Some of these died at Thebes
and at Troy; to others Zeus gave happy lives in an
abode apart from men in the Isles of the Blessed. The
last and fifth generation is that of Iron, the age of
Hesiod himself, who exclaims, " Would that I were not
of this generation, but either had died before or been
born later! Now truly is a race-of iron; men never
cease from toil and sorrow by day, nor from perishing
by night, and the gods shall give them grievous cares.
The father will not agree with his children, nor the
children with their father, nor guest with host, nor
friend with friend. Men will dishonor their parents
as they quickly grow old. Might shall make right,
and one man will sack another's city. Envy of evil
name, delighting in evil, with loathsome countenance,
will accompany wretched men. And then Reverence
and Nemesis, their lovely forms garbed in white, will
depart from the earth and abandon men, to be with the
race of the immortals. Grievous woes will be left for
mortals and there will be no defence against evil."

In general, the *Works and Days* marks an advance in
religious thought, as it is moral in its teaching, and insists upon the excellence and benefit of work, the necessity of the observance of justice, the desirability of
human concord, and the obligation of piety towards
the gods.

Of the lyric poets, Pindar, who was doubtless influenced by the Orphic doctrines later to be discussed,
proclaims the morality of the gods and asserts the happiness after death of those who have kept the faith.
In the *Second Olympian Ode* he sings: " The good,
having the sun shining for evermore, for equal nights
and equal days, receive the boon of a life of lightened
toil, not vexing the soil with the strength of their hands,
no, nor the water of the sea, to gain a scanty livelihood;
but, in the presence of the honoured gods, all who were
wont to rejoice in keeping their oaths, share a life that

knoweth no tears, while the others endure labour that none can look upon." (Translation by Sandys.)

It is, however, in the three great Athenian tragedians that we find most frequent and fullest utterance concerning questions of religion and morality. The plays of Aeschylus, the earliest of the tragedians, are especially permeated with religious and moral teaching. In fact, the trilogy called the *Oresteia* (the *Agamemnon, Libation-Bearers,* and *Eumenides*) may be regarded in a sense as sermons expounding the text that the "sinner must pay the penalty." And this penalty, as in the old Hebraic conception, pursues a guilty line and may be visited upon the children. In the tragedies of Aeschylus there is strongly emphasized the idea of *Moira* (Fate), of *Atê* (the infatuation of the sinner that leads him on to ruin), and of *Nemesis* (Heaven's punishment falling upon those who are guilty of *Hybris*, or arrogant insolence and excess in word, in thought, in deed). These ideas, to be sure, especially that of Nemesis, are found elsewhere in Greek literature, as for example, in the history of Herodotus, who represents the Persians, extravagant of word and deed, as meeting a just doom for their overweening conduct, struck down in all their vain and insolent pride by Nemesis. In Aeschylus there is truly a divine order ruling the cosmos and Zeus, at length, is supreme.

Sophocles, too, is a religious poet, but ideas of this character are not put so strongly in the foreground as in Aeschylus. Yet all through his plays, interwoven in the warp and woof of their fabric, are his conceptions of piety, of humility, of *sophrosyne* (the golden mean), and of reverence. In the Antigone, King Creon indignantly asks the heroine: " And didst thou indeed dare to transgress that law " (i.e., so as to give holy rites of burial to her brother, the so-called traitor, Polynices)? Antigone replies: " Yes: for it was not Zeus that had published me that edict; not such are the laws set among men by the Justice who dwells with the gods below; nor deemed I that thy decrees were of such force, that a mortal could over-ride the unwritten and unfailing statutes of heaven. For their life is not of today or yesterday, but from all time, and no man knows when they were first put forth " (Jebb).

Moving, too, is the prayer of the Chorus in the *Oedipus Tyrannus:*

> Toward God's great mysteries, oh, let me move
>   Unstained till I die
> In speech or doing; for the Laws thereof
> Are holy, walkers upon ways above,
>   Born in the far blue sky;
>
> Their father is Olympus uncreate;
>   No man hath made nor told
> Their being; neither shall Oblivion set
> Sleep on their eyes, for in them lives a great
>   Spirit and grows not old.
>
> — G. MURRAY.

In the *Electra* the Chorus thus consoles the impatient and suffering heroine: " Courage, my daughter, courage; great still in heaven is Zeus, who sees and governs all: to him commit thy bitter wrath."

Neither in Aeschylus nor in Sophocles do we find a clearly expressed idea of immortality, although the latter, in a fragment, affirms future happiness for those who have been initiated into the Eleusinian Mysteries.

Euripides, although a contemporary of Sophocles, seems to belong to a new age in religious thought. He is a pronounced sceptic of much in the old mythology and rejects as improbable many of the current stories dealing with the misconduct of the gods. In an interesting and important fragment (294), he says: " If the gods do aught that is base, then they are not gods." Again, in the *Iphigenia among the Taurians* (391), the heroine declares: " I think no one of the gods is evil." Often we see Euripides in efforts to rationalize. An interesting example is his treatment of the *Erinyes* (Furies). In the *Eumenides* of Aeschylus the Furies, who were in pursuit of the guilty Orestes, were represented as actual persons, members of the chorus, in fact, dread women of haggard countenance and snaky

locks. But Euripides, in the *Iphigenia among the
Taurians,* conceives them, in modern fashion, as but
terrifying hallucinations of a guilty conscience and a
temporarily disordered mind. Euripides was an ardent
pupil of the Sophists and the philosophers of his day
and their teachings and influence in general are clearly
reflected in his plays. He is, therefore, a product of a
new period in Athenian thought, a time of transition,
when the beliefs and the habits of men had been un-
settled by the rapidly changing social and political environment of the closing years of the fifth century.

Besides the poets and the playwrights there were
certain other agencies at work which were of potent
influence in affecting Athenian religious belief in the
Age of Pericles. These agencies were the Orphic doctrines, the Eleusinian Mysteries, and the speculations
and teachings of the philosophers and the Sophists.

Orphism was a product of the sixth century B.C. and
originated in connection with the worship of the god
Dionysus. It was Orpheus, the mythical, magical
Thracian lyre-player, who was credited with having
modified and rearranged the Bacchic rites. Accurate
and complete information of the origin of Orphism, its
history, its ritual, and its influence is unfortunately lacking. But of its general character we are certain.
Orphism was a religion of mysticism; the beliefs and
practices of this sect, so divergent in many particulars
from current religion, are remarkable. Pantheism, and
not polytheism, was at its basis. The body was regarded as an impeding material element imprisoning
the soul, which was divine and immortal. The Orphic
sect believed in the idea of prenatal sin and the possibility of redemption or atonement. Salvation was open
to initiates only. Transmigration of souls was likewise
a feature of the belief. It was thought that at death
the soul went to Hades to be reborn into another body,
and that the cycle caused by sin might be shortened by
virtuous conduct, by the practice of vegetarianism, and,

in short, by the observance of an elaborate ritual, which seems to have had its origin in Crete and in Asia Minor, especially Phrygia. The exact destination and lot of the finally purified soul are unknown, but blessedness and eternal happiness resulted. The members of the Orphic cult were not numerous in the classical period and failed to make any wide-spread popular appeal, although the direct or indirect influence of these striking doctrines was considerable, and may be seen in the Odes of Pindar, the dramas of Euripides, and especially in the schools of Pythagoras and Empedocles, and in the philosophy of Plato.

There are many striking aspects of Orphism which seem to anticipate later beliefs and practices, especially Christian. Orpheus himself, as leader of wild animals, is as Christ, shepherd of his flock. The doctrines of prenatal sin, of the necessity of purification and redemption and the pursuit of spiritual excellence, the belief in future life, the hope of immortality, the possibility of becoming one with the divine through purity — these are, indeed, remarkable doctrines, but the cult was unable to do more than to tinge the main stream of Hellenic religion. Orphism in its nature was not calculated to make a widespread popular appeal. It was hard for devotees of the Orphic sect themselves to keep the faith, for, as Plato (*Phaedo* 69c) says, quoting the Orphic text: " Many are wand-bearers, few *Bakchoi*."

In the latter part of the sixth century B.C. Pythagoras established at Croton in Italy a school of thought which bore great resemblance to Orphism. Pythagoras, too, taught the divine nature of the soul and the necessity of its purification and development through ethical discipline and a careful regimen. For example, meat, beans, and woolen garments were taboo. But Pythagoras emphasized the intellectual side of Orphism rather than the emotional, and stressed the value of number and harmony.

Another extremely important influence in connection with Athenian religion were the *Eleusinian Mysteries*. These rites, annually celebrated in the fall at Eleusis in Attica, were held in honor of the goddess Demeter, earth-mother and goddess of grain, and her daughter Persephone (Kore). The initiates of the Mysteries were sworn to secrecy and for the most part they have kept the vow so faithfully that we are baffled in obtaining complete or even satisfying information relative to them. As Pausanias says: " My dream forbade me to describe what is within the wall of the sanctuary; and surely it is clear that the uninitiated may not lawfully hear of that from the sight of which they are debarred."

The date of the origin of the Mysteries is uncertain. They are not mentioned in Homer or in Hesiod, but doubtless are as early as the eighth century B.C., since the interesting Homeric *Hymn to Demeter*, which is probably of the seventh century B.C., tells in charming verse the story of the cult and its beginnings. Persephone, while gathering flowers, was carried away by the chthonian god Hades (Pluto) to his kingdom below. For nine days her mother Demeter, disguised as an old woman, wandered over land and sea in search of her lost daughter. She came to Eleusis where, fatigued and distressed, she sat by a well. There she was accosted by the daughters of King Celeus. Through their influence Demeter was employed as nurse for the infant prince, the son of Metaneira and Celeus. That he might wax strong, by day she anointed him with ambrosia, and by night she hid him in the live coals of the fire. But the infant's mother, seeing this, cried aloud in her fear. Demeter, angered, assumed her immortal form, revealed her divine nature, and commanded the building of a temple and an altar and the establishment of the mystic rites and worship in her honor. Now Demeter, in her grief for her daughter, had caused the earth to remain barren and no seed sprouted in the soil and no fruit appeared until, at the behest of Zeus,

Hades restored Persephone to her mother. But Persephone had eaten of the food of the dead, the pomegranate seed, and must dwell in the world below for a third of the year. In the spring, however, she might go to the world above and join her mother.

In the words of the Hymn, Demeter caused the earth to bloom again and " to Triptolemus and Diocles the charioteer, and mighty Eumolpus, and Celeus, she showed the manner of the rites, and taught them her goodly mysteries, holy mysteries which none may violate, or search into, or noise abroad, for the great curse from the gods restrains the voice. Happy is he among deathly men who hath beheld these things! And he that is uninitiate, and hath no lot in them, hath never equal lot in death beneath the murky gloom."

The origin of the Mysteries is doubtless to be found in religious rites related to agriculture. In a sense, it was a harvest festival.

The chief facts known of the ritual may briefly be given. In March at Agrae there were held preliminary *Lesser Mysteries* in honor of Persephone and Dionysus. In the autumn, on the thirteenth of Boedromion (September), the ceremonies began; on the fifteenth, candidates for initiation assembled, and on the sixteenth, they, together with their animals, the pigs which were to be sacrificed, were purified by bathing in the sea. Sacrifices followed and on the nineteenth the procession to Eleusis, fourteen miles distant, started over the Sacred Way. The worshippers carried the image of the god Iacchus (a form of Dionysus), and also the sacred symbols which had been brought from Eleusis. At sunset the procession reached Eleusis, where for three days and nights the festival was celebrated with sacrifices, with initiations and purifications, and with performances of the sacred drama. Important features of the ritual of purification were the handling of the sacred symbols and the drinking, after fasting, of the mystic *kykeon* (barley meal, mint and water), even as Demeter had done. The culmination of the celebration were the dramatic and religious rites performed in the great hall (*telesterion*). The foundations of this great religious assembly-place, together with many other interesting archeological discoveries, have been disclosed by the modern excavations at Eleusis. Scenes were apparently enacted picturing various episodes in the story of Demeter and Persephone as told in the hymn above outlined. Dionysus, Iacchus, and Triptolemus, as personages in the religious ritual became more important in later times.

There are many references in the ancient writers to the remarkable influence of the Mysteries and their tremendous emotional and personal appeal. The chorus of Aristophanes' *Frogs* (455ff.) is composed of initiates who sing: " We alone have the sun and its gracious light, we who have been initiated into the Mysteries and have lived a pious life toward strangers and toward our own people."

In a fragment (114 [102]) from a dirge written by Pindar, in memory of an Athenian who had been initiated into the Mysteries, we read: " Blessed is he who hath seen those things before he goeth beneath the earth; for he knoweth the end of mortal life, and the beginning of that existence given of God." Similarly in Sophocles (Frag. 719): " Thrice blessed they of men who see these mystic rites before they go to Hades' realm. These alone have life there, for others there all things are evil." Isocrates (*Panegyricus* 28) refers to the Mysteries as " that mystic initiation, the partakers of which have hopes that are more pleasant, concerning both the end of life and all eternity."

One of the most illuminating passages relative to the Mysteries, although it is of late date, may be quoted:[1] " Then, in the moment of death, the soul is affected in like manner, as in the initiation into the Great Mysteries. At first, there are wanderings and weary coursings to and fro, and, until the consummation, a strange and

[1] Cited by Stobaeus, *Florilegium* 120.26; see Sandys, Edition of Isocrates, *Panegyricus,* 28.

doubtful marching through the gloom; and then, at the very verge of that consummation, there comes a blending of every horror, — 'tis all shivering, trembling, sweating, and affrightment; and after this, a wondrous light breaks forth; and the pure meadows and open plains give their welcome with minstrelsy and dances and the solemnity of hallowed sounds and saintly visions, wherein he who is now all-perfect and initiated obtains freedom and release at last. He ranges here and there engarlanded, he revels in the sacred mysteries, he shares the companionship of pure and holy men; and anon he looks on earth and contemplates the uninitiated and unpurified crowd of the living — all trampled down and huddled together in the depth of mire and mist, and abiding in their miseries through fear of death and through disbelief in the good things yonder."

As in Orphism, so in the Eleusinian Mysteries, we see emphasis placed on purification and the purging of the self of sins; there is likewise an effort to win redemption and salvation and a belief in the possibility of a happiness after death. Both Orphism and the Mysteries have obvious oriental aspects, and both anticipate certain features of Christian doctrines and ritual. While Orphism met with no popular response in Athens, the interest in the Mysteries was constant and widespread and was, furthermore, fostered by official sanction. The vitality of the Mysteries is shown by the fact that the worship was continued to the fourth century after Christ.

In Athens itself we find the worship of certain gods particularly emphasized and, as was generally the case throughout Greece, these gods were her protecting deities. Just as Hera was identified with Samos and Argos, Zeus with Olympia, and Apollo with Delos and Delphi, so Athena and Poseidon were especially venerated at Athens. For, according to the old belief, Athena had given to Attica the olive, ever sacred to her, while

Poseidon's gift was the horse. The early worship of these gods at Athens is attested by the myth which told of their contest for the land of Attica, a tale which found visible and artistic expression in the sculptured group on the western pediment of the Parthenon. It was Athena who was the protecting deity. This goddess granted increase to the land and prosperity to the people; in war, she gave victory, and in peace, skill and accomplishment in the arts, especially handicraft and weaving. Finally, Athena came to be identified with the Athenian genius and culture, and was venerated as the goddess of wisdom and enlightenment, and reason and art. On the Acropolis, the Parthenon, the Erechtheum (in part), and the temple of Wingless Victory were built in her honor, and the two magnificent statues by Phidias were set up to her glory. The great festival of the Panathenaea was instituted and celebrated as a form of worship of the patron goddess. The coins of Athens were adorned, on the obverse, with the head of Athena and, on the reverse, with her owl.

The worship of Dionysus was a striking development in Athenian religion in the sixth and fifth centuries B.C. Of no importance in Homer the cult of Dionysus grew amazingly. To native and primitive elements in Greek religion, which recognized the divine aspect of nature in respect to the growth and the development of life and the life-spirit, were added the orgiastic features of the cult of the Thracian Dionysus. Thebes was the early center of his cult in Greece proper. At Athens, we find that Dionysus is the god of generation and of wine and, in particular, of the theater and drama.

Apollo, a god of very great influence in other parts of the Greek world, held a place of lesser importance in Athenian religion, although the festival of the *Thargelia* was held in May to honor him as protector of the crops. The gymnasium of the Lyceum was located in a precinct sacred to him. Athenian drama is full of references and prayers to Apollo as god of light, of

healing, and of music. Chiefly, however, as the god of
Delphi and of oracles is Apollo famous. Athens, as
other Greek states, had at Delphi a treasure-house
which contained offerings to the god of prophecy;
Athenian officials regularly journeyed to Delphi to consult the oracle, and attended Apollo's games and festivals both at Delphi and Delos. Artemis, sister of
Apollo, goddess of the chase and of the moon, is his
feminine counterpart.

Hermes was a god of numerous attributes and functions. In Homer regarded as herald and messenger
of the gods, he was later identified with the flocks and
herds, with trade and gain, with youth, with eloquence,
and with the gymnasia. He was thought of as conduc-
tor of the souls of the dead to the world below. The delightful Homeric *Hymn to Hermes* represents him as a
precocious infant, the inventor of the lyre and the thief
of Apollo's cattle. In Athens, his statue, usually composed only of the head placed on a rectangular pillar,
was set up in many public places, such as cross-roads,
in front of houses, and in the stadium. These statues
were called *Hermae*. The wholesale mutilation of these
Hermae in Athens in 413 B.C., in which affair Alcibiades
and Andocides were implicated, was a great scandal.

Aphrodite was goddess of love, marriage, and the
family. Her worship, in which were blended various
oriental elements, was not of especial local import in
Athens.

The cult of the god Asclepius (Roman *Aesculapius*)
deserves brief characterization because of its interesting features. At Athens, on the southern side of the
Acropolis and just west of the theater, are the remains
of the sanctuary of Asclepius — a long colonnade, and
the foundations of a small temple. These remains seem
to be of the fourth century B.C., but the sanctuary
surely dates from the fifth. Here, patients in quest of
health, and worshippers came, slept, and sacrificed.
The chief scene of the worship of Asclepius, however,

was at Epidaurus in the Peloponnesus, and from here, no doubt, the cult of the god of healing had come to Athens. Excavations at Epidaurus have revealed a flourishing religious center, where there were built a beautiful theater (the best preserved today of all Greek theaters), the temple of Asclepius, the Rotunda (*Tholos*), the temple of Artemis, a great colonnade, and a stadium. These buildings are of the fourth century B.C., but the worship of the god on this site must have been of great antiquity. The colonnade served as a dormitory in which the patients slept and in a dream awaited as a revelation from the god the manner of their alleviation, or an actual cure during the night. In case of a cure the grateful suppliant might dedicate to the god a votive offering representing the part of the body healed, as, for example, ears or eyes or hands. Many inscriptions have been found which attest the cures effected by the god. A few examples of these follow (taken from Frazer, *Pausanias,* 3, p. 249):

"A man, whose fingers were all paralyzed but one, came as a suppliant to the god. But when he saw the tablets in the sanctuary with the miraculous cures recorded on them, he was incredulous and scoffed at the cures. However, he fell asleep in the dormitory and dreamed a dream. He thought he was playing dice in the temple and that as he was about to make a throw, the god seized his hand and straightened out his fingers. In the morning he went forth whole.

Alcetas of Halice, a blind man, had a dream. He thought that the god came and opened his eyes with his fingers, and so he saw the trees in the sanctuary for the first time; in the morning he went forth whole.

Thyson, a blind boy of Hermion, had his eyes licked by one of the dogs about the temple and went away whole.

A man who suffered much from an ulcer on the toe was brought forth by the attendants and placed on a seat. While he slept, a serpent came forth from the dormitory and healed the ulcer with his tongue. It then glided back into the dormitory. When the man awoke he was cured and declared that he had seen a vision; he thought a young man of goodly aspect had smeared a salve upon his toe.

Arata, a Lacedaemonian woman, came to Epidaurus on behalf of her daughter who was afflicted with dropsy and had been left behind in Lacedaemon. She slept in the sanctuary and dreamed a dream. She thought that the god cut off her daughter's head and hung up the headless trunk, neck down. When all

the moisture had run out, he took down the body, and put on
the head again. After she had dreamed this dream, the mother
returned to Lacedaemon, where she found that her daughter
was cured, and had seen the very same dream."

It is evident that sacred dogs and serpents were kept
in the sanctuary of Asclepius.

What shall we say regarding the authenticity of these
miraculous cures ascribed to the divine intervention
of the god? No doubt when the patient was suffering
from a malady more or less imaginary, amelioration
followed prayer, faith, auto-suggestion, and the advice
and consolation of the priests. Furthermore, these
priests were doubtless experienced healers and their
medical and surgical knowledge often must have been
employed in the sufferers' behalf.

Besides these positive influences — Orphism, the
Mysteries, and the traditional worship of the gods
of their fathers — Athenian religious belief of the fifth
and fourth centuries B.C. was subjected to powerful
forces of philosophical and scientific inquiry which
tended to produce uncertainty and scepticism. The old
mythology and the old beliefs were in many particulars
untenable, if faith were placed in the speculations of
the early philosophers and physicists and, later on, of
the Sophists.

How could one believe implicitly in the Homeric and
Hesiodic conceptions of the creation of the world, gods,
and men, if credence were given to those Ionian philosophers who explained the nature of things as originating in a *first principle*, apart from the gods? Thales
defined this first principle as water; Anaximenes as
air; Heraclitus as fire; Anaxagoras as *Nous* (Mind or
Reason). These early thinkers, to be sure, did not
actually disbelieve in the existence of the gods, yet
their speculations in effect were a negation of divine
omnipotence and importance. Certainly their teachings were popularly interpreted as being at variance
with the accepted religion, so that Anaxagoras was

compelled to leave Athens, partly, at least, because of his heterodox views. The resulting situation in the realm of religious thought may be compared with the confusion in the modern world during the previous generation, and even now far from ended, caused by a supposed conflict and incompatibility of science and the Christian religion.

Scepticism early shows itself in the striking protests and criticisms of Xenophanes, the Eleatic philosopher-poet, in the plays of Euripides, and in the queries and the teachings of the popular sophists, whose influence upon the younger generation was great.

The ideas and dialectic of Socrates and Plato should be studied in connection with philosophy and logic yet religious elements are potent in the teachings of these thinkers. Socrates was a student and expounder of ethics primarily, but his ethics were fundamentally religious, and his work in Athens he regarded as a divine mission, divinely guided. His teaching was largely spiritual, as can be seen from the dialogues of Plato where Socrates regularly is the chief speaker.

Summing up Plato's religious creed briefly, we may say that he believed in the practice of justice and of holiness which is righteousness; he held that real knowledge must be ascertained and, in consequence, virtue will be the inevitable result. He accepted to some extent the Orphic doctrines, in that he believed that the soul is divine and the body is as a prison-house; death therefore was to him a boon, an escape, which frees one from evil; the soul is immortal and after transmigration returns to God; God himself would seem to be the highest of the Ideas — the Idea of Good. In Plato we find a welcome given to all that is best and finest in previous Greek religious tradition and likewise a rejection of crude myth or palpable error.

From this brief survey of the origin and the nature of the diverse elements contributing to Greek religious thought it is evident that a dogmatic generalization relative to Athenian religion is hazardous. We read, for example, that Greek religion was largely a polytheistic worship of anthropomorphic gods through the medium of sacrifice; further, that these gods were powerful, but humanly fallible and even cruel, and sacrifice to them by worshippers was a matter of " give and take," or, as Plato states it, " an art of trafficking." And it is true that a general impression of this tenor is left upon the mind of the reader of Homer, Hesiod, and the lyric poets. We are informed, moreover, that a rather primitive and superstitious belief in an imaginative but conflicting mythology held sway over the Athenian mind. And substantiation of this assertion may be gained from countless references and passages throughout Greek literature. The popular view of Greek religion is, that it was lacking in a conception of sin, that it offered little or no hope of immortality, that it denied to humanity the expectation of a happy future existence, and that it considered improbable any approximation or kinship of the human with the divine.

To the correctness of this characterization candor compels answer that many proofs are forthcoming. And yet we find the early philosophers calmly ignoring the old cosmogonies and theogonies. Xenophanes, Euripides, and Plato reject anthropomorphism and the attribution of base deeds to the gods. We see Xenophanes and Plato, though not entirely shaking themselves free from polytheism, yet affirming and expounding an almost monotheistic conception of the deity; Orphism taught the divinity of the soul, the belief in immortality, the necessity of good conduct in this world, and the possibility of salvation in the next. The Eleusinian Mysteries, as Orphism, exhorted devotees to purification and righteous behavior, whereby a happy and blessed life after death would be obtained. Hesiod asserted the importance of hard work and justice towards all; Theognis emphasized thrift and industry; Socrates preached, year in and year out, ethi-

cal conduct which is, at its best, Christian; Aeschylus
and Sophocles in their great plays inculcated morality,
and proclaimed with assurance that there is a god in
his heaven and all will be well in the end.

It may be objected that the influences and ideals
above outlined were not far-reaching in their effects
and were of little importance in shaping the views and
affecting the conduct of the average Athenian. No
doubt this was true of the more ignorant and unthinking. Yet if Orphism and Plato won comparatively few
followers, the mass of the citizens, by nature keen-
witted, curious, and susceptible, were surely responsive
to the great moral teachings of Attic tragedy and the
sacred and emotional appeal of the Mysteries of
Eleusis.

In seeking to understand the nature of Greek religion, however, we must try to divest ourselves of modern religious conceptions which are largely Hebraic.
Greek religion is ethical rather than theological, and
was concerned far more with actual life in this world
than with preparation for the next. In consequence,
it was not calculated to give solace in adversity and in
old age, nor assurance regarding the hopes and aspirations of the future. But *sophrosyne* (temperance and
moderation) underlay Athenian thought and action
and, above all, *good taste* in all things, and a sense of
the fitting and of the beautiful. And these ideals, if
they are followed in the conduct of daily life, form no
mean religion.

It is highly important that the student of religion
should realize the Greek element in Christian religion.
The ethical teachings of Socrates and Plato are not dissimilar to those of Christ. The later Greek philosophy,
derived in large measure from Plato, profoundly influenced Christian thought and dogma. While Christianity had its origin in Palestine, yet it found expression and became universal only through the aid of
Greek rhetoric and philosophy.

CHAPTER XVIII

SCIENCE

"In science the Greeks had to build from the foundations. Other peoples had extensive knowledge and highly developed arts. Only among the Greeks existed the true scientific method with its characteristics of free inquiry, rational interpretation, verification or rectification by systematic and repeated observation, and controlled deduction from accepted principles." — SEDGWICK AND TYLER.

OUR modern age, in which physical science is so prominent, is prone to ignore Greek scientific achievements, which are, however, far more considerable than is generally thought. The scope of this volume, largely devoted to Athens in the classical period, precludes lengthy consideration of theories and discoveries in Greek science: the latter, in fact, were mostly products of the less creative, but scholarly, Alexandrian Age.

It is not surprising that the world today, which has brought to actual realization through miraculous inventions of the last few decades the mere dreams and myths of antiquity, should largely ignore the gropings in the physical sciences of the scientists of over two thousand years ago. Nor, in a sense, is our ignorance and indifference in the matter of Greek scientific attainments so serious as would be our neglect of Greek ideas, ideals, and art; all agree that in the latter fields modern materialism and commercialism have much indeed to learn from ancient Hellas, whereas in science we are supreme. However, a few of the most striking facts relative to Greek scientific knowledge, theories, and discoveries may find a place here and should be of interest. For extremely technical details the specialist is referred to the ample bibliography on this chapter to be found in the appendix.

It will be noted that the sciences which most of all appealed to the Greek mind were mathematics and mathematical astronomy. Medicine and anatomy came next, perhaps, then geography, botany, and the natural sciences in general. Chemistry was not considered or studied as a science apart, but rather as a handmaid of the practical arts, a necessary stock-in-trade of those who devoted themselves to manufactures.

The truth is that the Greeks were interested primarily in the study of man and in the investigation of Nature as man's environment. The intense study of Nature *per se* was not pursued unremittingly by them.

Early Greek science was so intimately associated with philosophy that it cannot be separated from it. In the chapter on Philosophy we saw the interest of the early pre-Socratic thinkers in the physical sciences and in mathematics. In the sixth century B.C., Thales, whose name comes first in the history of Greek philosophy, was a mathematician and astronomer; several theorems of elementary geometry are ascribed to him and he is said to have prophesied an eclipse of the sun (585 (?) B.C.). Anaximander thought that Man came into being from the fish; it is said, too, that for geographical science Anaximander drew the first map of the world, and that he introduced the sun-dial.

The first important Greek mathematician was Pythagoras (sixth century B.C.) who taught his Theory of Numbers and made numerous discoveries in arithmetic, geometry, and acoustics. In astronomy, many Pythagoreans believed that the globular earth moved in empty space while the sun, moon and stars remained immovable. They did not, however, urge the heliocentric theory; credit for this is to be given to Aristarchus.

For the striking theories of the early physicist-philosophers the reader should turn to the chapter on Philosophy, e.g., for Heraclitus and his doctrine of " Fire " and " Flux," for the views and notable achievements of the versatile Empedocles, for Anaxagoras and his " Seeds " and, finally, for the extremely interesting and tremendously important doctrines of the Atomists, Leucippus and Democritus.

Of Greek MATHEMATICS geometry was by far the most important branch. Plato was intensely interested in geometry, which had been studied by Thales and Pythagoras, and we are told that over the door of the Academy this motto was to be read: " Let no one ignorant of geometry enter within." The Platonic dialogues show that the great philosopher had a very considerable knowledge of geometry. Eudemus (about 330 B.C.), the pupil of Aristotle, wrote a history of geometry which is not now extant.

Alexandria in Egypt, founded by Alexander the Great in 332 B.C., grew with great rapidity. Under the patronage of the Ptolemies, the Museum and the large Library attracted numerous scholars and thousands of students — the first real University in the modern sense of the term. All branches of learning were there studied and furthered by distinguished scholars. In literature this scholarship was devoted, as we have seen, to the annotation and editing of the classical authors and few original compositions of literary excellence were produced. In science, however, Alexandria became a great center. After 300 B.C. the history of Greek science is, for the most part, the history of Alexandrian science. Pergamum and other cities were rivals, but were feeble by comparison.

The reputed founder of the Alexandrian school of mathematics was Euclid, the author of the epoch-making treatise on geometry. The *Elements* of Euclid (about 300 B.C.), in thirteen books, supplanted all former works on the subject and have remained the very basis of elementary geometry to the present day. In fact, Euclid and geometry have been synonymous terms for centuries.

Archimedes of Syracuse (about 287–212 B.C.), who

studied at Alexandria, was a more versatile mathematician than Euclid. Not only did he write a great work — now lost — on geometry, but there are extant treatises by him on the Sphere and the Cylinder, the Measurement of the Circle, On Conoids and Spheroids, and other works. Archimedes was specially interested in Statics and Hydrostatics. It was the successful solution of a problem in the latter subject which caused him, as the story relates, to leap from the bath and to run home naked, crying, " Eureka! Eureka! (I have found it)." To Archimedes, too, as pioneer in mechanics and the theory and practice of the lever, is ascribed the famous remark, " Give me a place to stand and I will move the earth."

Other prominent mathematicians were Apollonius of Perga " the Great Geometer " (born about 262 B.C.) and, much later, Pappus and Diophantus, of about 300 A.D. Diophantus of Alexandria has the distinction of being the author of the first extant treatise on algebra, although the original Greek work, in thirteen books, is now represented in a Latin translation of the first six books only.

As for the value and the accuracy of the mathematical investigation of the Greeks a competent critic [1] in this field, may be quoted: " Acquaintance with the original work of the Greek mathematicians is necessary for any mathematician worthy of the name. Mathematics is a Greek science. So far as pure geometry is concerned, the mathematician's technical equipment is almost wholly Greek. The Greeks laid down the principles, fixed the terminology, and invented the methods *ab initio:* moreover, they did this with such certainty that in the centuries which have since elapsed there has been no need to reconstruct, still less to reject as unsound, any essential part of their doctrine."

Many ingenious inventions and mechanical appliances, some of which we may think of modern origin, came from the researches of these men of science.

[1] Mr. T. L. Heath, in *The Legacy of Greece,* p. 98.

Archytas is said to have invented the screw and the pulley. Archimedes originated the water-screw, discovered the principle of the lever, and perfected new military engines.

Perhaps the most versatile inventive genius of the ancient Greek world was Hero (or Heron), of uncertain date, a mathematician, whose inventions are numerous. He wrote a work, *Pneumatica,* wherein ingenious devices are described. Among these contrivances were: the first penny-in-the-slot machine (a Holy-Water automaton); a steam-sphere which rotated by the retro-action of escaping-steam, and other steam appliances; Hero's Ball, from which water was forced out by compressed air, the principle of the fire-engine; a water-organ; and the *hodometer,* or road-measurer ("the wheel of a vehicle sets in motion a series of cog-wheels, like clock-work, which record the rotations of the carefully measured wheel, and so gives the distance passed over").

Greek ASTRONOMY had its beginnings in the studies of Thales and Pythagoras. It was further developed by Eudoxus of Cnidus (408–355 B.C.), who wrote a work called the *Phaenomena,* subsequently reproduced by Aratus (*ca.* 270 B.C.). As in the case of mathematics, Alexandria became the center of astronomical study and really great discoveries were made.

Copernicus was anticipated in the heliocentric theory by Aristarchus of Samos (*ca.* 270 B.C.). Archimedes states that Aristarchus conjectured that " neither the fixed stars nor the sun are subject to any motion; but the earth annually revolves round the sun in the circumference of a circle, in the center of which the sun remains fixed." This striking theory, however, did not win acceptance at the time.

Remarkable, too, were the researches of Eratosthenes (*ca.* 275–195 B.C.), librarian at Alexandria. He asserted that the earth is spherical, and, as Strabo tells us, that India might be reached by sailing westward from Iberia, if the immensity of the Atlantic Ocean did not prevent! That the earth is round is proved, he said, by the convexity of the sea. Distant lights at sea level can not be seen by sailors, but if these lights are elevated they are at once visible. To sailors approaching land the shore continually rises and objects that formerly seemed low grow in size (Strabo, 1. 1. 20, and 1. 4. 6). Eratosthenes also computed mathematically the circumference of the earth and found it to be 250,000 stades — there are between eight and nine stades in an English mile — which is amazingly close to the actual measurement of 25,000 English miles.

The last two great Greek astronomers were Hipparchus and Ptolemy. The former founded the science of trigonometry, catalogued the stars, and correctly established numerous important astronomical facts. Ptolemy is the author of the great work which forms the basis of the *Almagest*. His astronomical system was regarded as standard until the time of Copernicus.

In the natural sciences Aristotle, that master of learning, wrote important works on animals (*Historia Animalium*) and the *Parts of Animals* and these works, which show keen observation, survive from his investigations in the province of nature. Theophrastus, his pupil and successor in the Lyceum, composed a *Treatise on Plants*. This work, the most important study in botanical science produced by the Greeks, has recently been translated and is now available to all botanists.

The most important branch of science among the Greeks, after mathematics, was MEDICINE. Let us briefly trace the development and tendencies in this province of study.

The cult of Asclepius (Roman *Aesculapius*), the god of healing, and the cures effected by priests in the temples of that deity, especially at Epidaurus, are described in the chapter on Religion.

Greek medical science really begins in the sixth century B.C. with the School of the island of Cos, whose foremost representative is the great Hippocrates, who was born in 460 B.C. Alexandrian scholars collected the writings of this school — the *Hippocratic Corpus* or Collection — and these give us much information regarding its teachings and methods during the period from the sixth to the fourth centuries B.C. Although the Pythagoreans, as early as 500 B.C., had done some dissecting of animals the ignorance of anatomy, physiology, and pathology was profound and general before the Alexandrian Age, when dissection of the human body was first countenanced. The medical knowledge of Hippocrates, the Father of Medicine, was based on the recognition that disease is a natural phenomenon, on careful clinical observation, and the discovery that Nature herself is a beneficent healer. Medical treatment consisted of such sensible procedure as baths, massages, careful diet, and suffusions. Unfortunately the practice of bleeding — the curse of medicine for centuries — was also in vogue, although it was apparently employed in moderation. The Hippocratic School achieved proficiency in surgery, especially in the treatment of dislocations, fractures, and bandaging. Drugs were employed and some 265 kinds are mentioned in the Hippocratic Collection. This school held the theory that health and disease depend upon the four " humors " of the body — blood, phlegm, yellow bile, and black bile — and that the physical condition depends on the proportion in which these are mixed. This theory was popularized by Galen. The fame of Hippocrates was very great; he traveled much and his pupils were numerous. Of unimpeachable probity himself, his ideal of the good physician is the practitioner of high ethical standards and professional behavior. This ideal is incorporated in the well-known Hippocratic Oath, an oath which is still sworn to by graduates of our medical schools. The concluding words of this remarkable oath are: " With purity and holiness I will pass my life and practice my Art. Into whatever houses I enter, I will go there for the benefit of the sick and will abstain from every injurious act and corruption. Whatever in my professional practice — or even not in connection with it — I see or hear in the lives of men which ought not to be spoken of abroad, I will not divulge. While I keep this Oath unviolated, may it be granted me to enjoy life and the practice of the Art, always respected among men, but should I break or violate the Oath, may the reverse be my lot."

A new era of medicine dates from the Alexandrian Age when, in the city founded by Alexander the Great, great strides were taken. Discoveries in anatomy and physiology were stimulated by the fact that dissection of the human body was at last allowed. Cadavers were disemboweled for mummification and vivisection of criminals was legally permitted. The two greatest medical scientists of Alexandria were Herophilus and Erasistratus of the third century B.C. Herophilus named the *duodenum* and other structures which still bear his name. He discovered the importance of the brain, the nature of the nerves and, most important of all, the function of the arteries in conveying blood from the heart to all parts of the body. It had been previously supposed that the arteries contained air — hence their name. Herophilus also described the pulse and showed how its behavior affords indication of health and disease. Thus was Harvey (1578–1657) virtually anticipated in the discovery of the circulation of the blood.

Erasistratus made other discoveries in the anatomy of the brain, the valves of the heart, the epiglottis, and the nervous system.

Pliny tells us that " the ancients were accustomed to giving mandragora as an anaesthetic for injuries inflicted by serpents, and before incisions or punctures are made in the body in order to insure insensibility to pain."

In the treatise of Celsus (first century A.D.) on medicine, a Latin work, in eight books, probably translated from Greek, we have a complete account of medicine as it then existed. The sections of this work which treat of surgery and internal medicine are very good. Dioscorides wrote on drugs, Rufus of Ephesus on human anatomy, Soranus of Ephesus on gynaecology, and Aretaeus on clinical medicine.

Greatest in the bulk of his extant medical writings and in influence on the history of medicine, is Galen, who was born at Pergamum about 130 A.D. His writings, now published in twenty-two volumes, treat of all branches of medicine and surgery. Galen spent some years at Alexandria and also at Rome. The writings of Galen and of Hippocrates are at the very basis of medicine today. From the brief summary above presented it will be seen that the Greeks created modern medicine.

In concluding this chapter, another quotation from a scholar who has done much to interpret Greek science to this generation, Mr. T. L. Heath, is appropriate: " When we think of the debt which mankind owes to the Greeks, we are apt to think too exclusively of the masterpieces in literature and art which they have left us. But the Greek genius was many-sided; the Greek, with his insatiable love of knowledge, his determination to see things as they are and to see them whole, his burning desire to be able to give a rational explanation of everything in heaven and earth, was just as irresistibly driven to natural science, mathematics, and exact reasoning in general, or logic."

CHAPTER XIX

THE NEW STUDY OF ANCIENT GREECE

"Continually laid aside — it is too tremendous and fatiguing for the world to live up to; continually rediscovered — for the world cannot live without it: that is the history of the Greek genius." — R. W. LIVINGSTONE.

THE title of this chapter may seem paradoxical to the reader who is unfamiliar with ancient Greek civilization. How can there be a profitable *new* study of a civilization long since passed away and of a people whose life and achievements have been studied for centuries? Have not generations of scholars definitively established the ancient texts to the smallest detail? Has not the last word been said in the criticism and interpretation of Greek literature and Greek history? Surely all the facts must be known. In the very nature of the case, how can there be new evidence and new information of importance?

Let us try to answer some of these questions. It will not be difficult, I think, to show the real state of the case. The truth is that in recent years investigations, discoveries of all kinds, and archaeological excavations have thrown a flood of new light on ancient Greek lands and civilization. Fifty years ago even the exact site of the Homeric Troy was uncertain and the descriptive details of the advanced civilization portrayed in the Homeric poems were regarded by many as fictitious. But the excavations of 1871–1886, conducted by Schliemann and Dörpfeld, revealed Priam's actual city on the hill of Hissarlik in northwestern Asia Minor. Here by the waters of the Scamander, in the plain of the Troad, was waged an actual war, the ten years' siege — only a few miles distant from Gallipoli, the scene of a modern sanguinary struggle — in which armies of Greece and Asia fought, although these hosts contended not for lovely white-armed Helen, as the poet would have us believe, but more plausibly for causes designated by the modern historian which bear all too familiar names — economic rivalry, commercial supremacy, and the control of the Bosporus.

More remarkable were the results of investigations at Mycenae " rich-in-gold," Agamemnon's famous capital. Here were excavated tombs within the Gate of Lions below the Acropolis, and the spade revealed a remarkable and hitherto unknown age of which we have written briefly in another chapter. In the graves were elaborately and beautifully wrought treasures of gold and silver — masks, breast-plates, inlaid daggers, cups, and vases. This great civilization, called Mycenaean from the place of its original discovery, was prevalent also in the island of Crete (see Chapter II). This Cretan civilization is called Minoan in honor of King Minos, who is no longer a mythical potentate, as his extensive palace-labyrinth has been excavated at Cnossos. Not many years ago 1000 B.C. seemed an incredibly early date to use in speaking of Grecian lands, but now we possess abundant works of art of an era to be dated from about 2500–1500 B.C.

At Olympia, in Elis, the site of the great Greek Games, the Germans excavated the whole *Altis,* or sacred precinct, laying bare the foundations of many buildings, especially the temples of Zeus and Hera. A museum erected at Olympia contains the works of art discovered there, of which the most noteworthy are the Hermes of Praxiteles, and the sculptured pediment group from the temple of Zeus. Remarkable, too, and of great importance are the results of the work done by the French at Delphi and Delos, by the Americans at Argos, Corinth, Athens, and Sardes, and by the Greeks at Eleusis and Epidaurus.

The spade is still being actively wielded in all parts of the Greek world and every discovery serves to correct or to corroborate previous conceptions or to give us absolutely new and illuminating knowledge of the civilization that is the mother of our own. Our appreciation of Greek literature owes much to these revelations, while our understanding of Greek life and thought has been, and is being, revolutionized by the inspiring results of archaeological studies.

It is not alone new inscriptions, vases, coins, sculptures, and all the monuments found in excavations, however, which necessitate the constant revision of books on ancient Greek civilization. In recent years fate, which has deprived us of so much of the ancient literature, has made some amends. The tombs and rubbish-heaps of Egypt are constantly yielding papyri manuscripts of every kind. While the majority of these papyri are bookkeeping records, farm accounts, or documents of small consequence, certain of these lost works, unexpectedly recovered after the lapse of centuries from the sands of Egypt, are of first-rate importance and interest. A few of these are: several speeches of the Attic orator Hyperides, who was considered by some ancient literary critics to be a worthy rival of Demosthenes; a *Partheneion* (a lyric for a chorus of maidens) by Alcman; the *Constitution of Athens* by Aristotle, a work of great value to the serious student of Greek history and constitutional law; the *Mimes*, or Dramatic Sketches, of Herondas; the *Odes* of Bacchylides, a writer of great fame in antiquity, whose writings previously were unknown to us except through scanty fragments; and the *Persians*, a lyric poem of some 250 lines by Timotheus. But this is not all. An epoch-making find was the discovery in 1905 of large portions of four comedies of the celebrated Menander: these plays are *Hero, Arbitrants, Girl with the Shorn Locks*, and the *Samian Girl*. A large part of the *Trackers*, a satyric play by Sophocles, was found in 1912. The *Cyclops* of Euripides previously had been the only example of this form of dramatic composition. Several valuable fragments of poems of

Sappho have also been discovered, besides fragments of Pindar, Lysias, Callimachus and others. As a result of these discoveries, the major portion of which have been made since 1891, it has been necessary to rewrite our histories of Greek literature, and writers famous in antiquity, but known to us heretofore by name only, can now be read. And the end is not come, for each year brings something new.

How is it with the condition of the texts that we have long possessed? Is it true that they have been letter perfect for centuries? Far from it, unfortunately. Improvement of these faulty extant works is constantly being effected through their revision, emendation, and interpretation. Critical scrutiny and sifting of extant Greek compositions have resulted also in the purging of many documents of interpolations and the attribution of compositions to their rightful authors. Our knowledge in these matters is far greater than that of our fathers. It seems incredible to us, for example, that, through the centuries, Homer was thought to be the author of the mock-heroic epic the *Batrachomyomachia* (the Battle of the Frogs and Mice), which was written perhaps about 490 B.C. In fact, we know more about the early literature, so far as authorship is concerned, than the Athenians themselves. Aristotle, with all his acumen, thought that Homer was the author of the satirical poem *Margites,* and Thucydides believed that he was borrowing from Homer when he quoted some lines from the *Hymn to Delian Apollo,* which was written centuries later than the Homeric poems. Shelley called his delightful versions of the *Hymn to Hermes* and other Hymns, *Translations from Homer.* The extremely popular *Anacreontics* of Cowley and Moore were not originally written by the famous lyricist Anacreon of Teos, in the sixth century B.C., but are of late Alexandrian authorship.

Plagiarism and forgeries, more venial offenses in ancient times than with us, have been a source of confusion and error. An interesting example of literary forgery is presented by the documents found in the manuscripts in Demosthenes' famous speech *On the Crown*. In the course of the speech the orator frequently calls upon the Clerk of the Court to read important documents and letters bearing on the case. In the Alexandrian Period, as these documents had disappeared, some ingenious individual essayed to make good this deficiency by providing forgeries. His industry seems to have failed him, however, when he was half through the long discourse so that the interpolations are entirely wanting in the latter part of the oration. So clever are the substitutions that commentators were long imposed upon. Modern scholarship has easily revealed the falsity of the inserted documents.

The history of Homeric scholarship is a striking chapter in the study of Greek literature. The authenticity of the Homeric poems has been a vexed question since the Alexandrian Period and has given rise to a regrettably large literature. Following the lead of the Separatists in the second century B.C., and of F. A. Wolf in 1795, numerous scholars have attacked the great poems in an effort to prove that the *Iliad* and the *Odyssey* could not have been the work of one man, and that, in fact, the original *Iliad* and *Odyssey* were comparatively insignificant nuclei for the inconsistent verses and passages which were gradually added by later bards. Until the last few years, from the time of Wolf, it has been pretty generally believed that the Homeric poems are of extremely composite origin and the heterogeneous product of numerous individuals, and that the *Odyssey* in particular is much later than the *Iliad*. Appreciation and enjoyment of Homer as sublime poetry have been lost sight of because of the labors, often mischievous, of specialists who have been far more interested in pointing out supposed flaws and inconsistencies than in showing and teaching the beauty and power of the great poems. In the last ten or twenty years the pendulum has been swinging back. Today there are many believers in the essential unity of the poems. The arguments of the destructive critics have been shown to be largely groundless and the supposedly fatal inconsistencies of little or no consequence. At any rate, whatever may be the exact answer to every question suggested by Homer, as a result of this saner study students may now *directly* approach Homer. They may cease to read about the poet and may, as in ancient Hellas, actually enjoy him.

The reader of the above paragraphs will now appreciate, I think, the reason and the necessity for new interpretations of Greek history and literature. But even if discoveries of inscriptions, monuments, and manuscripts were not being made, has not our conception of the writing of history largely changed? History no longer consists of an apparently endless string of dates, battles, and names of generals. Due prominence is now given to the description of society, the people, their language and literature, their art and religion, their aspirations and achievements. So it is that the student of Greek history, as never before, now has the privilege of reading the fascinating story of the life and thought and genius of the people themselves in the light of fuller information and richer appreciation.

New translations, too, are constantly needed. The translations which pleased the taste of previous generations utterly fail to satisfy the modern reader. Pope's *Iliad*, in his own time so popular, to us is poetic, but highly artificial and un-Homeric. Keats waxed enthusiastic over Chapman's laborious *Homer*. All these versions, and others much more recent, excellent perhaps in themselves in certain particulars, are in general misrepresentative of the originals. Ever-changing taste, feeling, idiom, and more accurate scholarship make imperative new translations for those who are denied enjoyment at first-hand of the originals.

There is, then, a new study of ancient Greece. No one, to be sure, except the unfortunately ignorant, the hopelessly prejudiced, or the unregenerate Philistine, denies the beauty of the Greek language, the excellence of the Greek literature, the charm and originality of Greek art, the eternal achievements of the Greek genius, and the value of a realization of the Greek contribution to the modern world.   Greek studies can never die. The temporary Dark Age of the last few years which culminated in the Great War is giving way to a renaissance of classical studies.   And this is indeed fortunate for the world of today, which has great need of those eternal gifts of beauty and truth, of good taste and moderation, of imagination and idealism that Athens, ancient in name only, can bounteously give to those who have eyes to see, ears to hear, and heart and soul to appreciate.   As Shelley sings:

> " But Greece and her foundations are
>   Built below the tide of war,
>   Based on the crystalline sea
>   Of thought and its eternity;
>   Her citizens, imperial spirits,
>   Rule the present from the past;
>   On all this world of men inherits
>   Their seal is set."

CHAPTER XX

THE GENIUS OF THE GREEKS

"L'esprit classique est le culte de la raison claire et libre, la recherche de la beauté harmonieuse et simple dans toutes les manifestations de la pensée." — M. RIBOT.

THE preceding chapters, it is to be hoped, have furnished the material and the evidence whereby we may sum up some of the most important of the Greek characteristics, particularly as found in the Athenians. What were their chief virtues? What, of permanent value, did they accomplish? Wherein should the modern world emulate them? What faults did they have and what mistakes did they make which we should avoid?

Of all the Greeks the Athenians were the most highly gifted. To their native Ionian liveliness, versatility, imagination, and sense of humor — Gallic characteristics — they added the sterling qualities of the Dorians. Physically, they were comely and energetic; mentally, they were quick-witted and curious. In temperament they were generally cheerful and light-hearted. The conventional and popular conception of the Greeks is erroneous, however, that represents them as an utterly care-free and always joyous folk, singing, dancing, and feasting in sheer pagan abandon. Healthy in body and mind, they enjoyed life sanely; yet, as they lived largely in and for the present, a strain of melancholy and sadness is frequently to be observed in their views of sickness and old age, of death and the hereafter. Greek literature contains numerous passages that reveal a keen appreciation of the vicissitudes and the uncertainty, the pains and the sorrows that are inseparable from human existence. The Greeks took life seriously, but not, on the whole, sadly.

At the outset we are struck by the intellectuality of the Greeks and the quality and the power of their minds. Modern biologists affirm that mankind has made no advance, so far as mental powers and ability are concerned, in the 2300 years that separate us from Plato and Aristotle. Professor Conklin says (*Heredity and Environment*, p. 418): " There has been no perceptible improvement in human heredity within historic times. Indeed no modern race of men is the equal of certain ancient ones. In Attica in the space of two centuries there appeared such a galaxy of illustrious men as has never been found on the whole earth in any two centuries since that time. Galton concludes that the average ability of the Athenian race of that period was on the lowest possible estimate as much greater than that of the English race of the present day as the latter is above that of the African negro."

In Greece, and especially in Athens, for the first time in the ancient world, intellect and reason were operative in all the activities of life. As Herodotus says (1. 60): " The Greeks have been from very ancient times distinguished from the barbarians by superior sagacity and freedom from foolish simpleness. The Athenians have the credit of surpassing all other Greeks in cleverness." As a result of this rule of reason they achieved a freedom that had hitherto been unknown. They had freedom in religion, which meant independence of the compulsion of tradition, of the restraint of superstition in its worst aspects, and of the dictation of priests with their intellectually crippling dogmas and formal creeds. The winning of political freedom meant the rise of the Athenian democracy, and, for the first time in history, government by the people. Individual freedom meant the opportunity for self-development and self-expression in all the relations of life. For example, every Athenian youth was free to choose his own career and to make the most of it. In ancient Athens, as in modern America, there was ample opportunity for the "self-made " man.

This freedom of the Greek, however, was the freedom of the individual only and that of his own city-state unrelated to the rest of the world. The Athenian was an intense individualist. He had broken the shackles which prevent man from achieving independence of thought and action, but he never developed the ability to work successfully and harmoniously with his fellows. He was impatient of discipline; the Spartan education found no popular favor at Athens. The Athenian had no genius for organization. The government of Attica in many of its domestic features of administration, e.g., the financial system, seems to the modern mind amateurish and even childish.

This trait of extreme individualism and fierce love of independence, characteristic indeed of all the Greeks, explains the early break-down of the Athenian Empire which was founded upon the Delian Confederacy. The members of this Confederation were not generously allowed to withdraw when dangers were past nor were they treated as equals by the Athenians. The citizens of the allied states were not given Athenian citizenship. Disaffection naturally arose, followed by inevitable dissolution. It remained for Rome to give to the world an example of successful organization and administration.

Even in times of critical danger to the Greek race as a whole it seemed well-nigh impossible to achieve concerted action. This was the case during the Persian invasions when a united army of the Greeks never faced the barbarians. Despite this handicap Greece was fortunately saved, only later to fall a victim to Macedonia because of interstate jealousies and too dearly cherished independence of action. Greek teachers and philosophers who thought and spoke in terms of internationalism and racial unity were rare. Isocrates, throughout his long career, preached Panhellenism to deaf ears. Modern writers find difficulty in understanding this

Athenian characteristic. For example, Theodore Roosevelt, writing to Trevelyan (Bishop, *Theodore Roosevelt and his Time*, 2. 154) says: "What a strange thing it is that those wonderful Greeks . . . lacked the self-restraint and political common-sense necessary to enable them to hold their own against any strong aggressive power." The silence of Plato and Aristotle regarding international relations in their discussions of the ideal state seems inexplicable and regrettable to some moderns. But this silence is explained when it is realized that the Athenian thought only in terms of the individual city-state, which was to be entirely free, independent, and as self-sufficient as possible. And the manifest superiority of the Athenians in all things except the possession of a great military machine — a superiority of which they were not unaware — tended to increase their natural indifference and even intolerance toward foreigners outside of Attica and towards "barbarians."

The fearless and constant application of intellect and of reason to life in all its aspects resulted in the beginnings of science, the discovery of the scientific method, and the development of abstract thinking. While it has remained for the modern world to make marvelous discoveries and to develop physical science, practically all of philosophy in all its varying aspects we have inherited from the Greeks. With curiosity of mind, hunger for knowledge, and power of reason, they first pursued the truth, loving it for its own sake.

There is no more conspicuous feature of the genius of the Greeks than their originality. This is strikingly seen in their literature with its manifold types, which they not only invented but so far perfected that they have served ever since as models. This perfection of form was attained not only in epic, lyric, dramatic, and pastoral poetry, but also in the matured prose style, which was admirably suited for every need of expression. Greek literature, furthermore, both prose and poetry, is characterized by simplicity of handling, directness of treatment, lucidity of style, conciseness of expression, and objectivity.

The influence of this literature — what we owe to the Greeks in this field of human endeavor — is too great for adequate discussion here. The epic poetry of Homer inspired the great epics of Vergil, Dante, and Milton. The literature of Rome has formal beginning in the translation of the *Odyssey* by the Greek, Livius Andronicus. Hesiod's didactic poem, the *Works and Days,* was an incentive for the *Georgics* of Vergil, while the *Bucolics* of Rome's great poet and the pastorals of Shelley and Tennyson are strongly colored by the *Idylls* of Theocritus, Bion, and Moschus. Horace prides himself on having brought to Rome the Aeolic measures of Alcaeus and Sappho. Attic tragedy is the blood and sinew of the Roman Seneca, whose plays were the inspiration for French classical drama and profoundly influenced English dramatic literature. Without the Greek New Comedy of Menander and his fellows the Roman comedy of Terence and Plautus could hardly have existed. The prose style of Gorgias and Isocrates, the oratorical fire, earnestness and mastery of Demosthenes, the histories of Herodotus and Thucydides, the philosophical writings of Plato and Aristotle — all have given to Roman and modern writers and thinkers ideas for inspiration and models for imitation. Even the modern novel is not without prototypes in the romances of Achilles Tatius, Heliodorus, and Longus, and the dialogues and the *True History* of Lucian.

The originality and inventiveness of the Hellenes, so manifest in their literature, may be seen in the development of the Orders of Architecture and in the construction of their temples; these qualities may be admired in their sculpture and works of art of every type and description.

To the modern world the word Greek is almost synonymous with the word Beauty — truly a remarkable tribute to the ancient Hellenes. It may be that our conception in this matter is somewhat exaggerated, and that impatience and disgust with the imperfections and the ugliness about us influence us to idealize the beauty in the past. If, through the magic of Aladdin's lamp, it were granted us to walk the streets of Periclean Athens, no doubt we should observe much that would seem incompatible with our dreams. Ugliness and dirt are not of today only. And yet nothing is more certain than that in general the instinct for the creation of the beautiful was inherent in the genius of the Greek people and was the property of the many and not of the chosen or the trained few. This beauty is not a refined prettiness that loses its charm nor is it the beauty of opulence and ornateness that surfeits and cloys. Greek beauty is the achievement of good taste and is characterized by simplicity and strength. The numerous embodiments of it which the world fortunately still possesses are objects of universal admiration and imitation. This element of beauty is conspicuous in the temples on the Acropolis, in the Panathenaic frieze of the Parthenon, in the contours and decoration of the commonest vase, and in the coins of every-day trade and commerce. Beauty is an all-pervading characteristic of the Greek language itself and of the Greek literature, a beauty of form, expression, and ideas. Underlying Greek beauty in all its manifestations is the feeling for symmetry and harmony, for the golden mean, for good taste and for the becoming, in short, for *sophrosyne,* a quality which is at the very basis of Greek ethical standards and behavior. These characteristics are aptly called by Swinburne (*Essay on Chapman,* 147), " those Grecian gifts of perfect form, of perfect light, and of perfect measure."

The Greek ideal of beauty, as it may be seen expressed in their monuments and literature, seems to some moderns too cold and lacking in appeal. Why is this? It is because of different conceptions which themselves are due to inherent feeling and the influence of accumulated tradition. Greek civilization, largely self-

evolved and developed, was little influenced and affected by outside forces; modern civilization, the heir
of the ages, is complex in the extreme. Realism is at
the very basis of Hellenism; idealism has, until recently at any rate, dominated the modern world. Greek
literature and art are largely objective in the best sense;
modern literature and art are subjective. Greek classic
reserve, chaste and unemotional, may seem cold to modern taste formed and fed by emotionalism. The calm
ending of an Attic tragedy, the quiet and dignified close
of an oration of Demosthenes, the simple dignity of a
Greek statue, the severe lines of a Doric temple, the
conciseness of a Greek lyric — all these manifestations
of the Hellenic temperament, in their sanity and normality, may lack appeal to modern feeling and taste
which have been taught to love infinite variety and
complexity, restlessness, and even exaggeration. Thus
Homer writes with his eye upon the object, as Matthew
Arnold well says, and paints his vivid pictures with a
few telling strokes of the brush and colors of the palette.
Greek lyric poetry poignantly but simply expresses
human feeling without that analysis of the emotions
characteristic of the modern lyric. An Attic tragedy
is comparatively simple in conception and execution,
while a Shakespearian drama is varied and complex,
and an ultra-modern play may be and often is startling
and sensational. It is the essential normality, the simplicity, and the truthfulness of Greek works of art that
may cause them to lack appeal to jaded modern feeling.
Our craze for novelty in the arts is an invitation to the
portrayal of the excessively ornate or the elaborate,
even the representation of the ugly and the grotesque.
The simply beautiful has ceased to attract. This surely
is but a temporary aberration of the modern world —
it is a passing phase that will be followed by a return
to truth and beauty. And it is to the Greeks that we
shall return, insofar as we are indebted to them for
the standards and the canons by which these eternal
virtues are to be tested and measured.

Athens was far from being a perfect city nor were the Athenians free from grave faults. In Athenian history there are many examples of the fickleness of the populace and of their " restless meddlesomeness." Political venality, personal corruption, the blackmail of individuals by informers, juries swayed by prejudice, and instances of cruelty were not unknown. The Athenians tolerated slavery. They were not free from conceit. Not a few were the victims of superstitions and vices. They were far from having solved the many problems of the human race. The modern world is a richer and a better world in many respects than the Grecian. It would indeed be a cause for reproach, and even despair, if civilization had made no progress in two thousand years of living and struggling! We have added much, and done much, to make life safer and more comfortable for the individual, easier for the weak and infirm, and richer in material rewards for the successful and strong. Why, then, is it profitable for us to study Greek civilization? The answer is, that spiritual progress has not kept pace with material. In the very wealth and struggle of modern life we have forgotten, or we ignore, much that the Greeks knew and practiced whereby life was made happy, spiritually rich, and better worth the living. The Greeks were active and energetic, but they knew how to enjoy leisure. To live richly was more important to them than to get riches.

The truth is that we are in great need today of certain Greek virtues. The Greek sense of beauty must animate all the people, instead of the few. Greek simplicity, directness, and moderation must temper modern complexity, evasion, and extravagance. Greek insistence upon thoroughness and accuracy should replace superficiality and sham. Greek love and pursuit of the truth should be emulated. Last but not least Greek good taste and appreciation of the becoming in all of life's relationships the modern world desperately needs.

The words of Sir William Osler, scientist and physician, may fittingly close this chapter and this book:

" As true today as in the fifth century B.C. the name of Hellas stands no longer for the name of a race, but as the name of knowledge. The deep rooting of our civilization is in the soil of Greece — much of our dogmatic religion, practically all the philosophies, the models of our literature, the ideals of our democratic freedom, the fine and the technical arts, the fundamentals of science."

BIBLIOGRAPHICAL APPENDIX

The object of this Appendix is to give the titles of some of the most important, helpful, and recent books bearing on our subject. These books are mostly in English, although a number of important French and German works are included. The general bibliographical list is followed by titles of books and suggested readings of special value for the topics treated in the several chapters of this volume. For other titles see also Supplement on pages 318–20.

GENERAL

ART AND ARCHAEOLOGY

Fowler, H. N., and Wheeler, J. R., Handbook of Greek Archaeology (N. Y. 1909)

Gardner, E. A., Handbook of Greek Sculpture (2d ed. Macmillan, 1915)

Gardner, Percy, Principles of Greek Art (N. Y. 1904)

Murray, A. S., Handbook of Greek Archaeology (N. Y. 1892)

Perrot et Chipiez, Histoire de l'art dans l'antiquité (Paris, 1882–1914)

Tarbell, F. B., History of Greek Art (Macmillan, 1896)

For Vases and Sculpture see titles under Chapters V and VI

Blümner, H., Leben und Sitten der Griechen (Leipzig, 1887)

Botsford, G. W., and Sihler, E. G., Hellenic Civilization (N. Y. 1915)

British Museum Guide to the Exhibition Illustrating Greek and Roman life (2d ed. London, 1920)

Casson, S., Ancient Greece (Oxford Univ. Press, 1922)

Companion to Greek Studies, ed. by Whibley (3d ed. Cambridge, Eng., 1916)

Cotterill, H. B., Ancient Greece (N. Y. 1913)

DICTIONARIES, LEXICA, AND ATLASES

Baumeister, Denkmäler des klassischen Altertums (3 vols. Munich, 1884–88)

Daremberg et Saglio, Dictionnaire des antiquités grecques et romaines (Paris, beginning 1873)

Encyclopaedia Britannica (for many excellent articles)
Everyman Library Atlas
Harper's Dictionary of Classical Literature and Antiquities
Müller, Handbuch der klassischen Altertumswissenschaft (Munich)
Pauly-Wissowa, Real-Encyclopädie der klassischen Altertumswissenschaft (Stuttgart)
Roscher, Lexikon der griechischen und römischen Mythologie (Leipzig)
Schreiber's Atlas of Classical Antiquities (ed. by Anderson, London, 1895)
Shepherd, W. R., Atlas of Ancient History (2d ed. N. Y. 1921)
Sieglin, Schulatlas zur Geschichte des Altertums (Gotha, Perthes)
Smith, W., Dictionaries of Greek and Roman Antiquities, Biography and Mythology, and Geography
Emmanuel, M., La Danse grecque antique (Paris, 1896)
Fougères, G., La Vie publique et privée des Grecs et des Romains (Paris, 1894)
Frazer, J. G., Pausanias' Description of Greece (6 vols. 2d ed. London, 1913)
Gardner and Jevons, Manual of Greek Antiquities (2d ed. London, 1898)
Genius of the Greeks (see titles for Chapter XX)
Gercke und Norden, Einleitung in die Altertumswissenschaft (3d ed., Leipzig, 1923)
Giraud, La Vie privée et la vie publique des Grecs (Paris, 1890)
Guhl und Koner, Das Leben der Griechen und Römer (6th ed. Berlin, 1893)
Guhl and Koner, Life of the Greeks and Romans (N. Y. 1875)
Gulick, C. B., The Life of the Ancient Greeks (N. Y. 1909)
Hermann, K. F., Lehrbuch der griechischen Privataltertümer (3d ed. by Blümner, Freiburg, 1882)
Hicks, E. L., and Hill, G. F., Greek Historical Inscriptions (Rev. ed. Oxford, 1901)
HISTORIES OF GREECE
Beloch, K. J., Griechische Geschichte (2d ed. Strassburg, 1912–16)
Botsford, G. W., Hellenic History (N. Y. 1922)
Breasted, J. H., Ancient Times (N. Y. 1916)
Bury, J. B., History of Greece (2d ed. Macmillan, 1924)
Curtius, E., History of Greece (5 vols. N. Y. 1907)
Ferguson, W. S., Hellenistic Athens (Macmillan, 1911)
—— Greek Imperialism (Boston, 1913)
Freeman, E. A., History of Sicily (4 vols. Oxford, 1891–94)

Gardner, P., New Chapters in Greek History (N. Y. 1892)
Glover, T. R., From Pericles to Philip (2d ed. London, 1918)
Grote, G., History of Greece (12 vols. Everyman's Library, 1906)
Grundy, G. B., The Great Persian War (London, 1901)
—— Thucydides and the History of His Age (London, 1911)
Holm, A., History of Greece (4 vols. Macmillan, 1894–99)
Meyer, E., Geschichte des Altertums (5 vols. 3d ed. Berlin, 1910–13)
HISTORICAL ROMANCES
Davis, W. S., A Victor at Salamis (Macmillan, 1915)
Gaines, C. K., Gorgo: A Romance of Old Athens (Boston, 1903)
Robinson, C., The Days of Alkibiades (N. Y. 1916)
Snedeker, C. D., The Coward of Thermopylae (N. Y. 1911)
James, H. R., Our Hellenic Heritage (Vol. I, London, 1921; Vol. II, Athens, her Splendour and her Fall. 1922)
Literature, see titles under Chapter X
Müller, Die griechischen Privataltertümer (Munich, 1893)
Pater, W., Greek Studies (Macmillan, 1895)
Stobart, J. C., The Glory That Was Greece (2d ed. Philadelphia, 1915
Translations of Greek Literature, see titles under Chapter X
Tucker, T. G., Life in Ancient Athens (Macmillan, 1906)
Ure, P. N., The Origin of Tyranny (Cambridge, Eng., 1922)
Whibley, L., Companion to Greek Studies (3d ed. Cambridge, Eng., 1916)

CHAPTER I. SOURCES OF INFORMATION

Botsford and Sihler, Hellenic Civilization, Chapter I
Gardner, P., New Chapters in Greek History (N. Y. 1892)
Marshall, F. H., Discovery in Greek Lands: A Sketch of the Principal Excavations and Discoveries of the last 50 years (Cambridge, Eng., 1920)
See Bibliography under Chapter XIX

CHAPTER II. GREEK STATES APART FROM ATTICA

Gulick, C. B., Life of the Ancient Greeks, Chapter I
Botsford, G. W., Hellenic History, Chapter I
Companion to Greek Studies (ed. by L. Whibley), Chapter I. 1
James, H. R., Our Hellenic Heritage, I. Chapter II, pp. 16–34
Zimmern, A. E., The Greek Commonwealth (4th ed. Oxford, 1924)

TRAVEL AND DESCRIPTION
    Allinson, F. G., and A. C. E., Greek Lands and Letters (2d
        ed. N. Y. 1922)
    Baud-Bovy, D., and Boissonas, F., In Greece: Journeys by
        Mountain and Valley (with 40 plates. London, 1922)
    Hogarth, D. G., Accidents of an Antiquary's Life (Macmillan,
        1910)
    Manatt, J. I., Aegean Days (N. Y. 1914)
    Marden, P. S., Greece and the Aegean Islands (N. Y. 1907)
    Richardson, R. B., Vacation Days in Greece (N. Y. 1904)

CHAPTER III. ATTICA AND ATHENS

Bosanquet, Mrs. R. C., Days in Attica; Modern Life (London,
    1914)
Companion to Greek Studies, I. 1.
D'Ooge, M. L., The Acropolis of Athens (Macmillan, 1909)
Frazer, J. G., Pausanias (2d ed. 1913)
Gardner, E. A., Ancient Athens (Macmillan, 1902)
Gulick, C. B., Life of the Ancient Greeks, Chapter II
Judeich, W., Topographie von Athen (Munich, 1905)
Weller, C. H., Athens and Its Monuments (Macmillan, 1913)

CHAPTER IV. ARCHITECTURE AND MONUMENTS OF ATHENS

Anderson and Spiers, The Architecture of Greece, revised by
    W. B. Dinsmoor (N. Y. 1927)
Blomfield, R., Greek Architecture (in the Legacy of Greece, ed.
    by R. W. Livingstone)
Dinsmoor, W. B., The Entrance to the Acropolis (In Prepara-
    tion)
D'Ooge, M. L., The Acropolis of Athens (N. Y. 1909)
Erechtheum, Description of, with Atlas of Plates (Harvard Univ.
    Press, 1927)
Fowler and Wheeler, Handbook of Greek Archaeology (see also
    bibliographies therein)
Frazer, J. G., Pausanias.
Gulick, C. B., Life, Chapter IV
Harrison and Verrall, Mythology and Monuments of Ancient
    Athens (N. Y. 1894)
Jahn and Michaelis, Arx Athenarum a Pausania descripta in usum
    scholarum (Bonn, 1901)
Marquand, A., Greek Architecture (N. Y. 1909)
Springer, A., Die Kunst des Altertums (11th ed. Leipzig, 1920)

Vitruvius, Ten Books on Architecture, translated by Morgan, M. H., and illustrations by Warren, H. L., (Harvard Press, 1914)
Weller, C. H., Athens and Its Monuments (N. Y. 1913)

CHAPTER V. HOUSE, FURNITURE, AND VASES

Companion to Greek Studies, VII. 8
Dictionaries and Manuals of Antiquities
Gulick, C. B., Life, Chapter III
Rider, B. C., The Greek House (Cambridge, Eng., 1916)
FURNITURE AND UTENSILS
 Gulick, Life, Chapter X.
 Ransom, C. L., Studies in Ancient Furniture (Chicago, 1905)
VASES AND VASE-PAINTING
 Baumeister, Denkmäler, article Vasenkunde.
 Beazley, J. D., Attic Red-figured Vases in American Museums (Oxford, 1918)
 Buschor, E., Greek Vase-Painting (London, 1921)
 Companion to Greek Studies, IV. 5.
 Fairbanks, A., Athenian White Lekythoi (Macmillan, 1914)
 Fowler and Wheeler, Greek Archaeology, pp. 412–525 (and bibliography)
 Herford, M. A. B., Handbook of Greek Vase-Painting (N. Y. 1919)
 Hoppin, J. C., Handbook of Attic Red-figured Vases (2 vols. Oxford, 1919)
 Pottier, E., Catalogue des vases antiques de terre-cuite au Musée du Louvre (Pt. 1 Paris, 1896)
 —— Douris and the Painters of Greek Vases (N. Y. 1916)
 Richter, Gisela M. A., The Craft of Athenian Pottery (Yale Univ. Press, 1922)
 Walters, H. B., History of Greek Pottery (Murray, 1905)

CHAPTER VI. SCULPTURE

Arndt, P., Griechische und römische Porträts (Munich, 1909–)
Brunn, H., and Arndt, P., Denkmäler griechischer und römischer Sculptur (Munich, 1888–1902)
Carpenter, Rhys, The Esthetic Basis of Greek Art (Bryn Mawr, 1921)
Catalogue of the Acropolis Museum: Vol. I, G. Dickens; Vol. II, S. Casson (Cambridge, Eng., 1912–21)

Collignon, M., Les Statues funéraires dans l'art grec (Paris, 1911)
Conze, A. C. L., Die attische Grabreliefs (Berlin, 1893)
Dickins, G., Hellenistic Sculpture (Oxford, 1920)
Fowler, H. N., and Wheeler, J. R., Greek Archaeology (N. Y. 1909)
Furtwängler, A., Masterpieces of Greek Sculpture (N. Y. 1895)
Furtwängler, A., and Ulrichs, H. L., Greek and Roman Sculpture (N. Y. 1914)
Gardner, E. A., Handbook of Greek Sculpture (2d ed. N. Y. 1915)
—— Six Greek Sculptors (London, 1910)
Gardner, P., Sculptured Tombs of Hellas (N. Y. 1896)
—— The Lamps of Greek Art: in The Legacy of Greece, ed. by R. W. Livingstone
Hekler, A., Greek and Roman Portraits (N. Y. 1912)
Joubin, A., La Sculpture grecque entre les guerres médiques et l'époque de Phidias (Paris, 1901)
Hyde, W. W., Olympic Victor Monuments and Greek Athletic Art (Carnegie Institute of Washington, 1921)
Jex-Blake, K., and Sellers, E., The Elder Pliny's Chapters on the History of Art (London, N. Y. 1896)
Jones, H. S., Select Passages from Ancient Authors Illustrative of the History of Greek Sculpture (London, 1895)
Lechat, H., La Sculpture attique avant Phidias (Paris, 1904)
Loewy, E., Nature in Greek Art (London, 1907)
—— Die griechische Plastik (Leipzig, 1911)
von Mach, E., A Handbook of Greek and Roman Sculpture (Boston, 1905)
Overbeck, J. H., Geschichte der griechischen Plastik (3d ed. Leipzig, 1881–82)
Orbis Pictus, Band 3, Archaische Plastik der Griechen (Berlin)
Powers, H. H., The Message of Greek Art (N. Y. 1913)
Reinach, S., Répertoire de la statuaire grecque et romains (I–IV, Paris, 1897–1910)
—— Répertoire des reliefs grecs et romains (I–III, Paris, 1909–12)
Richter, G. M. A., Handbook of the Classical Collection of the Metropolitan Museum of Art of N. Y. (N. Y.)
Walters, H. B., The Art of the Greeks (Revised ed. N. Y. 1922.)
Warrack, J., Greek Sculpture, (London, 1912)

CHAPTER VII. ATHLETIC SPORTS AND FESTIVALS

Companion to Greek Studies, V. 2
Gardiner, E. N., Greek Athletic Sports and Festivals (Macmillan, 1910)
Gulick, Life, pp. 91–105

Hyde, W. W., Olympic Victor Monuments and Greek Athletic Art
(Washington, D. C., 1921. Carnegie Institution Publ.)

CHAPTER VIII. POLITICAL, SOCIAL AND ECONOMIC CONDITIONS OF THE ATHENIAN PEOPLE

Abrahams, E. B., Greek Dress (London, 1908)
Barker, E., Greek Political Theory; Plato and His Predecessors
(London, 1918)
Boeckh, A., Die Staatshaushaltung der Athener (3d ed. Berlin,
1886)
Caldwell, W. E., Hellenic Conceptions of Peace (N. Y. 1919)
Clerc, M., Les Métèques athéniens (Paris, 1893)
Companion to Greek Studies, ed. by Whibley
Croiset, M., Aristophanes and the Political Parties at Athens;
translated by Loeb (Macmillan, 1909)
Donaldson, J., Woman in Ancient Greece (Longmans, 1907)
Evans, M. M., Chapters on Greek Dress (Macmillan, 1893)
Ferguson, W. S., Greek Imperialism (Houghton Mifflin, 1913)
Fowler, W. W., The City-State of the Greeks and Romans (Mac-
millan, 1907)
Francotte, H., L'Industrie dans la Grèce ancienne (2 vols. Brus-
sels, 1900)
Gardner, P., A History of Ancient Coinage (700–300 B.C.) (Ox-
ford, 1918)
Gilbert, G., Constitutional Antiquities of Sparta and Athens
(1895)
Glotz, G., La Solidarité de la famille dans le droit criminel en
Grèce (Paris, 1904)
—— Études sociales et juridiques sur l'antiquité grecque (Paris,
1906)
Greenidge, A. H. J., Handbook of Greek Constitutional History
(Macmillan, 1902)
Guiraud, P., La Main d'oeuvre industrielle dans l'ancienne Grèce
(Paris, 1900)
Gulick, Life of the Ancient Greeks, pp. 60–70; 206–215; 227–
250
Lipsius, J. H., Das attische Recht und Rechtsverfahren, based on
Meier und Schömann (Leipzig, 1905)
Meier und Schömann, Der attische Prozess (Revised by Lipsius,
Leipzig, 1905)
Meyer, E., Die Sklaverei im Altertum (in *Kleine Schriften*)
Putnam, E. J., The Lady (N. Y. 1910)
Raeder, A. H., l'Arbitrage international chez les Hellènes (N. Y.
1912)
Roper, A. G., Ancient Eugenics (Oxford, 1913)

Tod, M. N., International Arbitration amongst the Greeks (Oxford, 1913)

Trever, A. G., History of Greek Economic Thought (Chicago, 1916)

Van Hook, La Rue, The Degradation in Meaning of Certain Greek Words (*Classical Journal*, May, 1916)

—— The Exposure of Infants in Ancient Athens (*Trans. Amer. Phil. Assoc.*, 1920)

Zimmern, A. E., The Greek Commonwealth (Oxford, 4th ed. 1924)

—— Greek Political Thought: in The Legacy of Greece, ed. by R. W. Livingstone (1921)

CHAPTER IX. WRITING AND BOOKS

Birt, T., Das antike Buchwesen (Berlin, 1882)

—— Die Buchrolle in der Kunst (Leipzig, 1907)

Companion to Greek Studies, Chapter VII. 4

Gulick, Life, pp. 108–112

Hall, F. W., Companion to Classical Texts (London, 1913)

Murray, G., The Tradition of Greek Literature (in Cooper, The Greek Genius and Its Influence)

Putnam, G. H., Authors and Their Public in Ancient Times (N. Y. 1894)

Thompson, E. M., An Introduction to Greek and Latin Palaeography (Oxford, 1912)

White, J. W., The Scholia on the *Aves* of Aristophanes: Introduction (Boston, 1914)

CHAPTER X. GREEK LITERATURE

HISTORIES OF GREEK LITERATURE

Capps, E., From Homer to Theocritus (Scribner, 1901)

Christ-Schmid, Geschichte der griechischen Litteratur (Munich, 1908–)

Columbia University Lectures on Greek Literature (N. Y. 1912)

Croiset, A. and M., Histoire de la littérature grecque (5 vols. Paris, 1896–99)

Fowler, H. N., Ancient Greek Literature (2d ed. N. Y., 1923)

Krumbacher, K., Geschichte der byzantinischen Litteratur (2d ed. Munich, 1897)

Murray, G., Ancient Greek Literature (N. Y. 1897)

Susemihl, F., Geschichte der griechischen Litteratur in der Alexandrinerzeit (2 vols. 1891)

Wright, W. C., A Short History of Greek Literature (N. Y. 1907)

OTHER WORKS

Arnold, M., On Translating Homer (in Essays Literary and Critical)

Blass, F., Geschichte der attischen Beredsamkeit (4 vols. 2d ed. 1887–93, Teubner)

Bruns, I., Das literarische Porträt der Griechen (Berlin, 1896)

Bury, J. B., The Ancient Greek Historians (Macmillan, 1909)

Dobson, J. F., The Greek Orators (N. Y. 1920)

Haigh, A. E., The Tragic Drama of the Greeks (Oxford, 1896)

Jebb, R. C., Classical Greek Poetry (Macmillan, 1893)

—— The Attic Orators (2 vols. 2d ed. Macmillan, 1893)

—— Essays and Addresses (Cambridge, Eng., 1907)

—— Homer (Boston, 1890)

Lang, A., The World of Homer (N. Y. 1910)

Livingstone, R. W., Greek Literature (in The Legacy of Greece, Oxford, 1921)

Lodge, G., Greek Influence on Latin Literature (in Columbia Univ. Lectures on Greek Literature)

Mackail, J. W., Lectures on Greek Poetry (new ed. Longmans, 1926)

Murray, G., The Rise of the Greek Epic (2d ed. Oxford, 1911)

Norden, E., Die antike Kunstprosa (2 vols. 2d ed., Leipzig, 1915–18)

Norwood, G., Greek Tragedy (Boston, 1920)

Perry, E. D., Greek Lyric Poetry (in Columbia Univ. Lectures on Greek Literature)

Powell, J. U., New Chapters in the History of Greek Literature (Oxford, 1921)

Rohde, E., Der griechische Roman (Leipzig, 1914)

Scott, J. A., The Unity of Homer (Berkeley, Cal., 1921)

Shorey, P., Chapter I in Columbia Univ. Lectures on Greek Literature

Stemplinger, E., Das Plagiat in der griechischen Litteratur (Leipzig, 1912)

Symonds, J. A., Studies of the Greek Poets (3d ed. London, 1902)

Teichmüller, G., Literarische Fehden (Breslau, 1881–84)

Tyrrell, R. Y., Essays on Greek Literature (London, 1909)

Van Hook, La Rue, Greek Literature (article in the Encyclopaedia Americana, vol. 13)

Volkmann, R., Rhetorik der Griechen und Römer (Munich)

ENGLISH LITERATURE AND THE CLASSICS

Amos, F. R., Early Theories of Translation (N. Y. 1920)

Bywater, F., Four Centuries of Greek Learning in England (Oxford, 1919)

Campbell, L., Tragic Drama in Aeschylus, Sophocles, and Shakespeare (N. Y. 1904)

Collins, J. C., Greek Influence on English Poetry (London, 1910)

Cooper, L., Aristotle on the Art of Poetry (N. Y. 1913)

—— Two Views of Education (New Haven, Conn., 1922)

Foster, F. M. K., English Translations from the Greek: A Bibliographical Survey (N. Y. 1918)

Goad, C., Horace in the English Literature of the 18th Cent. (New Haven, 1918)

Goldmark, R. I., Studies in the Influence of the Classics on English Literature: Jonson, Landor, Arnold (N. Y. 1918)

Gordon, G. S., English Literature and the Classics (Oxford, 1912)

Harrison, J. S., Platonism in English Poetry of the 16th and 17th Centuries (Columbia Univ. Press)

Kerlin, J. S., Theocritus in English Literature (Lynchburg, Va., 1910)

Mustard, W. P., Classical Echoes in Tennyson (N. Y. 1904)

Nitchie, E., Vergil and the English Poets (Columbia Univ. Press)

—— Browning's Use of the Classics (*Classical Weekly*, Jan. 31, 1921)

Osgood, C. G., The Classical Mythology of Milton's English Poems (N. Y. 1900)

Rohde, E., Der griechische Roman (Leipzig, 1914)

Root, R. K., Classical Mythology in Shakespeare (N. Y. 1903)

Shorey, P., Lecture I in Columbia Univ. Lectures on Greek Literature

Stapfer, P., Shakespeare and Classical Antiquity (London, 1880)

Thayer, M. R., The Influence of Horace on the Chief English Poets of the 19th Century (Cornell Diss.)

Tucker, T. G., The Foreign Debt of English Literature (N. Y. 1907)

Van Hook, La Rue, Metaphorical Terminology of Greek Rhetoric and Literary Criticism (Chicago, 1904)

—— Greek Rhetorical Terminology in Puttenham's Arte of English Poesie (in *Trans. Am. Phil. Assoc.* 45)

Van Hook, La Rue, Frigidity as a Vice of Style in the Ancient Literary Critics (*Classical Philology*, vol. 12)

Watt, L. M., Attic and Elizabethan Tragedy (N. Y. 1908)

Wolff, S. L., Romances in Elizabethan Prose Fiction (N. Y. 1912)

ENGLISH TRANSLATIONS OF THE CHIEF GREEK AUTHORS

Achilles Tatius, Gaselee, S. (Loeb Classical Library)

Aeschines, *Orations*, Adams, C. D. (Loeb Library)

Aeschylus, *Tragedies*, Way, A. S. (Verse); Morshead (Verse); Campbell (Verse); Plumptre (Verse). *Agamemnon*, Murray, G. (Verse); Browning, R. (Verse). *Prometheus*, Browning, E. B. (Verse); *Oresteian Trilogy*, Morshead, *The House of Atreus* (Verse); Smyth, H. W. (Prose, Loeb Library)

Alcaeus, in Lyra Graeca, Edmonds, J. M. (Loeb Library)

Anacreontics, Moore, T. (Verse)

Anthology, Paton, W. R. (5 vols. Loeb Library); Mackail, J., *Select Epigrams;* Leaf, W., *Little Poems from the Greek*

Apollonius of Rhodes, Coleridge, E. P. (Prose); Seaton, R. C. (Loeb Library)

Appian's *Roman History*, White, H. (4 vols.)

Aratus, Mair, G. R. (Loeb Library)

Aristophanes, *Comedies*, Text with Translation and Notes by Rogers, B. B., each play in separate vol. Hickie, W. J. (Prose, Bohn Library); Frere, J. H., *Select Plays* (Verse); *Frogs*, Murray, G. (Verse)

Aristotle, *Ethics*, Welldon; *Politics*, Jowett; *Rhetoric*, Jebb (Sandys); *Poetics*, Butcher, S. H.; Bywater, I.; Cooper, L.; *Constitution of Athens*, Kenyon, F. G.; *De Anima*, Wallace, E.; Hicks, R. D.; *Historia Animalium*, Thompson, D. W.

Athenaeus, Yonge, C. D. (3 vols. Bohn Library)

Bacchylides, Jebb, R. C. (Prose)

Bion and Moschus, and Theocritus, Lang, A. (Prose)

Callimachus, Mair, A. W. (Loeb Library)

Clement of Alexandria, Butterworth, G. W. (Loeb Library)

Daphne and Chloe, Thornley, rev. by Edmonds, J. M. (Loeb Library)

Demetrius, *On Style*, Roberts, W. R.

Demosthenes, Kennedy, C. R.; Public Orations, Pickard-Cambridge

Dio's *Roman History*, Cary, E. (Loeb Library)

Dionysius of Halicarnassus, *Three Literary Letters*, Roberts, W. R.; *On Literary Composition*, Roberts, W. R.

Empedocles, Leonard, W. E. (Verse)

Epictetus, Crossley, H.; Long, G.

Euripides, entire, Way, A. S. (Verse, Loeb Library); Murray, G. (Verse); *Cyclops*, Shelley, P. B.

Galen, *On the Natural Faculties*, Brock, A. J. (Loeb Library)

Greek Poets in English Verse, ed. by Appleton, W. H.

Greek Poets, An Anthology, Dole, N. H.

Herodotus, Rawlinson, G.; Macaulay, G. C.; Godley, A. D. (Loeb Library)

Hesiod, Mair, A. W.; Evelyn-White, H. G. (Loeb Library)

Homer, *Iliad*, Lang, Leaf, and Myers (Prose); Bryant (Verse); Derby (Verse); Way (Verse)

—— *Odyssey*, Butcher and Lang (Prose; Palmer, G. H.; Bryant (Verse); Way (Verse); Mackail (Verse); Murray, A. T. (Loeb Library)

Homeric Hymns, Evelyn-White, H. G. (Loeb Library); Shelley, P. B. (in part)

Hypereides, Kenyon, F. G.

Isaeus, Jones, W.

Isocrates, Dimsdale, J. (revised by Young); Freese, J. H. (vol. I); Norlin, G. (Loeb Library)

Julian, Wright, W. C. (Loeb Library)

Longinus, *On the Sublime*, Roberts, W. R.; Prickard, A. O.

Longus, *Daphnis and Chloe*, Edmonds, J. M. (Loeb Library)

Lucian, Fowler, H. W. and F. G.; Harmon, A. H. (Loeb Library)

Lyric Poets, Edmonds, J. M. (Loeb Library)

Marcus Aurelius Antoninus, Rendall, G. H.; Haines, C. R. (Loeb Library)

Meleager, Headlam, W.

Menander, Allinson, F. G. (Loeb Library)

Pausanias, Frazer, J. G.; Jones, W. H. S. (Loeb Library)

Philostratus and Eunapius, The Lives of the Sophists; Wright, W. C. (Loeb Library)

Pindar, Myers, E. (Prose); Sandys, J. (Prose, Loeb Library)

Plato, Jowett, B. (5 vols.): *Four Socratic Dialogues*, Jowett, with preface by Caird; *Republic*, Davies and Vaughan; *Euthyphro, Apology, Crito, Phaedo, and Phaedrus*, Fowler, H. N. (Loeb Library); *Theaetetus and Sophist*, Fowler, H. N. (Loeb Library)

Plutarch, Clough; Perrin, B. (Loeb Library)

Polybius, Shuckburgh, E. S.; Paton, W. R. (Loeb Library)

Procopius, Dewing, H. B. (Loeb Library)

Quintus Smyrnaeus, Way, A. S. (Verse, Loeb Library)

Sappho, Wharton, H. T. (Various Verse Translations); in Lyra Graeca, Edmonds, J. M. (Loeb Library)

Sophocles, Jebb, R. C. (Prose); Way (Verse); Campbell (Verse); Plumptre (Verse); Storr, F. (Loeb Library); Oedipus, King of Thebes, Murray, G. (Verse)

Strabo, Falconer and Hamilton; Jones, H. L. (Loeb Library)

Theocritus, Calverley (Verse); Lang, A. (Prose); Way, A. S. (Verse); Edmonds, J. M. (Loeb Library)

Theophrastus, Characters, Jebb, revised by Sandys; Enquiry into Plants, Hort, A. (Loeb Library)

Thucydides, Jowett, B.; Smith, C. F. (Loeb Library)

Xenophon, Dakyns, H. G. Cyropaedia, Miller, W. (Loeb Library); Hellenica, Brownson (Loeb Library)

CHAPTER XI. EDUCATION

Bosanquet, B., Education of the Young in Plato's Republic (Cambridge, 1908)

Capes, W. W., University Life in Ancient Athens: The Ephebes (London, 1877)

Companion to Greek Studies, Chapter VII. 3

Drever, J., Greek Education: Its Practice and Principles (Cambridge, 1912)

Freeman, K. J., The Schools of Hellas (Macmillan, 1907)

Girard, P., L'Éducation athénienne (2d ed. Paris, 1891)

Gulick, Life, pp. 71–90; 105–111

Monroe, P., Sourcebook of the History of Education: Greek and Roman (N. Y. 1902)

Nettleship, R. L., Theory of Education in Plato's Republic (in E. Abbott's Hellenica, pp. 67 ff.)

Walden, J. W. H., The Universities of Ancient Greece (N. Y. 1909)

CHAPTER XII. THEATER AND PRODUCTION OF PLAYS

THEATER, PHYSICAL ASPECTS

Allen, J. T., The Greek Theater of the Fifth Century B.C. (Berkeley, Cal., 1920)

Bieber, M., Die Denkmäler zum Theaterwesen im Altertum (Berlin, 1920)

Capps, E., The Stage in the Greek Theater According to the Extant Dramas (New Haven, 1893)

Dörpfeld, W., und Reisch, E., Das griechische Theater (Athens, 1896)

Flickinger, R. C., The Greek Theater and Its Drama, pp. 57–117; esp. 57–75 (3d ed. Chicago, 1926)

Fowler and Wheeler, Greek Archaeology, pp. 165–172

Haigh, A. E., The Attic Theatre (3d ed. Oxford, 1907)

Norwood, G., Greek Tragedy, pp. 49–59

Weller, C. H., Athens and Its Monuments, pp. 190–200

Whibley, L., Companion to Greek Studies, in Chapter on Religious Institutions

PRODUCTION OF PLAYS

Allen, J. T., Greek Acting in the Fifth Century B.C. (Univ. of California, Publ. in Class. Phil. Vol. 2, No. 5)

Flickinger, R. C., The Greek Theater and its Drama (3d ed. Chicago, 1926)

Gulick, C. B., Life, pp. 112–118

Haigh, A. E., The Attic Theatre (3d ed. Oxford, 1907)

Norwood, G., Greek Tragedy, pp. 48–83

O'Connor, J. B., Chapters in the History of Acting and Actors in Ancient Greece (Chicago, 1908)

Rees, K., So-called Rule of the Three Actors in Greek Drama (Chicago, 1908)

Smith, K. K., The Use of the Buskin (Harvard Studies in Classical Philology, XVI)

CHAPTERS XIII AND XIV. TRAGEDY

Aeschylus, Translations of: see Appendix, Chapter X

Aristotle, On Tragic Art: see Appendix, Chapter X

Barnett, L. D., The Greek Drama (London, 1900)

Bryan, W. R., The Conventions of the Chorus (Univ. of Wis. Class. Studies, 1922)

Campbell, L., A Guide to Greek Tragedy (N. Y. 1891)

Capps, E., The Stage in the Greek Theater According to the Extant Dramas (1893)

Companion to Greek Studies

Decharme, P., Euripides and the Spirit of His Dramas, trans. by Loeb (Macmillan, 1905)

Euripides, Translations of: see Appendix, Chapter X

Flickinger, R. C., Greek Theater and Its Drama (3d ed. Chicago, 1926)

Goodell, T. D., Athenian Tragedy, a Study in Popular Art (New Haven, 1920)

Haigh, A. E., The Tragic Drama of the Greeks (Oxford, 1896)

Jebb, R. C., see Introductions to his separate editions of the Plays of Sophocles (Cambridge, Eng.)

Leach, Abby, Fate and Free-Will in Greek Literature (in Cooper, The Greek Genius and Its Influence)

Mackail, J. W., Lectures on Greek Poetry (Sophocles)

Matthaei, L., Studies in Greek Tragedy (Cambridge, Eng., 1918)

Murray, A. T., Plot and Character in Greek Tragedy (T. A. P. A. 1916)

Murray, G., Euripides and His Age (N. Y. 1913)

—— in English Literature and the Classics, ed. by G. S. Gordon

Messer, W. S., The Dream in Homer and Greek Tragedy (N. Y. 1918)

Myers, E., Aeschylus: in E. Abbott's Hellenica

Nestle, W., Euripides, der Dichter der griechischen Aufklärung (Stuttgart, 1901)

Norwood, G., Greek Tragedy (Boston, 1920)

Patin, H., Études sur les tragiques grecs (Paris, 1885–94)

Post, C. R., Dramatic Art of Sophocles (Harvard Studies in Classical Philology, 23 (1912)

Rees, K., So-called Rule of the Three Actors in the Classical Greek Drama (Chicago, 1908)

Ridgway, W., The Origin of Tragedy (Cambridge, 1910)

—— The Dramas and Dramatic Dances of Non-European Races in Special Reference to the Origin of Greek Tragedy (Cambridge, 1915)

Sheppard, J. T., Greek Tragedy (Cambridge, 1920)

Sophocles, Translations of: see Appendix under Chapter X

Stuart, D. C., Foreshadowing and Suspense in the Euripidean Prologue (Univ. of North Carolina Studies in Classical Philology, Oct. 1918)

—— The Origin of Greek Tragedy in the Light of Dramatic Technique (Trans. of the Amer. Phil. Assoc. 1916, Vol. 47)

Van Hook, La Rue, The " Thought "-Motif of Wisdom versus Folly in Greek Tragedy (A. J. P. 39, pp. 393–401; see, in connection with this, C. Knapp, A. J. P. 37, 300–315)

Weil, H., Études sur le drame antique (2d ed. Paris, 1908)

Wheeler, J. R., Greek Tragedy (in Columbia Univ. Lectures in Greek Literature)

Wilson, Pearl C., Wagner's Dramas and Greek Tragedy (N. Y. 1919)

CHAPTER XV. COMEDY

Aristophanes, Translations of: see Appendix, Chapter X

Capps, E., Greek Comedy, in Columbia Univ. Lectures on Greek Literature

—— The Introduction of Comedy into the City Dionysia (Chicago, 1903)

Cornford, F. M., The Origin of Attic Comedy (London, 1914)

Couat, A., Aristophane et l'ancienne comédie attique (Paris, 1892)

Denis, J., La Comédie grecque (Paris, 1886)
Flickinger, R. C., The Greek Theater and Its Drama (3d ed. Chicago, 1926)
Haigh, A. E., The Attic Theatre (3d ed. Oxford, 1907)
Legrand, P. E., The New Greek Comedy, trans. by Loeb (Putnam, 1917)
Menander, Translations of: see Appendix, Chapter X
White, J. W., The Verse of Greek Comedy (1912)

CHAPTER XVI. PHILOSOPHY

Adam, J., The Vitality of Platonism and Other Essays (Cambridge, 1911)
Bakewell, C. M., Source-book in Ancient Philosophy (N. Y. 1909)
Benn, A. W., Greek Philosophers (2d ed. London, 1914)
Barker, E., Greek Political Theory; Plato and His Predecessors (London, 1918)
Brownson, C. L., Plato's Studies and Criticisms of the Poets (Boston, 1920)
Bevan, E. R., Stoics and Sceptics (Oxford, 1913)
Burnet, J., Early Greek Philosophy (3d ed. London, 1920)
—— Greek Philosophy: in The Legacy of Greece, ed. by R. W. Livingstone
Companion to Greek Studies
Gomperz, T., Greek Thinkers, 4 vols. (N. Y. 1901–05)
Grote, G., Plato and the Companions of Socrates (London, 1875)
Hicks, R. D., Stoic and Epicurean (N. Y. 1910)
Jowett, B., Translation of Plato and Analyses of the Platonic Dialogues (3d ed. N. Y. 1892)
Leonard, W. E., Socrates, Master of Life (Chicago, 1915)
More, P. E., Platonism (Princeton Univ. Press, 1917)
Pater, W. H., Plato and Platonism (Macmillan, 1908)
Shorey, P., Plato (in Library of World's Best Literature, ed. by Warner)
Windelband, History of Ancient Philosophy (N. Y. 1899)
Woodbridge, F., Greek Philosophy (in Columbia Univ. Lectures on Greek Literature)
Zeller, E., Greek Philosophy (Various works)

CHAPTER XVII. RELIGION

Adam, J., Religious Teachers of Greece (Edinburgh, 1908)
Campbell, L., Religion in Greek Literature (Longmans, 1898)
Companion to Greek Studies
Cook, A. B., Zeus (Cambridge, Eng., 1914)
Cumont, F., Astrology and Religion among the Greeks and Romans (Putnam, 1912)

Fairbanks, A., Handbook of Greek Religion (N. Y. 1908)
Farnell, L. R., Cults of the Greek States (5 vols. Oxford, 1896–1909)
—— Higher Aspects of the Greek Religion (London, 1912)
—— Greek Hero Cults and Ideas of Immortality (Oxford, 1921)
—— Outline-History of Greek Religion (London, 1921)
Fox, W. S., Greek and Roman Mythology (Boston, 1916)
Foucart, P., Les Mystères d'Eleusis (Paris, 1914)
Frazer, J. G., The Golden Bough: a Study in Magic and Religion (3d ed. London, 1911–20)
—— Abridged edition of foregoing title (N. Y. 1922)
Gardner, E. A., Religion and Art in Ancient Greece (N. Y. 1910)
Gruppe, O., Griechische Mythologie und Religionsgeschichte (Munich, 1906)
Gulick, C. B., Chapter XX, pp. 263–283
Harrison, J., Religion of Ancient Greece (London, 1913)
—— Ancient Art and Ritual (Holt, 1913)
—— Themis: a Study of the Social Origins of Greek Religion (Cambridge Univ. Press, 1912)
Hastings, J. H., Encyclopaedia of Religion and Ethics (N. Y. 1908–22)
Inge, W. R., Greek Religion (in The Legacy of Greece, ed. by R. W. Livingstone)
James, H. R., Our Hellenic Heritage, vol. I, chapters 3 and 4 (Gods and Heroes)
Mommsen, A., Feste der Stadt Athen im Altertum (Leipzig, 1898)
Moore, C. H., Religious Thought of the Greeks from Homer to the Triumph of Christianity (Harvard Univ. Press, 1916)
More, P. E., The Religion of Plato (Princeton Univ. Press, 1921)
Murray, G., Five Stages of Greek Religion (Columbia Univ. Press, 1925)
Philios, M. D., Eleusis: Her Mysteries, Ruins and Museums (Appleton, 1906)
Preller, L., Griechische Mythologie (4th ed. vol. II, Berlin, 1920–21)
Rohde, E. Psyche (Tübingen, 9th ed. 1921. Eng. trans. N. Y. 1925)
Roscher, W. H., Lexikon der griechischen und römischen Mythologie (Leipzig)

CHAPTER XVIII. SCIENCE

Albutt, T. C., Greek Medicine in Rome (London, 1911)
Apollonius Pergaeus, Treatise on Conic Sections, Heath, T. L. (Cambridge, 1896)

Archimedes, Works, Heath, T. L. (Cambridge, 1897)

Aristarchus of Samos, See Heath, T. L.

Ball, W. W. R., A Short Account of the History of Mathematics (1919)

Berger, H., Geschichte der wissenchaftliche Erdkunde der Griechen (2d ed. Leipzig, 1903)

Berry, A., Short History of Astronomy (London, 1910)

Botsford and Sihler, Hellenic Civilization, pp. 627–656

Buck, A. H., The Growth of Medicine (New Haven, 1917)

Bunbury, E. H., Ancient Geography (2 vols. London, 1883)

Cajori, F., History of Mathematics (2d ed. N. Y. 1919)

Companion to Greek Studies, ed. by Whibley; chap. on Science.

Dannemann, F., Grundriss einer Geschichte der Naturwissenschaften (2 vols. Leipzig, 1896–98)

Daremberg et Saglio, Dictionnaire

Diel, H., Antike Technik (2d ed. Leipzig, 1920); for review of the inventions therein described, see rev. by Humphreys in *Classical Weekly,* Oct. 17, 1921)

Diophantos of Alexandria: A Study in the History of Greek Algebra, Heath, T. L. (2d ed. Cambridge, 1910)

Elliott, J. S., Outlines of Greek and Roman Medicine (London, 1914)

Encyclopaedia Britannica, under Sciences and Names of great Scientists mentioned in the text

Euclid, Elements, trans. with Intro. and Commentary by Heath, T. L. (Cambridge, 1908)

Fink, K., A Brief History of Mathematics, trans. by Beman, W. W., and Smith, D. E. (3d ed. Chicago, 1910)

Galen, On the Natural Faculties, trans. by Brock, A. J., in Loeb Library

Garrison, F. H., History of Medicine (3d ed. Philadelphia, 1921)

Gomperz, T., The Greek Thinkers (3 vols. N. Y. 1901–5)

Gow, J., Short History of Greek Mathematics (Cambridge, 1884)

Guenther, S., Geschichte der Mathematik (2 vols. Leipzig, 1908–1921)

Heath, T. L., Aristarchus of Samos, the Ancient Copernicus (Oxford, 1912)

—— History of Greek Mathematics (2 vols. Oxford, 1921)

—— Greek Mathematics and Astronomy in the Legacy of Greece, ed. by Livingstone, R. W.

Hippocrates, Genuine Works, trans. by Adams, F. (2 vols. N. Y. 1891)

Hoppe, E., Mathematik und Astronomie im klassischen Altertum (Heidelberg, 1911)

Hoefer, F., Histoire des mathématiques (5th ed. Paris, 1902)

Josephson, A. G. S., A List of Books on the History of Science (Chicago, 1911)

Legacy of Greece, ed. by R. W. Livingstone, for articles on Medicine, Mathematics, Biology, and Natural Science

Lones, T. E., Aristotle's Researches in Natural Science (London, 1912)

Locy, W. A., Biology and its Makers (3d ed. N. Y. 1915)

Neuberger, M., Geschichte der Medizin (2 vols. Stuttgart, 1906–8)

Osler, W., The Evolution of Modern Medicine (New Haven, 1913)

Pauly-Wissowa, Real-Encyclopädie, under the names of the scientists

Puschmann, T., History of Medical Instruction (London, 1891)

Sedgwick and Tyler, A Short History of Science (N. Y. 1917)

Singer, C., Greek Biology and Medicine: in The Legacy of Greece, ed. by R. W. Livingstone

Smith, D. E., Mathematics (Boston, 1923)

Tannery, P., Mémoires scientifiques (Toulouse, 3 vols. 1912–15)

—— Recherches sur l'histoire de l'astronomie ancienne (Paris, 1893)

Theophrastus, Enquiry into Plants, trans. by Hort, A. (2 vols. in Loeb Classical Library)

Taylor, H. O., Greek Biology and Medicine (Boston, 1922)

Thompson, D. W., Greek Natural Science: in The Legacy of Greece, ed. by R. W. Livingstone

—— Glossary of Greek Birds (Oxford, 1895)

Tozer, H. F., History of Ancient Geography (Cambridge, 1897)

Williams, H. S., History of Science (5 vols. Harper, 1904)

CHAPTER XIX. THE NEW STUDY OF ANCIENT GREECE

American School of Classical Studies at Athens (see *Art and Archaeology*, American School Number, Oct., 1922)

Baikie, J., Sea-Kings of Crete (London, 1910)

Banerjee, G. N., Hellenism in Ancient India (Calcutta, 2d ed. 1920)

Botsford, G. W., Hellenic History (especially Chapters II and III)

Botsford and Sihler, Hellenic Civilization

Burrows, R. M., Discoveries in Crete (N. Y., 1907)

Dörpfeld, W., Troja und Ilion (Athens, 1902)

Dussaud, R., Les Civilisations prehelléniques dans le bassin de la mer Égée (2d ed. Paris, 1914)

Evans, A., The Palace of Minos at Cnossos: I The Neolithic and Early Minoan Ages (London, 1921)

Gardner, P., New Chapters in Greek History (Putnam, 1892)

Hall, H. R., The Oldest Civilization in Greece (Lippincott, 1901)

—— Aegean Archaeology (London, 1915)

Hawes, C. H. and H. B., Crete, the Fore-Runner of Greece (Harper, 1909)

Hogarth, D. G., The Ancient East (Home Univ. Library)

Lang, A., World of Homer (Longmans, 1916)

Leaf, W., Troy: a Study of Homeric Geography (Macmilian, 1912)

—— Homer and History (Macmillan, 1915)

Marett, R. R., Anthropology and the Classics (1908)

Marshall, F. H., Discoveries in Greek Lands: a Sketch of the Principal Excavations and Discoveries of the last 50 years (Cambridge, 1920)

Michaelis, A. T. F., A Century of Archaeological Discoveries, trans. by B. Kahnweiler (London, 1908)

Mosso, A., Palaces of Crete (Putnam, 1907)

—— Dawn of Mediterranean Civilization (London, 1910)

Poulsen, F., Delphi (London, 1920)

Powell, J. V., and Barber, E. H., New Chapters in Greek Literature (Oxford, 1921)

Sandys, J. E., History of Classical Scholarship (3 vols. 1908–1921)

Schuchhardt, K., Schliemann's Excavations (Macmillan, 1891)

Scott, J. A., The Unity of Homer (Berkeley, Cal. 1921)

Seager, R. B., Explorations in the Island of Mochlos (1912)

Seymour, T. D., Life in the Homeric Age (Macmillan, 1907)

Smith, Recovery of Lost Greek Literature (*Yale Review*, July, 1914)

Thomson, J. A. K., The Greek Tradition (Macmillan, 1915)

Tsountas and Manatt, Mycenaean Age (N. Y. 1897)

Waldstein, C., Argive Heraeum (N. Y. 1902)

CHAPTER XX. THE GENIUS OF THE GREEKS

Abbott, E., Hellenica

Billeter, G., Die Anschauungen vom Wesen des Griechentums (Teubner, 1911)

Burns, C. D., Greek Ideals (London, 1917)

Butcher, S. H., Harvard Lectures on Greek Subjects (N. Y. 1904)

—— Some Aspects of the Greek Genius (London, 1893)

Chapman, J. J., Greek Genius and Other Essays (N. Y. 1915)

Collins, J. C., Greek Influence on English Poetry (London, 1910)

Cooper, L., The Greek Genius and Its Influence (Yale Univ. Press, 1917)

Croiset, M., The Greek Race and Its Genius (in L. Cooper's Greek Genius and its Influence)

Dickinson, G. L., The Greek View of Life (15th ed. N. Y. 1915)

Gildersleeve, B. L., Hellas and Hesperia (N. Y. 1909)

Livingstone, R. W., The Greek Genius and Its Meaning to Us (2d ed. Oxford, 1915)

—— The Legacy of Greece (Oxford, 1921. " Essays which aim to give some idea of what the world owes to Greece in various realms of the spirit and intellect, and of what it can still learn from her.")

Low, W. H., The Debt of Modern Art to Ancient Greece (*Scribners Mag.*, May, 1920)

Mahaffy, J. P., What Have the Greeks Done for Modern Civilization? (Putnam, 1910)

Murray, G., The Value of Greece to the Future of the World: in The Legacy of Greece, ed. by R. W. Livingstone

—— Religio Grammatici (N. Y. 1918)

Our Debt to Greece and Rome, edited by Hadzsits, G. D., and Robinson, D. M. (Longmans, Green, N. Y.)

Shorey, P., The Assault on Humanism (Boston, 1917)

Tucker, T. G., The Foreign Debt of English Literature

Value of the Classics, edited by A. F. West (Princeton Univ. Press)

Zielinski, T., Our Debt to Antiquity (London, 1909).

SUPPLEMENT TO THE BIBLIOGRAPHICAL APPENDIX

GENERAL

Cambridge Ancient History (Cambridge Univ. Press)
Rostovtzeff, M. A., A History of the Ancient World (Oxford, 1926)
Tarn, W. W., Hellenistic Civilisation (London, 1927)

CHAPTER II

Dixon, W. M., Hellas Revisited (N. Y., 1929)

CHAPTER IV

Schede, M., The Acropolis of Athens (N. Y., 1924)

CHAPTER V

Hoppin, J. C., Handbook of Greek Black-figured Vases (London, 1924)

CHAPTER VI

Chase, G. H., and Post, C. R., A History of Sculpture (N. Y., 1925)

CHAPTER VII

Gardiner, E. N., Olympia (London, 1925)
Jüthner, J., Körperkultur im Altertum (Jena, 1928)

CHAPTER VIII

Bonner, R. J., Lawyers and Litigants in Ancient Athens (Chicago, 1927)
Calhoun, G. M., The Business Life of Ancient Athens (Chicago, 1927)
Glotz, G., Ancient Greece at Work
Gomme, A. W., The Position of Women in Athens in the Fifth and Fourth Centuries (*Classical Philology*, Jan. 1925)
Sargent, Rachel, The Size of the Slave Population at Athens (Univ. of Illinois Press, 1924)

Van Hook, La Rue, Crime and Criminals in the Plays of Aristophanes (*Classical Journal,* Jan. 1928)

Zimmern, A., Solon and Croesus (Essays, Oxford, 1928)

CHAPTER X

For translations of Greek authors consult the latest list of volumes published in the Loeb Classical Library Series (G. P. Putnam, N. Y.)

Baldwin, C. S., Ancient Rhetoric and Poetic (N. Y., 1924)

Howe, G., and Harrer, G. A., Greek Literature in Translation (N. Y. 1924)

Körte, A., Hellenistic Poetry, translated by Hammer, J., and Hadas, M. (Columbia Univ. Press, 1929)

Livingstone, R. W., The Pageant of Greece (Selections from Greek Literature, Oxford, 1923)

Roberts, W. Rhys, Greek Rhetoric and Literary Criticism (N. Y., 1928)

Robinson, D. M., Sappho (Boston, 1924)

Van Hook, La Rue, The Modernity of Greek Literature (*Classical Weekly,* Dec. 12, 1927)

CHAPTER XII

Allen, J. T., Stage Antiquities of the Greeks and Romans (N. Y. 1927)

CHAPTERS XIII, XIV, XV

Bates, W. N., Euripides (Univ. of Pennsylvania Press, 1929)

Pickard-Cambridge, A. W., Dithyramb, Tragedy, and Comedy (Oxford, 1927)

Smyth, H. W., Aeschylean Tragedy (Univ. of California Press, 1924)

Stuart, D. C., The Development of Dramatic Art: Chapters I–IV (N. Y. 1928)

Ten Greek Plays (in English verse, Oxford, 1929)

CHAPTER XVI

More, P. E., Hellenistic Philosophies (Princeton Univ. Press, 1923)

Patrick, M. M., The Greek Sceptics (Columbia Univ. Press, 1929)

Wenley, R. M., Stoicism and Its Influence (Boston, 1924)

CHAPTER XVII

Bevan, E., Later Greek Religion (N. Y. 1927)
Nilsson, M. P., History of Greek Religion (Oxford, 1925)
Rose, H. J., A Handbook of Greek Mythology (N. Y. 1929)
Zielinski, T., The Religion of Ancient Greece (Oxford, 1926)

CHAPTER XIX

Guide to the Excavations and Museum of Ancient Corinth (1928)
Myres, J. L., Who Were the Greeks? (Univ. of California Press, 1929)

CHAPTER XX

Greene, W. C., The Achievement of Greece (Harvard Univ. Press, 1923)
Gulick, C. B., Modern Traits in Old Greek Life

INDEX

abacus, 24
Academy, 20, 158, 235
acanthus, 26
Acarnania, 12
Acharnians, of Aristophanes, 214
Achelous, 7
Achilles, 10
Achilles Tatius, 148
action, in drama, 176
actors, 180, 181, 183; guilds, 183
acoustics, in theater, 177, 182
Acro-Corinth, 12
Acropolis, 22
Admetus, 193
admission to theater, 181
Aegean race, 8
Aegina, 20
Aeginetan marbles, 50
Aegisthus, 190
Aeolians, 8
Aeschines, 87, 145
Aeschylus, plays of, 187–8; as a tragic poet, 194–5; religious views, 256
Aetolia, 12
Agamemnon, King, 13
Agamemnon, of Aeschylus, 188, 205
Agathias, 149
Ages of Man, 254
Agias, statue of, 56
agon, 212
Agora, 21, 83
agriculture, 97
Agrigentum, 16
Ajax of Sophocles, 174, 189; dramatic value, 202
Akragas, 16
Alcaeus, 130
Alcestis, of Euripides, 193
Alcibiades, 39, 232
Alcidamas, 97, 169
Alcman, 133, 282
Alexander the Great, 9; tutored by Aristotle, 244; sarcophagus, 56
Alexandrian Period, in Literature, 145–8; in Science, 273
algebra, 274
Alpheus, 7, 70
Amasis, 98
Amazons, in art, 52
amentum, 76

American School at Athens, 22, 248; excavations, 12, 13
Amphictyonic Council, 69
Amphora, 44
Anacreon, 133; Anacreontics, 133
anaesthetics, 278
Anaxagoras, 223–4
Anaximander, 219 ff.
Anaximenes, 219 ff.
Andocides, 140
Andromache, 110
animals, in art, 51
Antenor, 49
Anthologies, 149–51
Anthropomorphism, 221, 253; in art, 62
Antigone, of Sophocles, 189
Antioch, 119
Antiochus Epiphanes, 29
Antiphon, 140
Antisthenes, 248
antitheses, 221
Anytus, 230
Apelles, 3
Aphaia, temple, 50
Aphrodite, of Melos, 59 f.; of Cnidus, 55; 265
Apollo, oracle of, 12; early statues of, 49; statue at Olympia, 50; Belvedere, 59; and Marsyas, 55; at Athens, 264; *Hymn to,* 72
Apollonius, 147, 274
Apology, of Plato, 230, 234, 236
Apoxyomenus, 56
Appian, 148
Aratus, 148, 275
Arcadia, 14
Arcesilas, 60
Archaic Period of Art, 49 f.
archaism, in art, 61
Archilochus, 129
Archimedes, 273
architecture, 23–34
architrave, 24
Archons, 85; 179
Areopagus, 22; Council of, 85
Aretaeus, 279
Arete, 110
Argolis, 13
Argos, 13
Arion, 134, 185

321